中国农业科学院外文文献资源需求与保障研究

卢 垚　王鸶飞　马 鑫　著

中国农业科学技术出版社

图书在版编目（CIP）数据

中国农业科学院外文文献资源需求与保障研究 / 卢垚，王鸶飞，马鑫著. —北京：中国农业科学技术出版社，2021.9
 ISBN 978-7-5116-5477-9

Ⅰ.①中… Ⅱ.①卢… ②王… ③马… Ⅲ.①中国农业科学院—外文—文献资源建设—研究 Ⅳ.① G253

中国版本图书馆 CIP 数据核字（2021）第 184052 号

责任编辑　倪小勋
责任校对　马广洋
责任印制　姜义伟　王思文

出 版 者	中国农业科学技术出版社 北京市中关村南大街 12 号　　邮编：100081
电　　话	（010）82109707（编辑室） （010）82109702（发行部） （010）82109709（读者服务部）
传　　真	（010）82109707
网　　址	http://www.castp.cn
经 销 者	各地新华书店
印 刷 者	北京建宏印刷有限公司
开　　本	170 mm×240 mm　1/16
印　　张	14
字　　数	270 千字
版　　次	2021 年 9 月第 1 版　2021 年 9 月第 1 次印刷
定　　价	65.00 元

※ 版权所有·翻印必究 ※

一 绪 论 / 001

（一）中国农业科学院文献资源保障现状 / 001

（二）农业学科文献资源需求与保障研究 / 002

（三）主要研究内容 / 003

二 数据来源与分析方法 / 004

（一）数据来源 / 004

（二）分析方法 / 004

三 中国农业科学院外文文献需求和保障分析 / 011

（一）文献需求概况 / 011

（二）需求学科分析 / 012

（三）需求数据库分析 / 016

（四）文献保障水平 / 018

（五）综合利用水平评估 / 020

四 各直属研究所需求和保障分析 / 022

（一）作物科学研究所 / 022

（二）植物保护研究所 / 028

（三）蔬菜花卉研究所 / 033

（四）农业环境与可持续发展研究所 / 039

（五）北京畜牧兽医研究所 / 045

（六）蜜蜂研究所 / 051

（七）饲料研究所 / 057

（八）农产品加工研究所 / 063

（九）生物技术研究所 / 069

（十）农业经济与发展研究所 / 075

（十一）农业资源与农业区划研究所 / 081

（十二）农业质量标准与检测技术研究所 / 087

（十三）农业农村部食物与营养发展研究所 / 093

（十四）农田灌溉研究所 / 099

（十五）水稻研究所 / 105

（十六）棉花研究所 / 111

（十七）油料作物研究所 / 117

（十八）麻类研究所 / 123

（十九）果树研究所 / 129

（二十）郑州果树研究所 / 135

（二十一）茶叶研究所 / 141

（二十二）哈尔滨兽医研究所 / 147

（二十三）兰州兽医研究所 / 153

（二十四）兰州畜牧与兽药研究所 / 159

（二十五）上海兽医研究所 / 166

（二十六）草原研究所 / 172

（二十七）特产研究所 / 178

（二十八）环境保护科研监测所 / 184

（二十九）沼气科学研究所 / 190

（三十）南京农业机械化研究所 / 196

（三十一）烟草研究所 / 202

（三十二）深圳农业基因组研究所 / 208

五　总结和讨论 / 215
（一）中国农业科学院学科资源需求与保障特点 / 215

（二）中国农业科学院外文文献资源保障策略 / 216

参考文献 / 217

绪 论

科技文献作为重要的科技基础资源,其查阅、引用、发表等利用行为贯穿科学研究活动的整个生命周期,论文发表是科研活动最主要的成果产出形式。分析科研用户的文献利用行为,把握其发文现状、使用偏好和需求特征对文献资源建设工作具有指导性意义。本书从中国农业科学院各直属研究所外文电子期刊文献全文获取、引用以及发表的维度,综合评估各直属研究所的文献保障和利用水平,分析其文献利用规律和需求特征,为优化电子资源建设内容和结构提供科学依据。

(一)中国农业科学院文献资源保障现状

中国农业科学院作为国家综合性农业科研机构,担负着全国农业基础与应用基础研究、关键技术攻关、高技术研究及产业化、宏观战略研究的任务,取得了一大批具有国际先进水平的重大科技成果。中国农业科学院现有文献资源保障体系囊括作物、园艺、畜牧、兽医、植物保护、资源与环境、机械与工程、质量安全与加工、信息与经济9个学科集群相关农业科技文献资源,利用"研究所共建"机制覆盖36个直属机构,并进一步通过全国农业科研系统电子资源共建共享体系和"国家农业大数据与信息服务联盟",将文献资源保障范围辐射至全国农业科研系统。

在中国农业科学院和国家科技图书文献中心(NSTL)的支持下,以及全院各直属研究所共同努力下,现有文献资源保障体系已具备稳定规模,馆藏印本文献238万余册,包括印本图书39万余册,印本期刊1.4万种;中外文电子文献数据库80种,涵盖中外文电子书18万种、中文全文期刊10 000余种和外文全文期刊 11 000 余种，以及 20 种分析工具型数据库和 9 种经济统计型数据库，为全院及全国的农业科技创新、管理决策和产业发展提供高质量科技文献保障。

过去十年全院文献保障水平得到大幅度提升，外文文献保障率从 2010 年的 60% 提升至超过 90%，达到国内一流。但当前全院文献资源保障仍面临很多问题，在中国农业科学院电子文献资源建设专家咨询委员会 2018 年咨询会议上，主任委员中国农业科学院梅旭荣副院长指出，全院各学科间文献保障水平不平衡，各研究所文献利用水平参差不齐，而解决这一系列问题的根本途径就在于深入文献需求分析研究、优化文献保障分析评估方法，更精准客观地掌握用户需求和保障现状，从而指导保障体系结构和内容的调整。

（二）农业学科文献资源需求与保障研究

农业科学因其研究对象多样，涉及的学科范围广泛、门类繁多，其中既有侧重基础理论的，也有侧重应用技术的，具有很强的学科交叉属性。农业学科科技文献资源，远远超出了作物学、园艺学、兽医学等经典农业学科的范畴，涉及生物学、化学等基础学科，工程学、计算机科学等应用学科，经济学等人文社会学科。因此，多元化的需求给农业学科资源需求分析造成了一定的难度，尤其是体现在与其他学科相交叉的学科需求上。

中国农业科学院文献资源建设团队利用问卷调查、引文分析、目标机构对比等手段持续开展文献资源需求分析，直接影响着文献资源建设工作策略。王婷等[1]通过对农业科技人员进行问卷调研，发现其对电子期刊资源依存度很高，需求旺盛，提出应当提高电子资源保障水平；续玉红等[2]、王婷等[3]利用引文分析得出结论，中国农业科学院外文引文中 88.9% 的引文来源于外文期刊，确定了外文期刊在文献需求和建设中的主导地位。同时团队在国内也率先开展农业文献资源需求与保障分析相关方法研究。王婷等[4]针对农业交叉学科国外期刊需求，提出了期刊关联分析法，通过该方法对某一学科最具代表性期刊的参考文献进行共引分析，量化共引期刊间引证强度，判断其相互联系紧密度，从而找到相关期刊资源。面对用户越来越个性化、精准化的需求发展趋势，卢垚等[5]将文献按主题进行组织，通过文献主题分析进行更细粒度的需求分析，打破按学科进行分析的制约。随着资源保障体系中数字资源成为主流，农业科技文献需求和保障分析研究也逐步向着数据驱动的方向发展。

(三) 主要研究内容

本书将围绕中国农业科学院"建成世界一流农业科研院所"的发展目标和"服务产业重大科技需求、跃居世界农业科技高端"的定位,深入开展农业科技文献资源需求与保障研究,主要研究内容包括以下几部分。

(1)针对中国农业科学院和各研究所的外文文献需求进行分析,具体包括四个方面。首先是需求学科分析,电子文献信息资源建设一直以学科规划和发展作为准绳,对学科需求的把握一直是进行需求分析的基石。其次是需求主题分析,将利用文献主题分析来研判信息精准需求。再次是需求期刊分析,明确到具体文献资源品种。最后还将落实到需求数据库分析,作为资源订阅和推介的直接依据。

(2)评价中国农业科学院整体及各直属研究所外文全文保障水平,通过计算外文全文保障率对电子资源建设的成效进行评估,进一步发现现有保障体系中的薄弱环节,提出针对性调整意见。

(3)评估各直属研究所外文文献综合利用水平,客观了解各研究所文献利用能力,为各所借助文献资源充分利用,促进科技创新能力提升提供参考。

数据来源与分析方法

（一）数据来源

1. 文献使用数据来源

本书中文献使用数据来源于中国农业科学院已订阅外文电子期刊全文数据库 2019 年度 COUNTER 标准使用统计报告的期刊访问请求量报告（Journal Report 1），采集各数据库 2019 年全院及各直属研究所具有访问权限的用户的外文期刊全文获取次数进行分析统计。

2. 发文引文数据来源

发文引文数据来源于爱思唯尔 Scopus 数据库，其作为全球最大的外文文摘引文数据库，收录的出版物范围广，除 98% 的 SCI 收录期刊外，还涵盖了 EI 工程索引期刊，共计 23 000 余种，为进行文献需求和保障分析提供了较全面的数据范围。本书在 Scopus 数据库中通过机构检索中国农业科学院及各直属研究所 2017—2019 年发表的外文文献，经清洗、机构规范后，共计采集发文 10 845 篇，随后又采集了 10 845 篇发文相应的 52.2 万篇引用文献的元数据。

（二）分析方法

1. 文献学科分类分析

中国农业科学院文献资源建设始终围绕全院学科规划和发展，为了把握全院及各直属研究所学科资源需求，对发表的文献进行学科分类分析。在分析过程中，首先将全院发文按照学科进行分类，分类组织体系采用 Scopus 数据库的文献分类方法。Scopus 的文献分类法分为生命科学、社会科学、自然科学和医学四个大类，包括 27 个一级学科和 334 个二级学科。为了使文献分类与中国农业科学院学科设置相符，将 Scopus 文献分类体系与中国农业科学院学科体系（当前规划形成 9 个学科集群，包括 57 个学科领域和 302 个重点方向）进行了映射。就一级学科而言，与中国农业科学院学科相关紧密的有农业和生物科学，生物化学、遗传学和分子生物学，环境科学等类别；就二级学科而言，农学和作物科学、动物科学与动物学、食品科学、园艺学、兽医学、土壤科学、昆虫科学等类目与中国农业科学院学科设置较为接近，能够很好地映射（图 1）。并且一篇文献可被归入多个类别，即出现复分的现象，从研究对象、研究技术等不同的层面对其进行描述。本书中从一级学科和二级学科对全院及各直属研究所发文进行了统计分析。

2. 主题组织和遴选

除将文献按学科分类之外，本书还按照主题来组织发文引文，进行更细粒度的文献需求分析。主题组织作为图书馆信息资源管理常用的组织方式，将具有相同主题特征的文献以表示其主题的受控词汇作为标识标引和描述。本书利用 Scopus 数据库对文献按照引用关系自动聚类生成文献合集，并用学科主题词表标引的文献组织方法，对全院及各直属研究所发文、引文按照主题进行了组织。随之设计了一系列遴选指标，对各直属研究所发文、引文涉及的主题进行遴选，通过比较直属研究所发文在各主题的分布数量，来判断研究所自身侧重的研究方向；比较发文在主题内全球论文中的占比，反映研究所对该主题的贡献程度；分析引文在各主题的分布数量，反映研究所对主题文献的需求强度；比较主题显示度说明主题被关注度和发展势头；领域权重引用影响力指数（FWCI 值）说明研究所在主题内论文的引文影响力（图 2）。最终遴选出各研究所发/引文集中度、贡献度相对较高，引文影响力表现好，并且在全球范围内被关注程度较高、发展势头较好的主题，从而把握各所的精细需求。

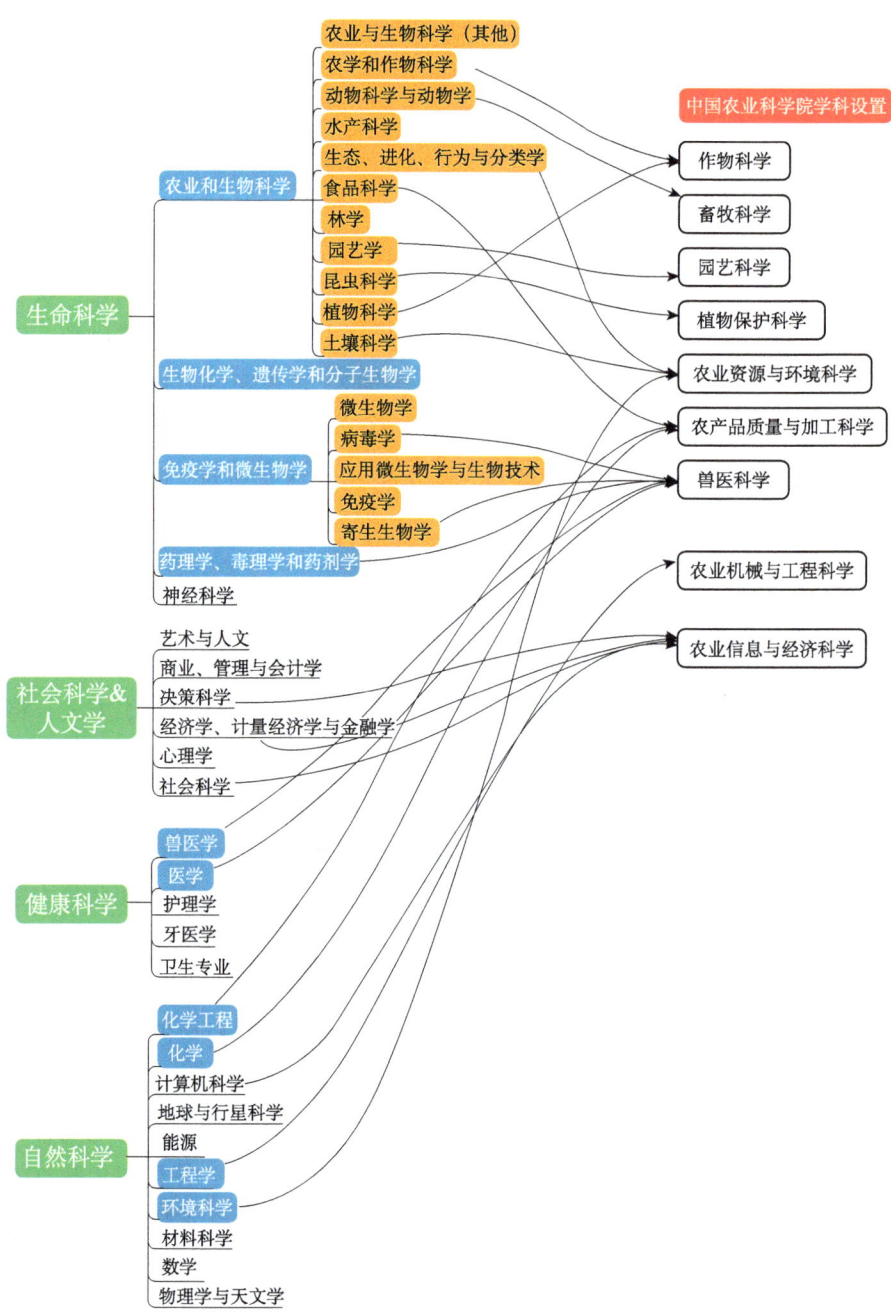

图 1　Scopus 文献分类与中国农业科学院学科设置

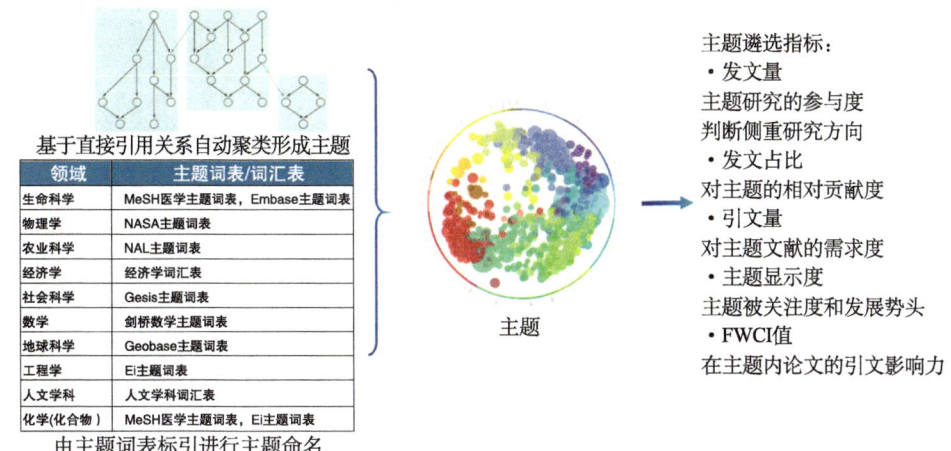

图2 主题组织和遴选

3. 引文分析

引文分析法作为一种基于客观引用数据的文献定量分析方法，被广泛应用于各种文献信息需求调查和分析，其利用数学和统计学的方法以及比较、归纳、概括等逻辑方法，对引文的数量特征及内部信息进行分析，以研究用户的文献利用规律、研究活动特征和学科资源需求等。本书在采集管理大量引文篇级元数据的基础上，在引用文献和施引文献间建立关联关系，从引文来源期刊、文献发表年份、文献类型、文献语种等多个维度对结构化引文数据开展分析，研判用户文献资源需求特征，并评估相应资源保障情况。

4. 资源定位与期刊规范

本书中文献需求和保障分析的结果，具体体现为机构用户需求的期刊种类、需求的数据库和外文电子期刊全文保障率。因此就需要将学科分析、主题分析、引文分析结果，分别从期刊和数据库层面，定位到具体资源（图3）。将分析所得需求期刊品种与农业学科相关的28个电子期刊全文型数据库（表1）期刊清单进行匹配，梳理期刊和数据库对应关系，按数据库级别对需求进行组织；同时，进一步梳理各库中已订阅期刊品种，再加之由NSTL建设的外文现刊品种，和主要的开放获取资源PLOS、BMC、DOAJ等期刊品种，形成统一的外文电子期刊全文保障范围，将其与需求刊种进行匹配，评估资源保障水平。而在上述分析需求刊种、需求数据库和评估保障水平的过程中，都以规范的期刊信息为依据，因此在进行各项分析之前还完成了期刊母体数据规范的工作。

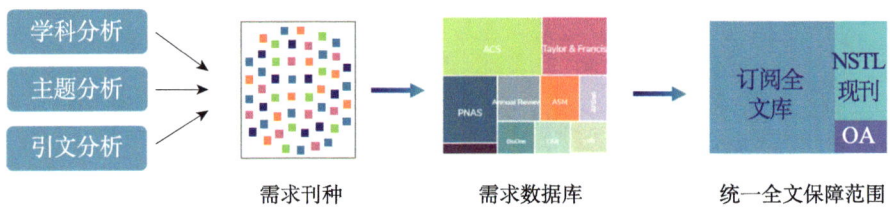

图 3　资源定位工作路线

表 1　纳入分析范围的外文电子期刊全文数据库

数据库简称	数据库全称	性质
ACM	Association for Computing Machinery	商业资源
ACS	American Chemical Society	商业资源
Annual Reviews	Annual Reviews	商业资源
APS	American Physiological Society	商业资源
APSnet	American Phytopathological Society	商业资源
ASBMB	American Society for Biochemistry and Molecular Biology	商业资源
ASCE	American Society of Civil Engineers	商业资源
ASM	American Society Microbiology	商业资源
ASME	American Society of Mechanical Engineers	商业资源
BioOne	BioOne Complete	商业资源
BMJ	British Medical Journal	商业资源
CABPlus	CABPlus	商业资源
Cell	Cell	商业资源
CUP	Cambridge University Press	商业资源
Emerald	Emerald	商业资源
IEEE	IEEE	商业资源
ISHS	International Society for Horticultural Science	商业资源
Jstor	Jstor	商业资源
MS	Microbiology Society	商业资源
NPG	Nature NPG	商业资源
OUP	Oxford University Press	商业资源
PNAS	PNAS	商业资源

续表

数据库简称	数据库全称	性质
RSC	Royal Society of Chemistry	商业资源
Science	Science	商业资源
ScienceDirect	ScienceDirect	商业资源
Springer	Springer	商业资源
Taylor & Francis	Taylor & Francis	商业资源
Wiley	Wiley	商业资源
ASHS	American Society of Horticultural Science	开放资源
BMC	BioMed Central	开放资源
DOAJ	Directory of Open Access Journals	开放资源
PLoS	The Public Library of Science	开放资源

5. 指标测算及说明

（1）文献保障率　文献保障率反映已建设电子资源对用户文献资源需求的保障情况。本书计算了中国农业科学院外文电子期刊全文保障率，以及各直属研究所的外文电子期刊全文保障率，是指对分析对象进行引文需求分析，所得外文期刊引文总次数中，已订阅电子期刊全文型资源所覆盖的引文次数所占的比例，反映馆藏资源对实际需求的满足和保障情况，计算公式如下。

$$外文电子期刊全文保障率 = \frac{订阅外文电子期刊覆盖的引文数量}{需求外文期刊文献引文数量总和}$$

（2）文献综合利用指数　文献综合利用指数反映各直属研究所的文献综合利用水平。该指标是以32个直属研究所为评估对象，将其在科研活动中3个主要文献利用环节，即文献引用、文献发表和文献使用（全文获取）的相应数量作为3个变量，利用相关分析法和复相关系数赋权法进行计算而得。在计算过程中，通过复相关分析，研究文献引用、发表和电子期刊数据库访问及全文获取之间的相关关系，并依据变量之间的独立性确定其权重，若某一变量与其他两者的复相关系数越大、共线性越强、重复信息越多，越容易由其他2个变量的线性组合表示，该变量的权重就应越小，反之亦然。因此取变量与其他2个变量的复相关系数绝对值的倒数作为其各自权重，综合计算各直属研究所的文献利用指数，计算公式如下。

$$\text{文献综合利用指数} = \text{发文量} \times |R_{发文}|^{-1} + \text{引文量} \times |R_{引文}|^{-1} + \text{使用量} \times |R_{使用}|^{-1}$$

（3）主题显示度　主题显示度用于主题遴选，反映主题的被关注度及发展势头，是对每一主题中文献的被引次数、浏览次数和平均期刊影响力加权求和的结果，计算公式如下：

$$Pj = 0.495[Cj - \text{mean}(Cj)]/\text{stdev}(Cj) + 0.391[Vj - \text{mean}(Vj)]/\text{stdev}(Vj) + 0.114[CSj - \text{mean}(CSj)]/\text{Stdev}(CSj)$$

（4）领域权重引用影响力指数　领域权重引用影响力指数（Field-Weighted Citation Impact，FWCI）是规范化的引文影响力指标，指论文被引频次与同类型论文平均被引次数的比值，消除了出版年、学科领域与文献类型的影响。在本书中用以反映主题文献合集的引文影响力。

中国农业科学院外文文献
需求和保障分析

（一）文献需求概况

英文期刊一直是中国农业科学院外文文献利用和建设的重点，本研究分别从文献语种和文献类型分析引文分布特征，继而分析全院外文电子文献资源需求基本概况。通过分析发现，中国农业科学院2017—2019年发表的外文文献中，99.16%的引文原始语言为英语，原始语言为汉语的文献仅占引文总量的0.7%，法语、日语等其他语种占比极低（图4），充分说明中国农业科学院科研用户利用外文文献以英文文献为主。在文献类型上，89%的引用来源于期刊，2%来源于图书，9%来源于会议、学位论文、网页和软件等其他类型的学术资源（图5）。依据这一分析结果，将继续保持英文期刊在中国农业科学院外文文献资源建设中的主导地位。而在本次文献需求和保障分析中，将来自图书、会议、数据库、软件等资源类型的引文以及来自国内期刊的引文排除，重点分析来源于外文期刊的引文，着重讨论对外文期刊的文献需求。

除文献语种和文献类型之外，还进行了引文发表年份分析（图6），发现中国农业科学院过去三年发文的引用文献数量分别在1997年、2000年和2007年形成三个阶梯，这也为订阅数据库选择资源回溯年限时，提供了重要的参考依据。

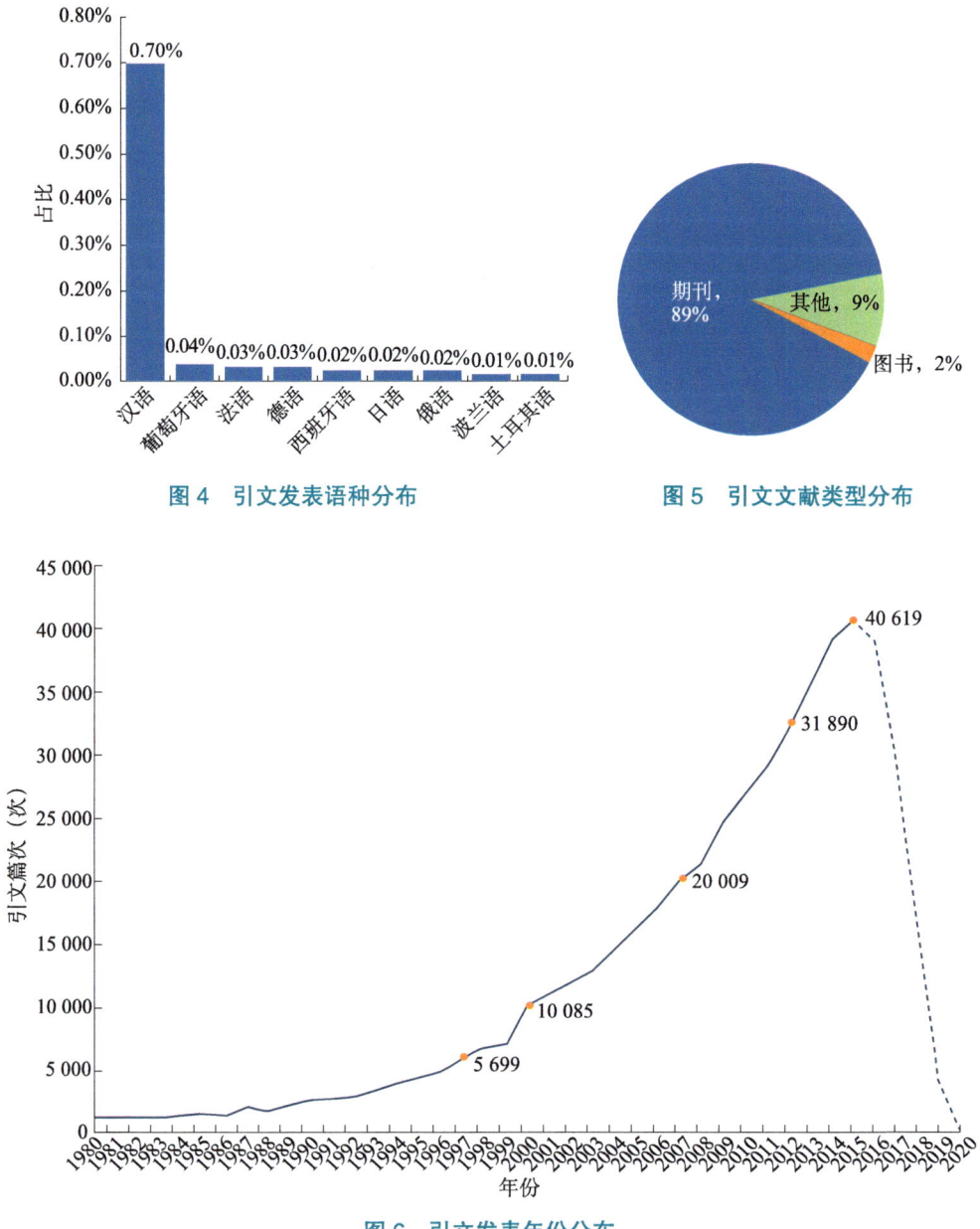

图4 引文发表语种分布

图5 引文文献类型分布

图6 引文发表年份分布

（二）需求学科分析

国家农业图书馆文献资源建设一直以支撑中国农业科学院学科发展作为导

向,因此掌握全院科研用户研究所涉学科领域及其布局是开展农业学科资源建设的基本准则。本书对采集的中国农业科学院 2017—2019 年发表的 10 845 篇外文论文进行学科分析,发现涉及的主要学科有农业和生物科学(64.94%)、生物化学、遗传学和分子生物学(37.83%)、环境科学(20.40%)、免疫学和微生物学(15.42%)和化学(14.05%)等(图 7)。除此之外,还有一定数量的发文涉及工程学、地球与行星科学、计算机科学、药理学、毒理学和药剂学、材料科学等学科(表 2)。

就农业和生物科学而言,涉及的二级学科主要包括植物科学(22.35%)、农学和作物科学(20.63%)、综合农业和生物科学(11.53%)、食品科学(11.52%)、动物科学和动物学(7.51%)、土壤科学(6.94%)、生态、进化、行为与系统学(6.83%)以及昆虫科学(4.41%)(图 7)。生物化学、遗传学和分子生物学的发文则主要集中在遗传学(11.58%)、分子生物学(9.06%)、生物化学(8.17%)、生物技术(8.02%)、综合生物化学、遗传学和分子生物学(4.87%)等亚类。

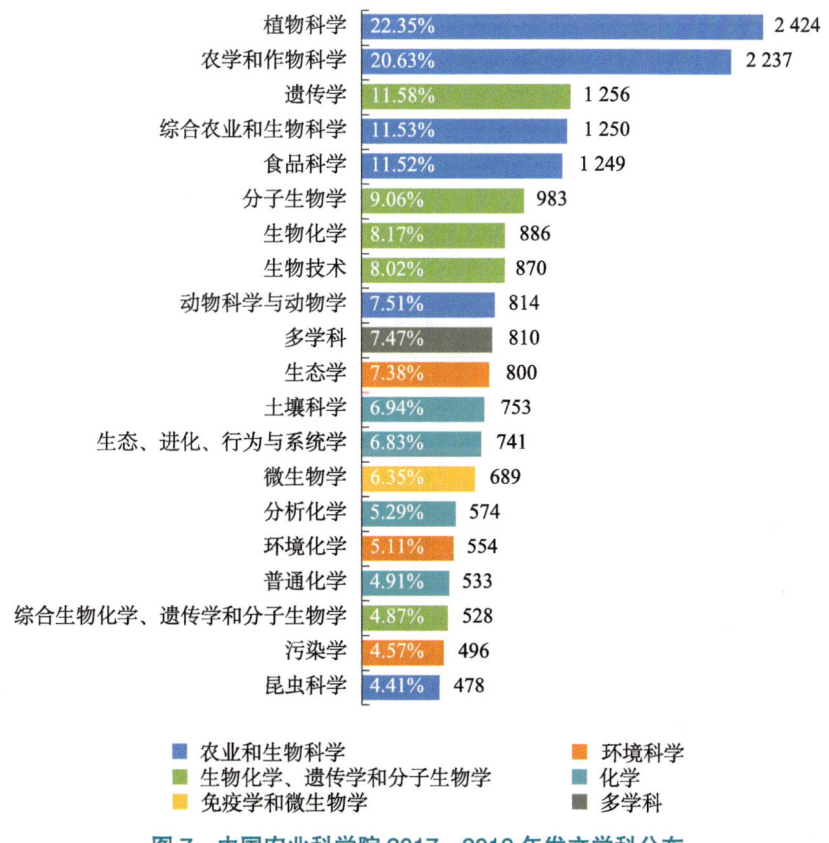

图 7　中国农业科学院 2017—2019 年发文学科分布

表 2　中国农业科学院 2017—2019 年发文学科分布

学科名称	发文量	占比 (%)
植物科学 Plant Science	2 424	22.35
农学和作物科学 Agronomy and Crop Science	2 237	20.63
遗传学 Genetics	1 256	11.58
综合农业和生物科学 General Agricultural and Biological Sciences	1 250	11.53
食品科学 Food Science	1 249	11.52
分子生物学 Molecular Biology	983	9.06
生物化学 Biochemistry	886	8.17
生物技术 Biotechnology	870	8.02
动物科学与动物学 Animal Science and Zoology	814	7.51
多学科 Multidisciplinary	810	7.47
生态学 Ecology	800	7.38
土壤科学 Soil Science	753	6.94
生态、进化、行为与系统学 Ecology, Evolution, Behavior and Systematics	741	6.83
微生物学 Microbiology	689	6.35
分析化学 Analytical Chemistry	574	5.29
环境化学 Environmental Chemistry	554	5.11
普通化学 General Chemistry	533	4.91
综合生物化学、遗传学和分子生物学 General Biochemistry, Genetics and Molecular Biology	528	4.87
污染学 Pollution	496	4.57
昆虫科学 Insect Science	478	4.41

续表

学科名称	发文量	占比(%)
传染病学 Infectious Diseases	468	4.32
有机化学 Organic Chemistry	453	4.18
生理学 Physiology	448	4.13
健康、毒理学和突变 Health, Toxicology and Mutagenesis	444	4.09
病毒学 Virology	407	3.75
普通兽医学 General Veterinary	384	3.54
物理与理论化学 Physical and Theoretical Chemistry	333	3.07
机械工程 Mechanical Engineering	329	3.03
计算机科学应用 Computer Science Applications	324	2.99
环境工程 Environmental Engineering	323	2.98
食用动物 Food Animals	320	2.95
园艺学 Horticulture	310	2.86
应用微生物学与生物技术 Applied Microbiology and Biotechnology	303	2.79
细胞生物学 Cell Biology	299	2.76
光谱学 Spectroscopy	298	2.75
综合环境科学 General Environmental Science	269	2.48
管理监测与政策法规学 Management, Monitoring, Policy and Law	269	2.48
废物管理和处置 Wasle Managemenl and Dispusal	269	2.48
免疫学 Immunology	265	2.44
微生物学（医学）Microbiology (medical)	259	2.39
通用化学工程 General Chemical Engineering	254	2.34
寄生生物学 Parasitology	248	2.29

（三）需求数据库分析

数据库使用情况反映对各数据库最直接的需求，对 2019 年全院访问外文电子期刊全文数据库使用统计数据进行分析，发现用户获取外文期刊全文次数较多的数据库有 ScienceDirect、Nature 和 Springer，其中 ScienceDirect 的全文获取次数超过总量四成，占 44.82%，Nature 和 Springer 的全文获取次数占比为 10.57% 和 10.29%。其他数据库全文获取情况见图 8。

另一方面，从文献引用的角度，利用引文分析法分析了中国农业科学院用户引文来源数据库分布。分析发现，全院及各直属研究所 2017—2019 年发文引用外文期刊 8 991 种，将引用所需刊种与全院订阅的 27 种外文全文数据库期刊目录进行比对，发现来自 ScienceDirect、Springer、Wiley 数据库的引用最多，分别占全部引文量的 28.32%、9.50% 和 9.59%，说明中国农业科学院直属研究所总体对这三个数据库的需求较高。其他数据库引用需求参见图 9。

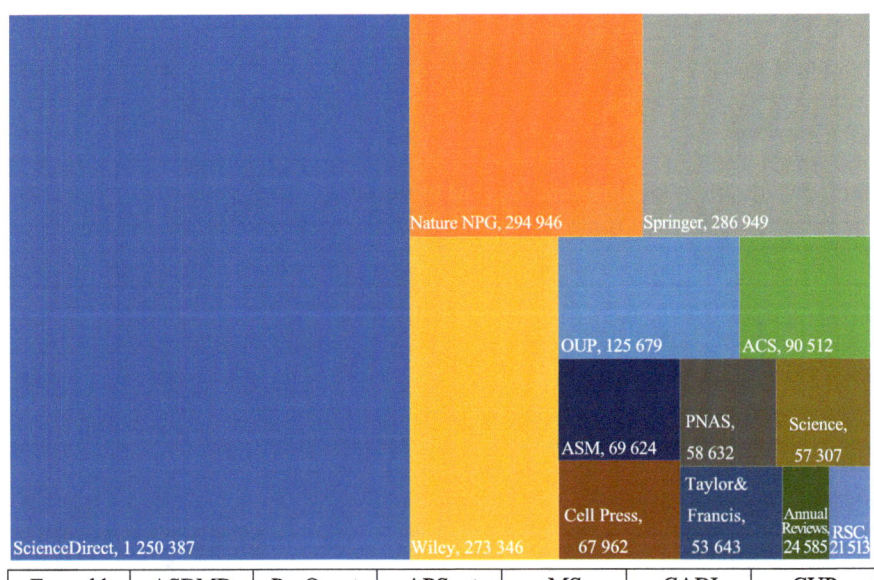

图 8　2019 年中国农业科学院获取外文期刊全文来源数据库分布

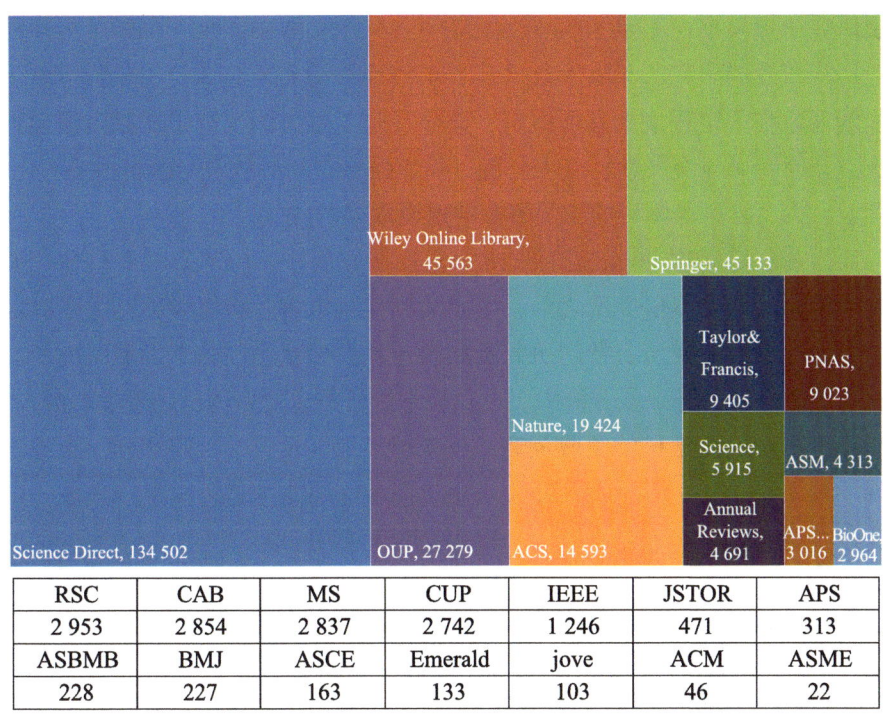

图9 中国农业科学院2017—2019年引文来源数据库分布

（四）文献保障水平

对全院以及各直属研究所外文电子期刊全文保障率进行计算，计算公式如下。

$$外文电子期刊全文保障率 = \frac{订阅外文电子期刊覆盖的引文数量}{需求外文期刊文献引文数量总和}$$

结果表明，全院总体引文保障率达91.03%，32个直属研究所中（表3）有22个单位的保障率在90%以上，保障情况较好的单位有作物科学研究所、水稻研究所、茶叶研究所和环境保护科研监测所等；北京畜牧兽医研究所等9个直属单位的保障率在80%～90%；仅南京农业机械化研究所的保障率低于80%。相较《中国农业科学院外文文献需求和保障分析报告（2018年版）》的分析结果，环境保护科研监测所、农田灌溉研究所、蜜蜂研究所、麻类研究所4个单位保障率由不足90%提升至90%以上，特产研究所和农业农村部食物与营养发展研究所保障率由不足 80% 分别提升至 84.27% 和 83.42%，保障较为薄弱的农业经济与发展研究所保障率也提升了 4.15 个百分点。各单位文献保障水平不平衡的现象在一定程度上有所缓解，充分反映了过去两年电子文献资源建设工作重点开展新兴与交叉学科需求分析，并加强与农业科学研究密切相关的化学、工程学、人文社科等学科的相关资源的建设取得的成效。

而当前保障率在 90% 以下的 10 个直属研究所中，除南京农业机械化研究所和农业经济与发展研究所之外，主要集中在从事畜牧兽医学科相关研究的研究所，以及饲料研究所、特产研究所和农业农村部食物与营养发展研究所。在针对这些研究所的进一步分析中，也发现它们所需求的资源已随着学科的发展，逐渐超出传统农业学科的领域范畴，越来越多地涉及医学、药理学、毒理学和药剂学等学科，针对这部分需求应当通过何种保障措施进行满足，也成为中国农业科学院电子文献资源建设中值得关注和研究的问题。

表 3　各直属研究所外文电子期刊全文保障率

研究所名称	需求刊种	保障率 (%)
作物科学研究所	1 916	93.81
植物保护研究所	2 774	91.09
蔬菜花卉研究所	1 536	92.33
农业环境与可持续发展研究所	2 025	90.35
北京畜牧兽医研究所	2 992	87.23
蜜蜂研究所	1 981	90.54
饲料研究所	1 737	86.87
农产品加工研究所	2 303	90.70
生物技术研究所	1 492	91.70
农业经济与发展研究所	557	84.44
农业资源与农业区划研究所	2 707	91.41
农业质量标准与检测技术研究所	1 556	92.52
农业农村部食物与营养发展研究所	777	83.42
农田灌溉研究所	723	91.83
水稻研究所	1 452	93.58
棉花研究所	1 427	92.85

续表

研究所名称	需求刊种	保障率 (%)
油料作物研究所	1 941	92.61
麻类研究所	1 492	90.12
果树研究所	695	91.42
郑州果树研究所	654	90.62
茶叶研究所	1 414	93.32
哈尔滨兽医研究所	1 636	86.07
兰州兽医研究所	2 028	84.41
兰州畜牧与兽药研究所	1 537	84.48
上海兽医研究所	1 481	85.59
草原研究所	1 136	91.21
特产研究所	1 770	84.27
环境保护科研监测所	1 362	93.50
沼气科学研究所	1 025	91.89
南京农业机械化研究所	643	67.85
烟草研究所	1 514	92.98
深圳农业基因组研究所	1 283	91.99

（五）综合利用水平评估

计算各直属研究所的文献综合利用指数以表示其文献综合利用水平，计算公式如下。

$$\text{文献综合利用指数} = \text{发文量} \times |R_{发文}|^{-1} + \text{引文量} \times |R_{引文}|^{-1} + \text{使用量} \times |R_{使用}|^{-1}$$

结果表明（表4、表5），作物科学研究所、农业资源与农业区划研究所、哈尔滨兽医研究所和北京畜牧兽医研究所的综合文献利用指数大于50，具有很强的文献利用能力，在各直属研究所中属于第一梯队。油料作物研究所、兰州兽医研究所、植物保护研究所、蔬菜花卉研究所、农产品加工研究所的文献综合利用指数在 40~50，对外文电子期刊文献的利用水平也较高，在各直属研究所中属于第二梯队。另外有半数的单位，即包括水稻研究所、棉花研究所、沼气科学研究所等在内的 16 家单位的外文文献综合利用指数在 10~40，处于中等水平。麻类研究所、南京农业机械化研究所等 7 家单位的外文文献综合利用指数在 10 以下，对外文文献的利用还有待提升。

表 4　各直属研究所外文文献综合利用水平

外文文献利用水平	直属单位
高（指数 >50）	作科所、资划所、哈兽研、牧医所
较高（指数 40~50）	油料所、兰兽研、植保所、蔬菜所、加工所
中（指数 10~40）	水稻所、棉花所、环发所、生物所、基因组所、质标所、茶叶所、环保所、饲料所、上兽研、烟草所、特产所、兰兽研、蜜蜂所、郑果所、沼科所
低（指数 <10）	麻类所、灌溉所、草原所、果树所、农经所、营养所、农机化所

表 5　各直属研究所外文文献综合利用指数

研究所名称	发文数	引文次数	下载次数	综合利用指数
作物科学研究所	872	39 688	256 008	96
植物保护研究所	1 202	44 588	92 876	44
蔬菜花卉研究所	382	16 158	120 763	44
农业环境与可持续发展研究所	450	18 413	85 705	34
北京畜牧兽医研究所	786	30 780	145 508	57
蜜蜂研究所	272	11 645	34 519	15
饲料研究所	277	10 806	57 407	22
农产品加工研究所	517	18 749	112 727	42
生物技术研究所	280	11 934	84 558	31
农业经济与发展研究所	51	1 545	8 693	3
农业资源与农业区划研究所	986	37 942	194 261	75
农业质量标准与检测技术研究所	289	11 054	71 726	27
农业农村部食物与营养发展研究所	48	1 827	5 957	2
农田灌溉研究所	84	3 378	22 002	8

续表

研究所名称	发文数	引文次数	下载次数	综合利用指数
水稻研究所	446	18 441	90 477	35
棉花研究所	351	17 827	90 373	35
油料作物研究所	399	18 811	132 857	49
麻类研究所	189	7 080	21 592	9
果树研究所	90	3 050	15 720	6
郑州果树研究所	128	4 808	40 599	15
茶叶研究所	281	10 790	67 542	25
哈尔滨兽医研究所	473	16 576	159 503	57
兰州兽医研究所	526	19 497	49 429	45
兰州畜牧与兽药研究所	160	5 229	42 486	15
上海兽医研究所	299	11 068	48 524	19
草原研究所	163	6 629	17 260	8
特产研究所	213	7 227	46 781	17
环境保护科研监测所	283	12 294	63 056	24
沼气科学研究所	157	6 270	26 840	11
南京农业机械化研究所	119	2 180	1 466	1
烟草研究所	265	10 716	47 001	19
深圳农业基因组研究所	173	8 596	79 736	29

四 各直属研究所需求和保障分析

（一）作物科学研究所

1. 需求学科分析

采集作物科学研究所（简称作科所）2017—2019年发表的外文期刊论文共计872篇，对其进行学科分析，可以看出该所发文主要集中在农业和生物科学（80.02%），生物化学、遗传学和分子生物学（51.79%）这两大学科（图10）。除此之外，也涉及化学、环境科学等学科。

对农业和生物科学，生物化学、遗传学和分子生物学两大学科的亚学科进行分析（图10），发现在农业和生物科学中，发文主要集中在植物科学（53.88%），农学和作物科学（40.26%），综合农业和生物科学（11.13%），土壤科学（5.27%），食品科学（2.78%），生态、进化、行为与系统学（2.58%）等亚学科中。生物化学、遗传学和分子生物学学科的发文主要集中在遗传学（21.67%），生物技术（18.99%），分子生物学（10.24%），生理学（7.55%），综合生物化学、遗传学和分子生物学（5.96%），生物化学（3.78%）和细胞生物学（2.39%）等亚学科。

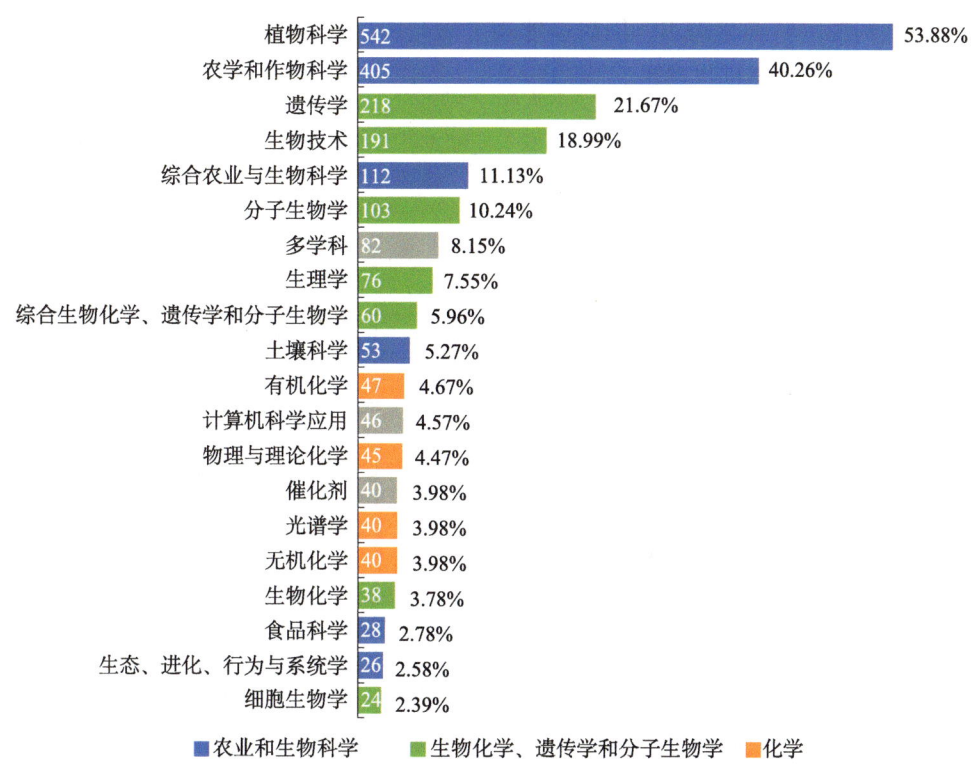

图 10　作物科学研究所 2017—2019 年发文学科分布

2. 发文和引文主题分析

将文献按照主题组织，进行更细粒度的需求分析，是为了解决单纯按照学科为单元进行分析，针对性不强，导致资源建设成本高、利用不充分的问题。2017—2019 年作物科学研究所发文共涉及 352 个主题，通过相应的遴选指标，遴选出发文、引文涉及的主要主题（表 6）。可以看出作科所在"Rice; *Oryza sativa*; Cultivated rice"这个主题的发文和引文最多，由此判断该研究所较为侧重这个领域的研究，在该领域文献的需求强度也最高；该所在"Corn; *Zea mays*; Physiological maturity"这个主题的发文占该主题全球同期论文的 33.33%，说明其在全球范围内对该领域的研究有较为突出的贡献；该所参与的最受关注、发展势头最好的主题为"Genome; Genes; Single guide"，主题显示度值为 99.987；而该所发文具有较高引文影响力的主题为"Brassinosteroids; Arabidopsis; BR biosynthesis"和"Genome; Genes; Single guide"，发文 FWCI 值是同类论文的 2.72 倍和 2.33 倍。综上，通过主题分析的结果不仅从各个角度反映出作科所学科文献资源的精细化需求，同时也体现了研究所研究领域的分布态势，能够为其学科规划和发展提供参考。

表6 作物科学研究所发文引文主要主题

主题	发文量	发文占主题同期论文比(%)	引文量	主题显示度	FWCI值
Rice; *Oryza sativa*; Cultivated rice	82	6.66	2 348	98.470	1.78
Genome; Genes; Single guide	33	0.52	1 209	99.987	2.33
Corn; Hybrids; Plant densities	31	5.06	594	94.926	1.02
Soybeans; Glycine max; Soybean breeding	30	7.50	838	92.258	1.08
Triticum; Wheat; Substitution line	25	11.42	524	90.002	1.20
Starch; Endosperm; Starch biosynthetic	14	3.11	432	94.777	2.13
Droughts; Transcription factors; Freezing tolerance	14	1.20	610	98.632	1.04
Wheat; Triticum; Adult plant	13	1.57	506	97.364	1.63
Rice; Drought; Lowland rice	12	2.04	275	95.657	1.96
Flowering; Rice; Long-day conditions	12	2.70	350	94.544	1.56
Corn; *Zea mays*; Spring maize	12	9.30	53	73.988	1.17
Micrornas; RNA; Degradome sequencing	11	0.53	580	99.589	1.55
RNA editing; Genome, Mitochondrial; Editing factors	11	2.08	455	96.083	1.45
Brassinosteroids; Arabidopsis; BR biosynthesis	11	1.42	483	97.909	2.72
Corn; *Zea mays*; Maize breeding	11	3.75	305	90.199	0.83
Paddy field; Nitrous oxide; Rice paddy	11	1.75	331	95.938	2.63
Corn; *Zea mays*; Physiological maturity	11	33.33	2	51.028	1.29
Fusarium; Scab diseases; DON content	10	1.18	170	97.277	1.75
Chloroplasts; Plastids; Chloroplast gene	10	5.05	254	90.641	1.05
Senescence; Transcription factors; Leaf senescence	10	1.58	251	96.753	0.64
Powdery mildew; Wheat; Single dominant	10	9.80	252	81.739	1.83
Setaria viridis; C4 photosynthesis; Millets	10	10.64	118	69.904	0.94
Salinity; Salt tolerance; Salt tolerant	9	0.51	351	98.949	1.31
Anthocyanins; Transcription factors; Anthocyanin biosynthetic	9	0.58	255	98.997	1.85
Phytochrome; Arabidopsis; Shade avoidance	9	1.40	347	98.457	1.76
Genomics; Breeding; Genomic predictions	9	0.60	425	99.072	0.64
Glutenins; Triticum; Glutenin subunit	8	1.41	140	93.688	1.59

续表

主题	发文量	发文占主题同期论文比 (%)	引文量	主题显示度	FWCI值
Rice; Temperature; Night temperature	8	2.90	142	89.540	1.25
Abscisic acid; Arabidopsis; Guard cells	7	0.80	408	98.300	0.58
Nitrates; Nitrogen; Nitrate transporters	7	1.35	185	97.199	1.18
Wheat; Triticum; Heading time	7	3.32	194	91.139	0.43
Transcription factors; Genes; Factors TFs	7	1.33	339	95.156	1.77
Triticum; Genome; Wheat genome	7	3.13	473	96.143	2.30
Soybeans; *Phytophthora sojae*; Rot PRR	7	11.11	157	70.519	0.97
Panicum; *Panicum miliaceum* subsp. *miliaceum*; Proso millet	7	18.42	22	53.327	1.27
Jasmonic acid; Oxylipins; Jasmonate signaling	6	0.90	321	98.285	2.52
Rice; Xanthomonas; Blight BB	6	2.33	208	90.299	1.51
Sprouting; Wheat; Sprouting PHS	6	4.38	228	81.880	0.93
Lodging; Lodging resistance; Corn	6	3.21	116	84.938	0.83

3. 需求期刊及保障情况

经引文分析得知作物科学研究所发文引用了 1 916 种外文期刊，与国家农业图书馆已订阅外文电子期刊品种进行比对，测算出其外文电子期刊全文保障率达到 93.81%，引文量前 40 的期刊见表 7。

表7 作物科学研究所引文量前40期刊

编号	期刊名称	引用数量	是否保障
1	Theoretical and Applied Genetics	2 056	是
2	Plant Physiology	1 856	是
3	Plant Cell	1 812	是
4	Plant Journal	1 545	是
5	Proceedings of the National Academy of Sciences of the United States of America	1 416	是
6	PLoS ONE	1 141	是
7	Crop Science	1 079	是

续表

编号	期刊名称	引用数量	是否保障
8	Journal of Experimental Botany	1 043	是
9	Science	898	是
10	Nature	844	是
11	Frontiers in Plant Science	745	是
12	Nature Genetics	698	是
13	Field Crops Research	651	是
14	Euphytica	624	是
15	Genetics	601	是
16	Molecular Breeding	572	是
17	Plant Molecular Biology	551	是
18	Plant Biotechnology Journal	535	是
19	Molecular Plant	512	是
20	Nucleic Acids Research	487	是
21	Bioinformatics	448	是
22	BMC Genomics	442	是
23	Journal of Physiology	431	是
24	BMC Plant Biology	427	是
25	Trends in Plant Science	421	是
26	Plant and Cell Physiology	415	是
27	Nature Biotechnology	391	是
28	Scientific Reports	369	是
29	Planta	348	是
30	Current Opinion in Plant Biology	327	是
31	Cell	312	是
32	Annual Review of Plant Biology	312	是
33	Nature Communications	299	是
34	Plant Science	294	是
35	Genome	261	是
36	PLoS Genetics	259	是
37	Plant Breeding	248	是
38	Journal of Biological Chemistry	244	是

续表

编号	期刊名称	引用数量	是否保障
39	Agronomy Journal	243	是
40	Journal of Integrative Plant Biology	239	是

4. 需求数据库分析

分析各直属研究所引用外文文献的来源数据库，从数据库层面把握各直属研究所需求，是外文全文数据库建设的重要依据，同时也为各直属研究所参与电子资源共建选择数据库提供参考。根据各直属研究所需求期刊分析结果，将其与国家农业图书馆订阅的 27 种外文全文数据库期刊目录进行比对，2017—2019 年作物科学研究所引文主要来源数据库如图 11 所示，其中来源于 ScienceDirect（24.51%）、Springer（23.55%）、Wiley（15.26%）和 OUP（10.98%）的引用最多。

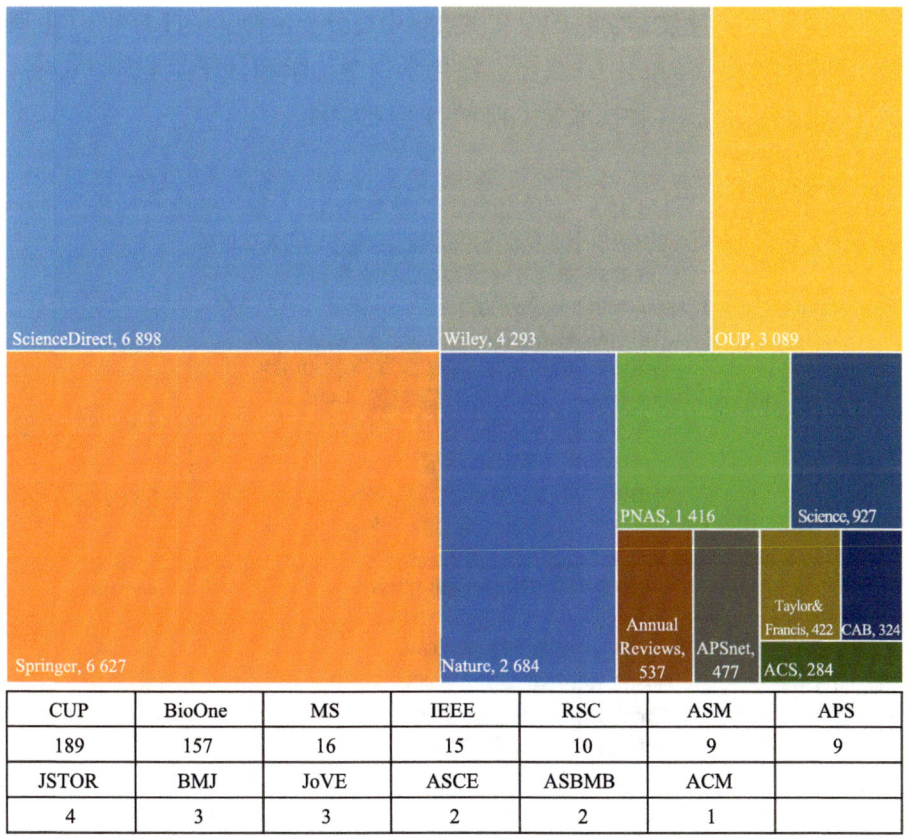

图 11 作物科学研究所引文来源数据库分布

（二）植物保护研究所

1. 需求学科分析

采集植物保护研究所（简称植保所）2017—2019 年发表的外文期刊论文共计 1 202 篇，对其进行学科分析，可以看出该所发文主要集中在农业和生物科学（56.91%），生物化学、遗传学和分子生物学（34.03%）这两大学科（图 12）。除此之外，在环境科学和免疫与微生物学也有一定数量的发文，说明植保所的研究在这些领域也有涉足。

对农业和生物科学，生物化学、遗传学和分子生物学两大学科的亚学科进行分析，结果如图 12 所示，在农业和生物科学中，发文主要集中在农学和作物科学（20.05%），昆虫科学（19.88%），植物科学（12.06%），生态、进化、行为与系统学（11.56%），综合农业和生物科学（8.40%）等亚学科中。生物化学、遗传学和分子生物学学科的发文主要集中在分子生物学（11.56%），生理学（6.82%），遗传学（6.66%），综合生物化学、遗传学和分子生物学（6.49%），生物化学（5.74%），生物技术学（4.58%）等亚学科。

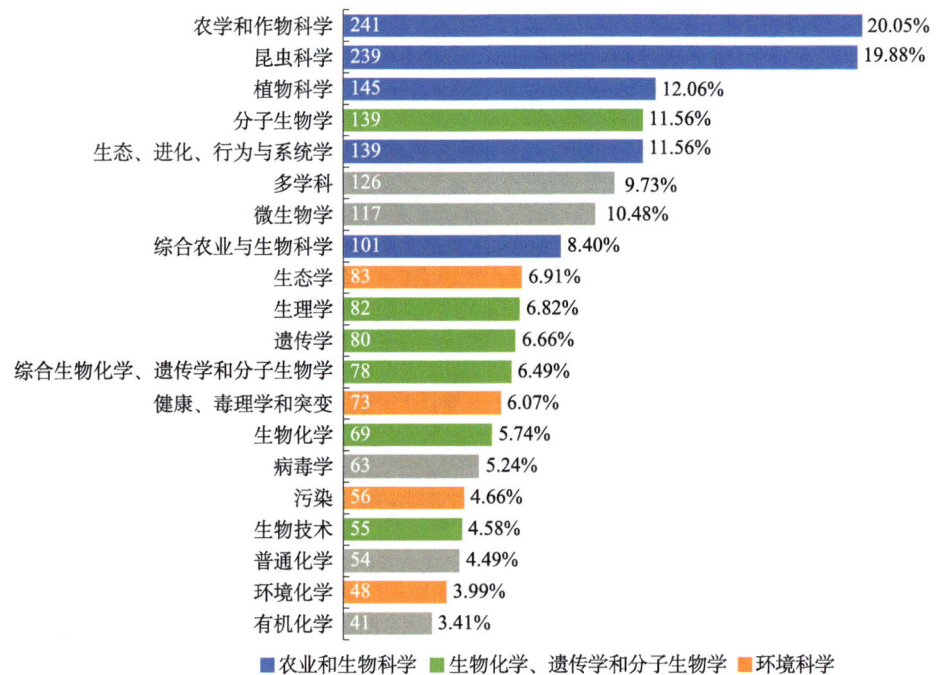

图 12　植物保护研究所 2017—2019 年发文学科分布

2. 发文和引文主题分析

将文献按照主题组织，进行更细粒度的需求分析，是为了解决单纯按照学科为单元进行分析，针对性不强，导致资源建设成本高、利用不充分的问题。2017—2019 年植物保护研究所发文共计涉及 399 个主题，通过相应的遴选指标，遴选出发文、引文涉及的主要主题（表 8）。可以看出植保所在 "Vitamin K 2; Bacterial typing techniques; Designated strain" 和 "Odor compounds; Carrier proteins; Chemosensory proteins" 这 2 个主题的发文最多，由此判断该研究所较为侧重这 2 个领域的研究，在 "Odor compounds; Carrier proteins; Chemosensory proteins" 主题的引文最多，表明在该领域文献的需求强度最高；该所在 "Fumigant; Fumigation; Soil fumigants" 这个主题的发文占该主题全球同期论文的 18.13%，说明其在全球范围内对该领域的研究有较为突出的贡献；该所参与的最受关注、发展势头最好的主题为 "Vitamin K 2; Bacterial typing techniques; Designated strain" 和 "Pesticides; Pesticide residues; Quick easy"，主题显示度值分别为 99.020 和 99.141；而该所发文具有较高引文影响力的主题为 "Bee; Pollinator; Wild bee"，发文 FWCI 值是同类论文的 10.35 倍。综上，通过主题分析的结果不仅从各个角度反映出植保所学科文献资源的精细化需求，同时也体现了研究所研究领域的分布态势，能够为其学科规划和发展提供参考。

表 8　植物保护研究所发文引文主要主题

主题	发文量	发文占主题同期论文比(%)	引文量	主题显示度	FWCI 值
Vitamin K 2; Bacterial typing techniques; Designated strain	55	2.27	853	99.020	0.74
Odor compounds; Carrier proteins; Chemosensory proteins	51	12.38	1 661	93.839	1.66
Bacillus thuringiensis; Proteins; Thuringiensis strain	38	6.71	1 135	94.640	0.91
Fumigant; Fumigation; Soil fumigants	29	18.13	539	81.694	0.79
Herbivores; Herbivory; Volatiles HIPVs	29	3.01	847	98.624	1.01
Bacillus thuringiensis; Genetically modified organisms; Non-target organisms	22	6.47	605	91.786	0.78
Bacillus thuringiensis; Noctuidae; Zea Boddie	20	4.30	957	94.565	1.50
Pesticides; Pesticide residues; Quick easy	20	1.48	301	99.141	0.85

续表

主题	发文量	发文占主题同期论文比 (%)	引文量	主题显示度	FWCI值
Planthopper; *Nilaparvata lugens*; Population dynamics	19	10.05	255	81.831	0.41
Begomovirus; Geminiviridae; Curl disease	19	2.41	620	95.420	1.04
Bemisia tabaci; Aleyrodidae; Tabaci biotype	18	4.65	611	90.621	1.72
Thysanoptera; Thripidae; Western flower	17	7.08	389	80.933	1.36
Heat tolerance; Temperature; Chill coma	17	2.80	429	97.389	0.87
Receptors, Odorant; Culicidae; Ionotropic receptors	15	2.85	683	96.217	1.33
Beauveria bassiana; Entomopathogenic fungi; Bassiana strain	15	1.69	230	96.500	0.75
Miridae; Hemiptera; Tarnished plant	14	14.58	283	66.959	0.63
Oryza sativa; Viruses; Black-streaked dwarf	14	7.29	283	82.326	1.48
Wolbachia; Symbionts; Cytoplasmic incompatibility	14	1.07	523	99.267	0.83
Bee; Pollinator; Wild bee	12	0.49	388	99.814	10.35
Viruses; Fungi; Blight fungus	11	2.52	210	94.027	0.92
Wheat; Triticum; Adult plant	11	1.33	184	97.364	0.69
Genome; Genes; Single guide	11	0.17	270	99.987	5.19
Enantiomers; Enantioselectivity; Chiral pesticides	10	3.25	205	93.364	1.36
Tylenchoidea; Nematoda; Cyst nematodes	10	2.65	236	94.738	1.25
Plant immunity; Kinases; Receptors PRRs	10	1.40	387	98.829	1.09
Chitinase; Chitin; Chitinase production	9	2.33	188	92.777	0.86
Phytoseiidae; Predatory mites; Californicus McGregor	9	2.16	148	90.225	1.06
Cyst nematodes; Grain crops; Cereal cyst	8	6.02	137	74.083	0.82
Pesticides; Herbicides; Encapsulation efficiency	8	4.06	127	90.863	1.89
Viruses; Apple stem grooving virus; Virus ACLSV	8	3.16	94	84.048	0.70
RNA Interference; RNA, Double-stranded; Insect pest	8	1.59	237	97.476	1.20
MicroRNAs; RNA; Degradome sequencing	8	0.38	291	99.589	1.64
Climate change; Carbon dioxide; Ambient CO_2	7	4.29	130	83.881	0.38

续表

主题	发文量	发文占主题同期论文比(%)	引文量	主题显示度	FWCI值
Viruses; Luteoviridae; Yellow dwarf	7	2.87	160	88.723	0.61
Insecticides; Receptors, Nicotinic; Neonicotinoid insecticide	7	1.70	201	95.564	1.60
Coccinellidae; Harmonia axyridis; Harlequin ladybird	7	1.60	241	90.366	1.58
Genes; Gene expression; Stable genes	7	0.67	482	96.751	0.76

3. 需求期刊及保障情况

经引文分析得知植物保护研究所发文引用了 2 774 种外文期刊，与国家农业图书馆已订阅外文电子期刊品种进行比对，测算出其外文电子期刊全文保障率达到 91.09%，引文量前 40 的期刊见表 9。

表 9　植物保护研究所引文量前 40 期刊

编号	期刊名称	引用数量	是否保障
1	PLoS ONE	1 641	是
2	Proceedings of the National Academy of Sciences of the United States of America	1 320	是
3	Annual Review of Entomology	803	是
4	Journal of Economic Entomology	778	是
5	Scientific Reports	759	是
6	Insect Biochemistry and Molecular Biology	759	是
7	Nature	748	是
8	Science	746	是
9	Pest Management Science	726	是
10	Journal of Insect Physiology	596	是
11	Applied and Environmental Microbiology	539	是
12	Environmental Entomology	538	是
13	International Journal of Systematic and Evolutionary Microbiology	516	是
14	Journal of Chemical Ecology	502	是

续表

编号	期刊名称	引用数量	是否保障
15	Journal of Agricultural and Food Chemistry	488	是
16	Journal of Biological Chemistry	488	是
17	Nucleic Acids Research	453	是
18	Plant Physiology	446	是
19	Biological Control	444	是
20	Plant Cell	435	是
21	Crop Protection	433	是
22	Plant Disease	419	是
23	Entomologia Experimentalis et Applicata	403	是
24	Molecular Plant-Microbe Interactions	389	是
25	Insect Molecular Biology	372	是
26	Molecular Biology and Evolution	362	是
27	Journal of Virology	361	是
28	BMC Genomics	339	是
29	Phytopathology	333	是
30	Bioinformatics	329	是
31	Plant Journal	300	是
32	Virology	282	是
33	Bulletin of Entomological Research	280	是
34	Pesticide Biochemistry and Physiology	277	是
35	Nature Biotechnology	270	是
36	Cell	267	是
37	Journal of Invertebrate Pathology	266	是
38	Journal of Bacteriology	264	是
39	Annual Review of Phytopathology	263	是
40	International Journal of Systematic Bacteriology	251	是

4. 需求数据库分析

分析各直属研究所引用外文文献的来源数据库，从数据库层面把握各直属

研究所需求，是外文全文数据库建设的重要依据，同时也为各直属研究所参与电子资源共建选择数据库提供参考。根据各直属研究所需求期刊分析结果，将其与国家农业图书馆订阅的 27 种外文全文数据库期刊目录进行比对，发现 2017—2019 年植物保护研究所引文主要来源数据库如图 13 所示，其中来源于 ScienceDirect（29.80%）、Wiley（18.08%）、Springer（13.58%）和 OUP（10.02%）的引用最多。

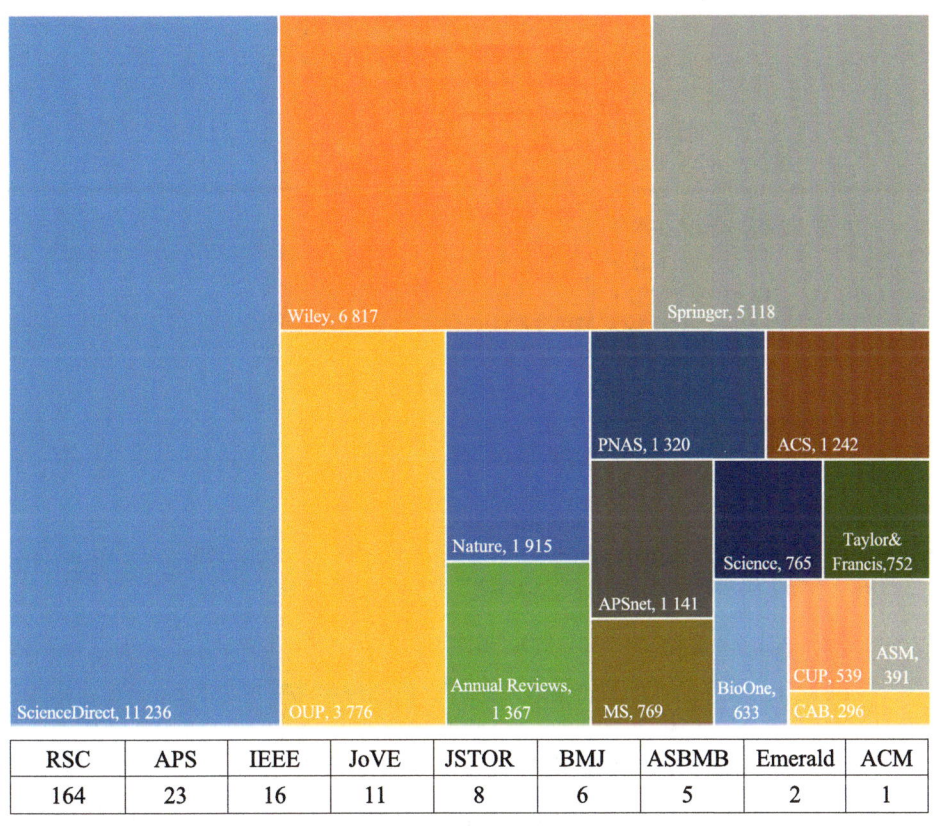

图 13　植物保护研究所引文来源数据库分布

（三）蔬菜花卉研究所

1. 需求学科分析

采集蔬菜花卉研究所（简称蔬菜所）2017—2019 年发表的外文期刊论文共

计382篇，对其进行学科分析，可以看出该所发文主要集中在农业和生物科学（68.61%），生物化学、遗传学和分子生物学（40.48%）这两大学科（图14）。除此之外，在化学、化学工程和环境科学也有一定数量的发文，说明蔬菜所的研究在这些领域也有涉足。

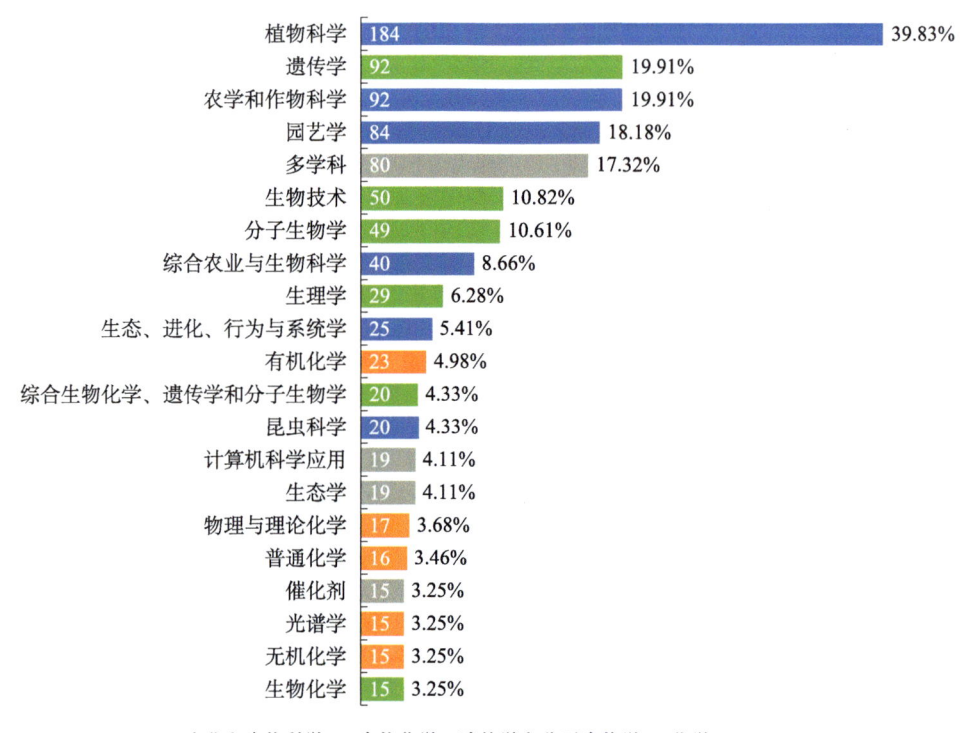

图14　蔬菜花卉研究所2017—2019年发文学科分布

对农业和生物科学，生物化学、遗传学和分子生物学两大学科的亚学科进行分析，结果如图14所示，在农业和生物科学中，发文主要集中在植物科学（39.83%），农学和作物科学（19.91%），园艺学（18.18%），综合农业和生物科学（8.66%），生态、进化、行为与系统学（5.41%），昆虫科学（4.33%）等亚学科中。生物化学、遗传学和分子生物学学科的发文主要集中在遗传学（19.91%），生物技术（10.82%），分子生物学（10.61%），生理学（6.28%），综合生物化学、遗传学和分子生物学（4.33%），生物化学（3.25%）等亚学科。

2. 发文和引文主题分析

将文献按照主题组织，进行更细粒度的需求分析，是为了解决单纯按照学科为单元进行分析，针对性不强，导致资源建设成本高、利用不充分的问题。2017—2019年蔬菜花卉研究所发文共计涉及232个主题，通过相应的遴选指标，遴选出发文、引文涉及的主要主题（表10）。可以看出蔬菜所在"*Bemisia tabaci*; Aleyrodidae; Tabaci biotype"这个主题的发文和引文最多，由此判断该研究所较为侧重这一领域的研究，在该领域文献的需求强度也最高；该所在"*Brassica*; Agrobacterium; Hypocotyl explants"这个主题的发文占该主题全球同期论文的7.55%，说明其在全球范围内对该领域的研究有较为突出的贡献；该所参与的最受关注、发展势头最好的主题分别为"Solid Phase Extraction; Nanomagnetics; Extraction MSPE"和"MicroRNAs; RNA; Degradome sequencing"，主题显示度值分别为99.360和99.589；而该所发文具有较高引文影响力的主题为"Tomatoes; *Lycopersicon esculentum*; Tomato varieties"，发文FWCI值是同类论文的2.66倍。综上，通过主题分析的结果不仅从各个角度反映出蔬菜所学科文献资源的精细化需求，同时也体现了研究所研究领域的分布态势，能够为其学科规划和发展提供参考。

表10 蔬菜花卉研究所发文引文主要主题

主题	发文量	发文占主题同期论文比(%)	引文量	主题显示度	FWCI值
Bemisia tabaci; Aleyrodidae; Tabaci biotype	21	5.43	524	90.621	1.92
Brassica napus; *Brassica rapa*; Linkage map	16	3.76	311	94.999	1.96
Anthocyanins; Transcription factors; Anthocyanin biosynthetic	15	0.96	437	98.997	1.10
Melons; *Cucumis melo*; Melon Accessions	13	5.86	194	84.275	1.48
Solid Phase Extraction; Nanomagnetics; Extraction MSPE	10	1.13	114	99.360	1.52
Tomatoes; *Lycopersicon esculentum*; Tomato varieties	8	2.36	196	95.701	2.66
Micrornas; RNA; Degradome sequencing	8	0.38	235	99.589	0.30
Waxes; Epicuticular wax; Wax biosynthesis	7	1.33	196	95.627	0.68
Glucosinolates; Brassica; Glucosinolate biosynthesis	7	0.82	246	97.826	0.28
Genes; Gene expression; Stable genes	7	0.67	363	96.751	1.81
Paeonia; *Paeonia lactiflora*; Tree peony	6	4.29	30	59.845	1.02
Potatoes; *Solanum tuberosum*; Cultivated potato	6	2.52	99	87.619	2.34
Phytophthora infestans; Potatoes; Infestans isolates	5	1.71	66	85.640	1.01

续表

主题	发文量	发文占主题同期论文比 (%)	引文量	主题显示度	FWCI 值
Pollen; Anthers; Tapetal cells	5	1.25	125	94.342	0.84
Gibberellins; Plant growth regulators; Gibberellic acid	5	0.97	132	95.769	0.58
Brassinosteroids; Arabidopsis; BR Biosynthesis	5	0.64	214	97.909	0.92
Brassica; Agrobacterium; Hypocotyl explants	4	7.55	41	57.143	0.36
Brassica juncea; *Brassica napus*; Cytoplasmic male sterility	4	5.71	50	64.605	0.46
Fusarium oxysporum; Fusarium; Vascular wilt	4	1.95	69	84.794	1.29
Potyvirus; Mosaic viruses; Virus PPV	4	0.86	92	91.703	0.32
Fungicides; *Botrytis cinerea*; Cinerea isolates	4	0.76	33	93.275	0.87
Polyploidy; Allopolyploidy; Diploid progenitors	4	0.66	132	97.489	0.70
Flowers; Genes; Organ identity	4	0.53	113	96.989	0.96
Lipopeptides; Bacillus; Amyloliquefaciens strain	4	0.52	22	97.454	0.61
Indoleacetic acids; Auxins; Auxin efflux	4	0.41	46	98.907	0.45
Herbivores; Herbivory; Volatiles HIPVs	4	0.41	178	98.624	1.67
Starch; Amylose; Digestible starch	4	0.17	68	99.536	0.45
Genome; Genes; Single guide	4	0.06	174	99.987	2.18
Rootstocks; Scions; Graft incompatibility	3	3.57	33	75.572	1.44
Cucumbers; *Cucumis sativus*; Female flower	3	3.53	69	73.587	1.26
Solanum tuberosa L.; Potatoes; Microirrigation	3	2.50	37	82.701	0.03
Gene silencing; Viruses; Rattle virus	3	2.07	39	78.052	0.70
Plasmodiophora brassicae; Plasmodiophorida; Clubroot resistance	3	1.72	117	80.049	0.54
Thanatephorus cucumeris; Rhizoctonia; Solani anastomosis	3	1.29	19	79.721	0
Gene duplication; Genome; Duplicate gene	3	1.13	142	93.301	2.53
Echinocandins; Candida; Echinocandin resistance	3	0.84	73	94.567	0.67
Arabidopsis; Histones; Imprinted genes	3	0.45	113	98.094	0.34
Droughts; Transcription factors; Freezing tolerance	3	0.26	111	98.632	0.97
Genome; Algorithms; Novo genome	3	0.15	137	99.448	1.92

3. 需求期刊及保障情况

经引文分析得知蔬菜花卉研究所发文引用了 1 536 种外文期刊，与国家农业图书馆已订阅外文电子期刊品种进行比对，测算出其外文电子期刊全文保障率达到 92.33%，引文量前 40 的期刊见表 11。

表 11　蔬菜花卉研究所引文量前 40 期刊

编号	期刊名称	引用数量	是否保障
1	Plant Physiology	575	是
2	Plant Cell	487	是
3	PLoS ONE	461	是
4	Proceedings of the National Academy of Sciences of the United States of America	450	是
5	Plant Journal	435	是
6	Theoretical and Applied Genetics	383	是
7	Journal of Experimental Botany	341	是
8	Nucleic Acids Research	325	是
9	Frontiers in Plant Science	296	是
10	Science	262	是
11	Bioinformatics	257	是
12	Nature	255	是
13	BMC Genomics	243	是
14	Scientific Reports	230	是
15	Nature Genetics	211	是
16	Journal of Physiology	167	是
17	Euphytica	164	是
18	Trends in Plant Science	158	是
19	Genetics	154	是
20	BMC Plant Biology	151	是
21	PCR Methods and Applications	149	是
22	Journal of Agricultural and Food Chemistry	149	是

续表

编号	期刊名称	引用数量	是否保障
23	Plant Disease	149	是
24	Molecular Biology and Evolution	140	是
25	Scientia Horticulturae	137	是
26	Genome Biology	131	是
27	Planta	129	是
28	Annual Review of Plant Biology	122	是
29	Plant Cell Reports	119	是
30	Nature Biotechnology	118	是
31	Molecular Breeding	117	是
32	Current Opinion in Plant Biology	117	是
33	Journal of Economic Entomology	113	是
34	Cell	111	是
35	Insect Biochemistry and Molecular Biology	110	是
36	Pest Management Science	110	是
37	Plant Molecular Biology	109	是
38	Food Chemistry	107	是
39	Nature Communications	100	是
40	Plant Science	99	是

4. 需求数据库分析

分析各直属研究所引用外文文献的来源数据库，从数据库层面把握各直属研究所需求，是外文全文数据库建设的重要依据，同时也为各直属研究所参与电子资源共建选择数据库提供参考。根据各直属研究所需求期刊分析结果，将其与国家农业图书馆订阅的27种外文全文数据库期刊目录进行比对，发现2017—2019年蔬菜花卉研究所引文主要来源数据库如图15所示，其中来源于ScienceDirect（28.45%）、Springer（17.51%）、Wiley（14.81%）和OUP（13.13%）的引用最多。

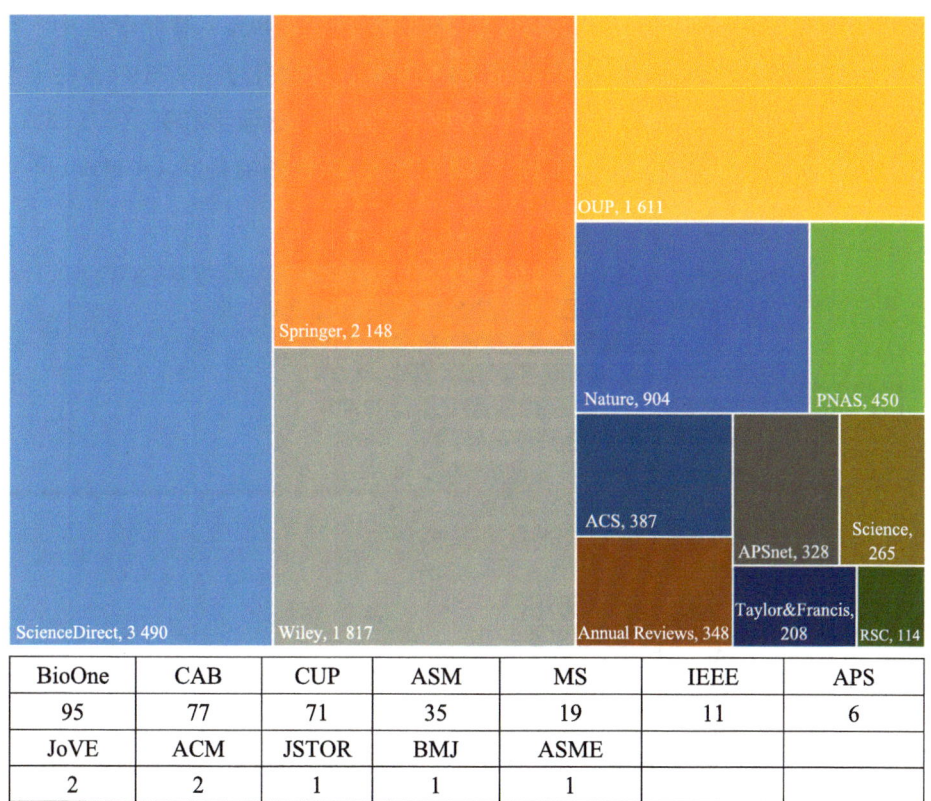

图15　蔬菜花卉研究所引文来源数据库分布

（四）农业环境与可持续发展研究所

1. 需求学科分析

采集农业环境与可持续发展研究所（简称环发所）2017—2019年发表的外文期刊论文共计450篇，对其进行学科分析，可以看出该所发文主要集中在农业和生物科学（62.79%），环境科学（38.62%）这两大学科（图16）。除此之外，在地球与行星科学，工程学，化学，生物化学、遗传学和分子生物学也有一定数量的发文，说明环发所的研究在这些领域也有涉足。

对农业和生物科学，环境科学两大学科的亚学科进行分析，结果如图16所示，在农业和生物科学中，发文主要集中在农学和作物科学（27.63%），土壤科学（17.11%），综合农业和生物科学（12.72%），生态、进化、行为与系统学（12.40%），植物科学（11.46%），林业科学（10.99%）等亚学科中。环境科学学科的发文主要集中在生态学（13.19%），环境化学（9.73%），污染学（7.22%），管理监测与政策法规学（5.97%），健康、毒理学和突变（5.65%），水科学与技术（5.02%），环境工程学（4.71%），综合环境科学（4.24%）等亚学科。

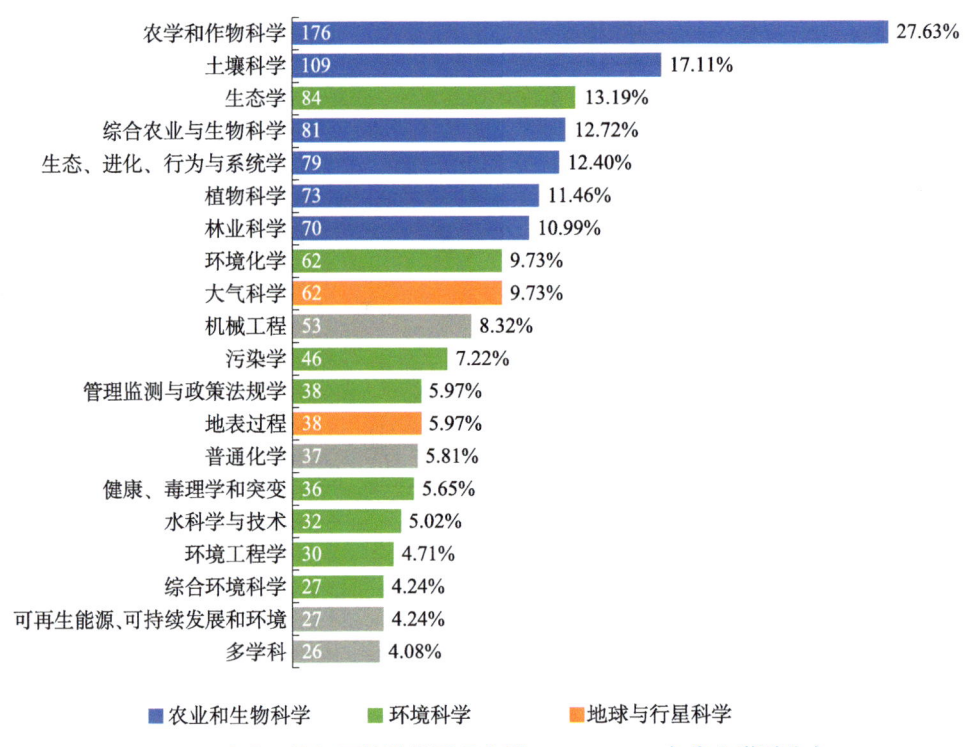

图 16　农业环境与可持续发展研究所 2017—2019 年发文学科分布

2. 发文和引文主题分析

将文献按照主题组织，进行更细粒度的需求分析，是为了解决单纯按照学科为单元进行分析，针对性不强，导致资源建设成本高、利用不充分的问题。2017—2019 年农业环境与可持续发展研究所发文共计涉及 286 个主题，通过相应的遴选指标，遴选出发文、引文涉及的主要主题（表 12）。可以看出环发所在 "Mulching; Plastic film; Residual plastic" 这个主题的发文最多，由此判断该研究所较为侧重这一领域的研究，在 "Soil organic carbon; Organic carbon; Soil aggregation" 主题的引文最多，表明在该领域文献的需求强度最高；该所在 "Carbon capture; Leakage; CO_2 leakage" 这个主题的发文占该主题全球同期论文的 7.41%，说明其在全球范围内对该领域的研究有较为突出的贡献；该所参与的最受关注、发展势头最好的主题为"Pyrolysis; Soil amendment; Biochar amendment"和"Soil organic carbon; Organic carbon; Soil aggregation"，主题显示度值分别为 99.968 和 99.574；而该所发文具有较高引文影响力的主题为"Diseases; Crops; Disease recognition"，发文 FWCI 值是同类论文的 5.796 倍。综上，通过主题分析的结果不仅从各个角度反映出环发所学科文献资源的精细化需求，同时也体现了研究所研究领域的分布态势，能够为其学科规划和发展提供参考。

表 12　农业环境与可持续发展研究所发文引文主要主题

主题	发文量	发文占主题同期论文比 (%)	引文量	主题显示度	FWCI 值
Mulching; Plastic film; Residual plastic	27	4.49	268	94.587	1.01
Pyrolysis; Soil amendment; Biochar amendment	23	0.42	235	99.968	1.05
Light; Lighting; Photosynthetic photon	19	2.04	175	96.626	1.59
Soil organic carbon; Organic carbon; Soil aggregation	17	0.70	428	99.574	1.80
Evapotranspiration; Penman-monteith equation; Evapotranspiration ET0	14	1.95	330	95.416	3.64
Soil respiration; Respiration; Heterotrophic respiration	12	1.29	181	96.825	1.23
Climate change; Crop; Crop models	12	0.49	227	99.758	3.26
Antibiotic resistance; Drug resistance, Microbial; Antibiotic-resistant bacteria	10	0.47	297	99.881	1.17
Nitrous oxide; Soil emission; Oxide emissions	9	0.63	269	99.321	1.14
Pesticides; Herbicides; Encapsulation efficiency	9	4.57	130	90.863	1.97
Composting; Compost; Thermophilic phase	8	0.54	156	99.479	0.53
Net primary production; Productivity; Annual NPP	8	1.20	109	96.869	0.53
Solar radiation; Solar energy; Daily global	7	0.34	214	99.679	2.62
Phosphorus; Organic phosphorus; Moderately labile	6	1.12	118	96.670	0.72
Soil; Microbial community; Soil fungal	6	0.43	109	99.229	1.01
Arsenic; Arsenites; Arsenate reductase	6	1.46	91	95.497	0.56

续表

主题	发文量	发文占主题同期论文比 (%)	引文量	主题显示度	FWCI 值
Soil organic carbon; Soil carbon; Crop yield	6	3.21	39	76.673	1.07
Alkalis; Seedlings; Alkaline stress	6	5.83	54	78.576	1.41
Anaerobic digestion; Biogas; Methane yields	5	0.14	73	99.935	1.01
Greenhouses; Humidity control; Greenhouse climate	5	0.60	57	95.731	0.53
Arsenic; Pollution control; Arsenic adsorption	5	0.34	79	99.494	0.68
Eddy covariance; Net ecosystem exchange; Carbon flux	5	0.56	152	98.486	1.01
Trend analysis; Rainfall; Slope estimator	5	0.44	123	97.803	0.70
Paddy field; Nitrous oxide; Rice paddy	5	0.79	159	95.938	2.57
Nanoparticles; Pharmaceutical preparations; Media milling	5	0.59	89	98.647	1.00
China; Corn; Accumulated temperature	5	2.55	37	76.899	0.12
Solar heating; Greenhouses; North wall	5	4.50	33	72.078	0.68
Phenology; NDVI; Vegetation phenology	4	0.19	142	99.441	0.75
Allelopathy; Weeds; Allelopathic effects	4	0.55	22	93.844	1.26
TRMM; Rain gages; Satellite-based precipitation	4	0.31	143	99.295	2.53
Antibiotics; Oxytetracycline; Veterinary antibiotics	4	0.18	140	99.816	2.07
Drought; Stream flow; Evapotranspiration index	4	0.21	89	99.361	0.95
Desalination; Solar heating; Slope solar	4	0.31	68	99.203	1.76
Hydrogels; Acrylics; Water absorbency	4	0.45	35	98.115	1.47
Stoichiometry; Phosphorus; Stoichiometric ratios	4	0.48	62	96.249	0.89
Irrigation; Deficit irrigation; Root-zone drying	4	1.33	102	90.822	2.16
Diseases; Crops; Disease recognition	4	0.55	14	93.475	5.76
Grassland; Headwater; Alpine meadows	4	2.26	49	83.274	1.72
Carbon capture; Leakage; CO_2 leakage	4	7.41	11	70.219	0.39

3. 需求期刊及保障情况

经引文分析得知农业环境与可持续发展研究所发文引用了 2 025 种外文期刊，与国家农业图书馆已订阅外文电子期刊品种进行比对，测算出其外文电子期刊全文保障率达到 90.35%，引文量前 40 的期刊见表 13。

表 13 农业环境与可持续发展研究所引文量前 40 期刊

编号	期刊名称	引用数量	是否保障
1	Agricultural Water Management	435	是
2	Soil Biology and Biochemistry	434	是
3	Global Change Biology	381	是
4	Environmental Science and Technology	332	是
5	Science of the Total Environment	302	是
6	Plant and Soil	281	是
7	Soil and Tillage Research	280	是
8	Agricultural and Forest Meteorology	270	是
9	Agriculture, Ecosystems and Environment	269	是
10	Nature	254	是
11	Proceedings of the National Academy of Sciences of the United States of America	252	是
12	Soil Science Society of America Journal	252	是
13	Journal of Experimental Botany	244	是
14	Bioresource Technology	238	是
15	Science	229	是
16	Journal of Hydrology	227	是
17	Field Crops Research	223	是
18	PLoS ONE	211	是
19	Plant Physiology	202	是
20	Geoderma	196	是
21	Chemosphere	189	是
22	Journal of Physiology	172	是

续表

编号	期刊名称	引用数量	是否保障
23	Environmental Pollution	156	是
24	Water Research	149	是
25	Applied and Environmental Microbiology	142	是
26	Journal of Hazardous Materials	137	是
27	Plant, Cell and Environment	126	是
28	Scientific Reports	124	是
29	Biology and Fertility of Soils	107	是
30	European Journal of Agronomy	106	是
31	Rangeland Journal	104	是
32	Journal of Geophysical Research	104	是
33	Frontiers in Plant Science	103	是
34	Applied Energy	101	是
35	Catena	100	是
36	Journal of Environmental Quality	100	是
37	Journal of Agricultural and Food Chemistry	96	是
38	Renewable and Sustainable Energy Reviews	95	是
39	Scientia Horticulturae	87	是
40	Chemical Engineering Journal	86	是

4. 需求数据库分析

分析各直属研究所引用外文文献的来源数据库，从数据库层面把握各直属研究所需求，是外文全文数据库建设的重要依据，同时也为各直属研究所参与电子资源共建选择数据库提供参考。根据各直属研究所需求期刊分析结果，将其与国家农业图书馆订阅的27种外文全文数据库期刊目录进行比对，发现2017—2019年农业环境与可持续发展研究所引文主要来源数据库如图17所示，其中来源于ScienceDirect（50.81%）、Wiley（14.61%）和Springer（12.62%）的引用最多。

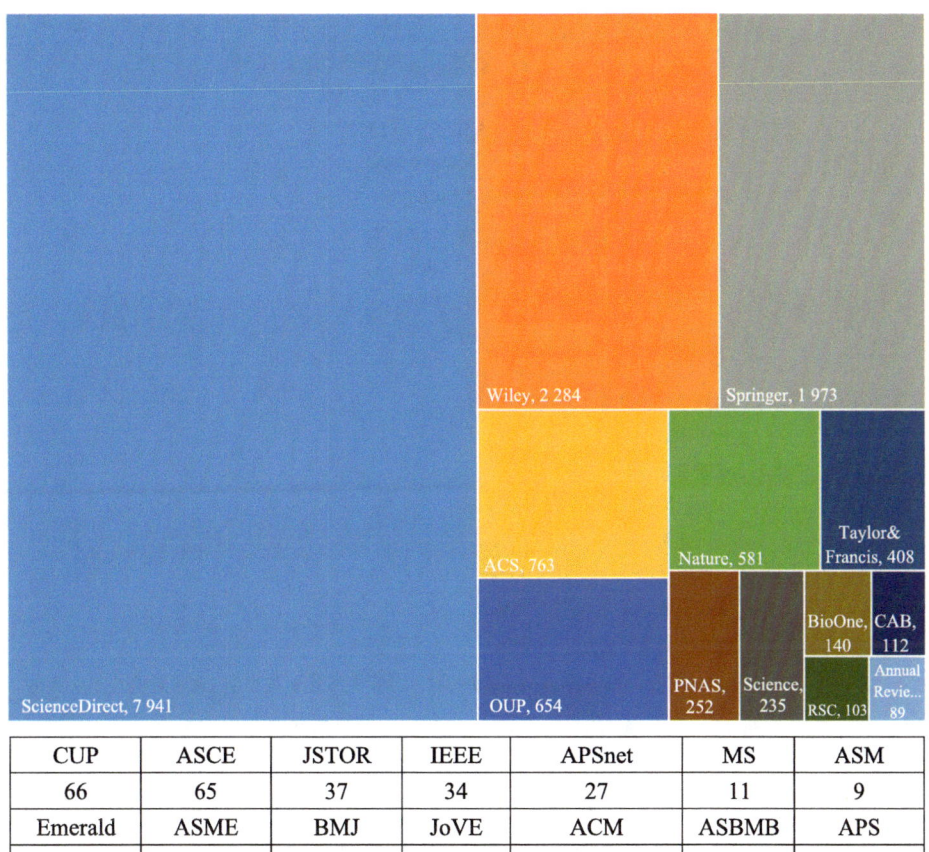

图17 农业环境与可持续发展研究所引文来源数据库分布

（五）北京畜牧兽医研究所

1. 需求学科分析

采集北京畜牧兽医研究所2017—2019年发表的外文期刊论文共计786篇，对其进行学科分析，可以看出该所发文主要集中在农业和生物科学（52.83%），生物化学、遗传学和分子生物学（41.62%），兽医学（10.98%）这三大学科（图18）。除此之外，在医学、化学、环境科学、免疫与微生物学也有一定数量的发文，说明北京畜牧兽医研究所的研究在这些领域也有涉足。

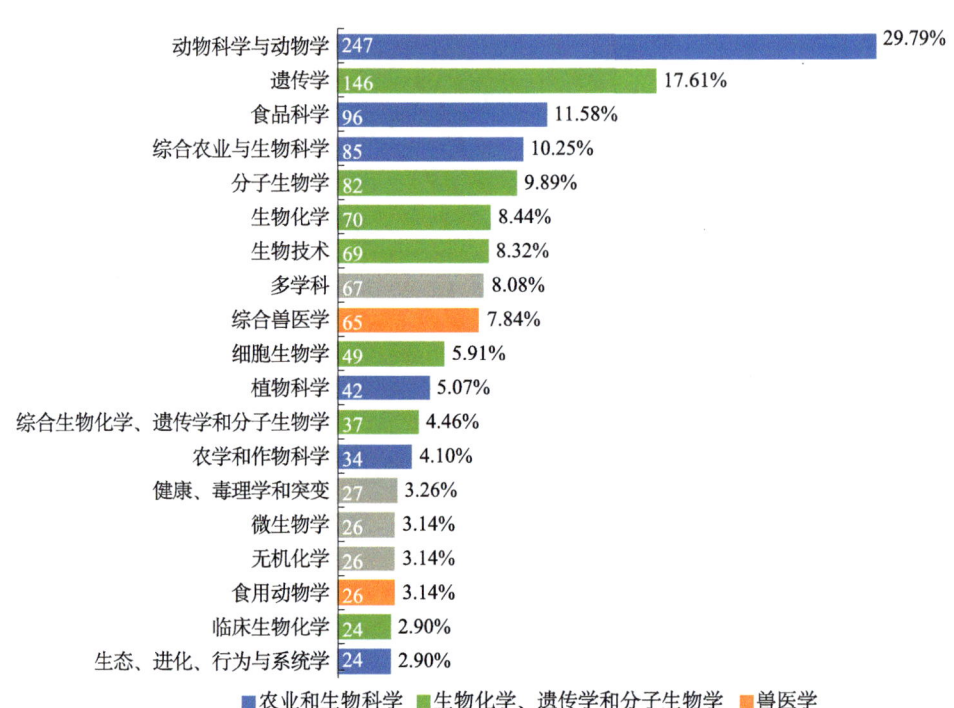

图 18　北京畜牧兽医研究所 2017—2019 年发文学科分布

对农业和生物科学，生物化学、遗传学和分子生物学和兽医学三大学科的亚学科进行分析，结果如图 18 所示，在农业和生物科学中，发文主要集中在动物科学与动物学（29.79%），食品科学（11.58%），综合农业和生物科学（10.25%），植物科学（5.07%），农学和作物科学（4.10%），生态、进化、行为与系统学（2.90%）等亚学科中。生物化学、遗传学和分子生物学学科的发文主要集中在遗传学（17.61%），分子生物学（9.89%），生物化学（8.44%），生物技术（8.32%），细胞生物学（5.91%），综合生物化学、遗传学和分子生物学（4.46%），临床生物化学（2.90%）等亚学科。兽医学学科的发文主要集中在综合兽医学（7.84%）和食用动物学（3.14%）等亚学科。

2. 发文和引文主题分析

将文献按照主题组织，进行更细粒度的需求分析，是为了解决单纯按照学科为单元进行分析，针对性不强，导致资源建设成本高、利用不充分的问题。2017—2019 年北京畜牧兽医研究所发文共计涉及 414 个主题，通过相应的遴选指标，遴选出发文、引文涉及的主要主题（表 14）。可以看出北京兽医研究所在"Zinc; Copper; Mg Zn/kg"这个主题的发文最多，由此判断该研究所较为侧重这一领域的研究，在"Genomics; Breeding; Genomic predictions"主题的引文最多，表明在该领域文献的需求强度最高；该所在"Fats; Swine; IMF content"这个主题的发文占该主题全球同期论文的 11.36%，说明其在全球范围内对该领域的研究有较为突出的贡献；该所参与的最受关注、发展势头最好的主题为"Genome; Genes; Single guide"和"Genomics; Breeding; Genomic predictions"，主题显示度值分别为 99.987 和 99.072；而该所发文具有较高引文影响力的主题为"Swine; Arginine; Weaned piglets"，发文 FWCI 值是同类论文的 5.53 倍。综上，通过主题分析的结果不仅从各个角度反映出北京畜牧兽医研究所学科文献资源的精细化需求，同时也体现了研究所研究领域的分布态势，能够为其学科规划和发展提供参考。

表14 北京畜牧兽医研究所发文引文主要主题

主题	发文量	发文占主题同期论文比(%)	引文量	主题显示度	FWCI值
Zinc; Copper; Mg Zn/Kg	18	4.81	300	89.157	0.78
Oocytes; Granulosa cells; Ovarian follicle	14	2.07	322	95.596	1.05
Heat stress; Hot temperature; Temperature-humidity index	13	1.27	292	96.366	2.00
RNA, Long untranslated; Neoplasms; Proliferation migration	13	0.10	300	99.984	1.11
Goats; Microsatellite repeats; Goat populations	12	4.29	240	82.907	0.70
Genomics; Breeding; Genomic predictions	12	0.80	449	99.072	0.99
Broiler chickens; Heat stress; Acute heat	11	2.21	136	89.743	1.44
Genome; Genes; Single guide	11	0.17	337	99.987	0.96
Micrornas; Adipocytes; Adipocyte differentiation	10	1.19	159	98.674	0.78
Metagenome; Obesity; Microbial composition	10	0.12	205	99.985	2.77
Broiler chickens; Lysine; Digestible lysine	9	3.20	173	82.344	1.21
Cattle; Cattle breeds; Cattle populations	9	2.80	194	86.404	1.39
Cattle; Polymorphism, Single nucleotide; Growth traits	8	5.71	150	81.278	0.91
Genome; Polymorphism, Single nucleotide; CNV Regions	8	1.83	213	91.704	0.88

续表

主题	发文量	发文占主题同期论文比 (%)	引文量	主题显示度	FWCI 值
Mycotoxins; Trichothecenes; DON exposure	8	1.30	111	97.690	2.29
Broiler chickens; Probiotics; Growth promoters	8	0.75	179	97.310	1.73
Clenbuterol; Food additives; Swine urine	7	2.05	92	95.281	0.70
Proteomics; Droughts; Protein spots	7	1.94	90	90.931	1.26
MicroRNAs; Muscle, Skeletal; Myogenic differentiation	7	1.62	149	94.784	0.33
Lactoferrin; Milk; Iron-binding glycoprotein	7	1.50	185	94.472	1.01
Chickens; Toll-Like receptors; Receptors TLRs	6	3.61	71	78.771	0.62
Sus scrofa; Swine; Pig domestication	6	3.09	169	77.791	1.09
Swine; Genome-Wide Association Study; Pig breeds	6	2.31	180	86.712	0.51
Oocytes; Blastocyst; Maturation IVM	6	1.94	123	88.981	2.67
Meat; Meat quality; Longissimus thoracis	6	1.20	44	94.648	0.14
6-Phytase; Phytases; Phytase production	6	0.91	149	94.892	3.11
RNA; MicroRNAs; Expression profile	6	0.23	112	99.861	2.20
Fats; Swine; IMF Content	5	11.36	39	54.955	0.67
Milk; Trace elements; Cow milk	5	3.18	62	84.057	0.90
Chickens; Genetic variation; Native chickens	5	2.91	31	68.829	0.54
Aflatoxin M1; Aflatoxins; UHT Milk	5	1.60	219	92.179	0.78
Efficiency; Cattle; Intake RFI	5	1.54	98	91.159	1.33
Swine; Arginine; Weaned piglets	5	1.03	65	92.417	5.53
Genome-Wide Association Study; Methods; Kernel association	5	0.67	114	96.955	0.73
Porcine respiratory and reproductive syndrome virus; Porcine reproductive and respiratory syndrome; Pathogenic porcine	5	0.62	138	96.354	0.60

3. 需求期刊及保障情况

经引文分析得知北京畜牧兽医研究所发文引用了 2 992 种外文期刊，与国家农业图书馆已订阅外文电子期刊品种进行比对，测算出其外文电子期刊全文保障率达到 87.23%，引文量前 40 的期刊见表 15。

表 15 北京畜牧兽医研究所引文量前 40 期刊

编号	期刊名称	引用数量	是否保障
1	Poultry Science	986	是
2	PLoS ONE	916	是
3	Journal of Dairy Science	801	是
4	Journal of Animal Science	740	是
5	Proceedings of the National Academy of Sciences of the United States of America	554	是
6	Nature	519	是
7	Scientific Reports	480	是
8	BMC Genomics	445	是
9	Science	435	是
10	Journal of Biological Chemistry	414	是
11	Cell	357	是
12	Nucleic Acids Research	356	是
13	Animal Genetics	332	是
14	Bioinformatics	316	是
15	Nature Genetics	278	是
16	Journal of Nutrition	267	是
17	Biology of Reproduction	223	是
18	Animal Feed Science and Technology	196	是
19	Journal of Pineal Research	194	是
20	Genetics	188	是
21	Meat Science	187	是
22	PLoS Genetics	186	是

续表

编号	期刊名称	引用数量	是否保障
23	PCR Methods and Applications	182	是
24	Molecular Biology and Evolution	176	是
25	Biochemical and Biophysical Research Communications	175	是
26	American Journal of Physiology	172	是
27	Genetics, Selection, Evolution	170	是
28	Nature Biotechnology	168	是
29	Journal of Agricultural and Food Chemistry	167	是
30	Food Control	166	是
31	Journal of Virology	164	是
32	British Poultry Science	158	是
33	Theriogenology	154	是
34	Genome Biology	153	是
35	Asian-Australasian Journal of Animal Sciences	145	是
36	American Journal of Human Genetics	142	是
37	Biological Trace Element Research	142	是
38	Food Chemistry	141	是
39	Fungal Diversity	140	是
40	British Journal of Nutrition	137	是

4. 需求数据库分析

分析各直属研究所引用外文文献的来源数据库，从数据库层面把握各直属研究所需求，是外文全文数据库建设的重要依据，同时也为各直属研究所参与电子资源共建选择数据库提供参考。根据各直属研究所需求期刊分析结果，将其与国家农业图书馆订阅的27种外文全文数据库期刊目录进行比对，发现2017—2019年北京畜牧兽医研究所引文主要来源数据库如图19所示，其中来源于ScienceDirect（41.11%）、OUP（13.76%）和Wiley（12.53%）的引用最多。

四　各直属研究所需求和保障分析　051

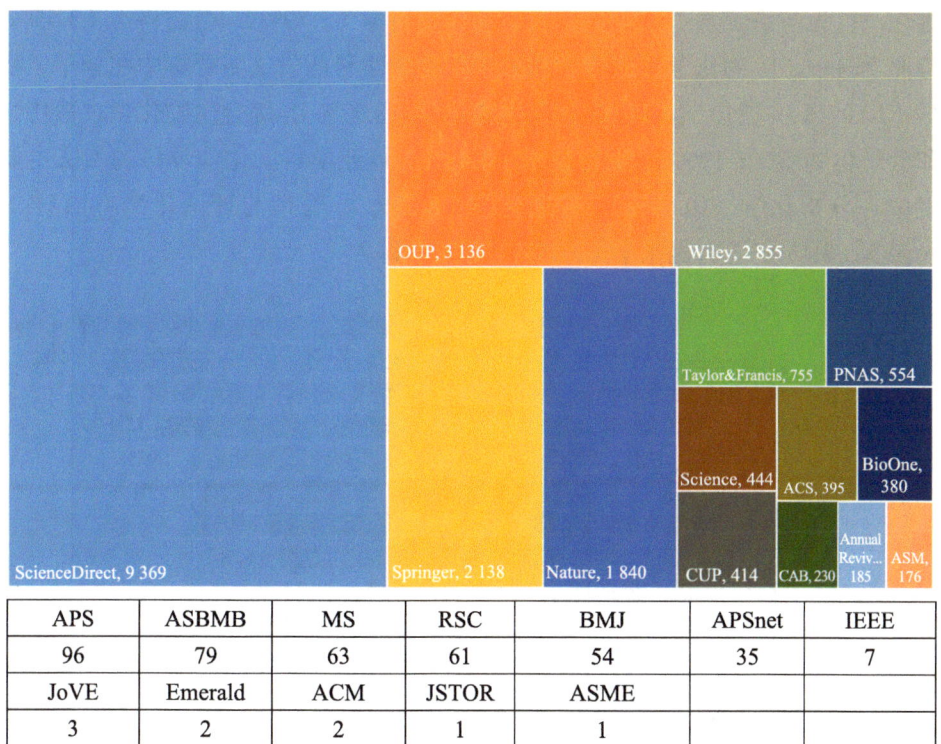

图 19　北京畜牧兽医研究所引文来源数据库分布

（六）蜜蜂研究所

1. 需求学科分析

采集蜜蜂研究所 2017—2019 年发表的外文期刊论文共计 272 篇，对其进行学科分析，可以看出该所发文主要集中在农业和生物科学（51.72%），生物化学、遗传学和分子生物学（33.45%），化学（24.14%）这三大学科（图20）。除此之外，在环境科学、医学、免疫与微生物学也有一定数量的发文，说明蜜蜂研究所的研究在这些领域也有涉足。

对农业和生物科学，生物化学、遗传学和分子生物学和化学三大学科的亚学科进行分析，结果如图 20 所示，在农业和生物科学中，发文主要集中在昆虫科学（14.14%），食品科学（13.45%），综合农业和生物科学（12.41%），生态、进化、行为与系统学（7.24%），农学和作物科学（3.79%），植物科学（3.45%）等亚学科中。生物化学、遗传学和分子生物学学科的发文主要集中在分子生物学（12.07%），遗传学（11.03%），生物化学（8.97%），综合生物化学、遗传学和分子生物学（5.17%），生物技术（4.48%）等亚学科。化学学科的发文主要集中在分析化学（10.69%），普通化学（8.62%），物理与理论化学（4.14%），光谱学（3.45%），有机化学（3.45%）等亚学科。

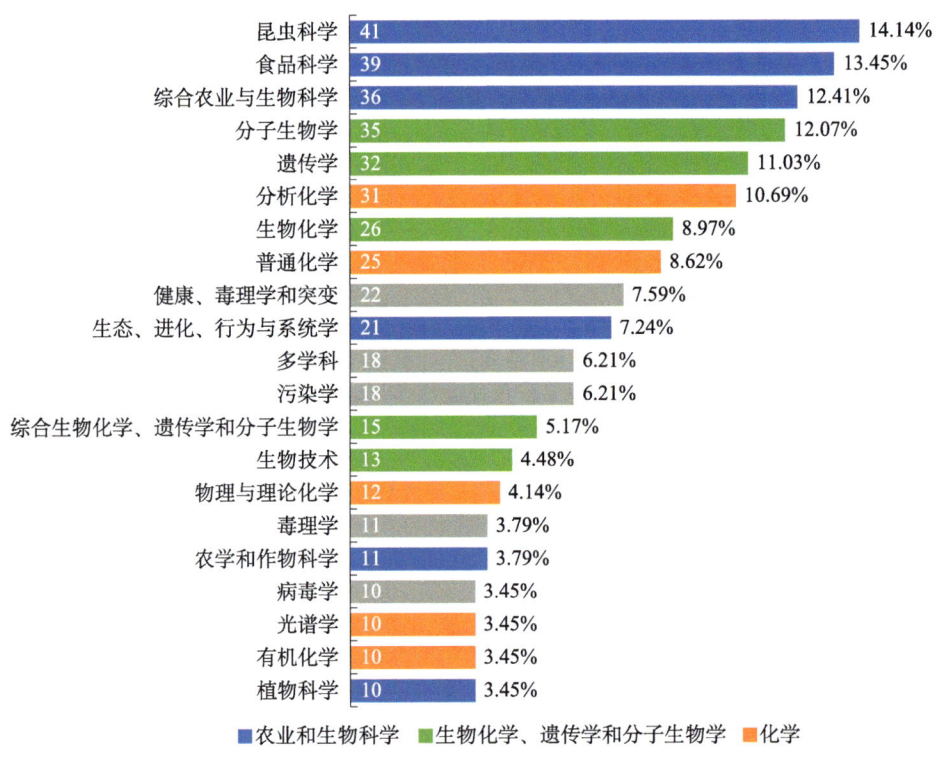

图 20 蜜蜂研究所 2017—2019 年发文学科分布

2. 发文和引文主题分析

将文献按照主题组织，进行更细粒度的需求分析，是为了解决单纯按照学科为单元进行分析，针对性不强，导致资源建设成本高、利用不充分的问题。2017—2019 年蜜蜂研究所发文共计涉及 150 个主题，通过相应的遴选指标，遴选出发文、引文涉及的主要主题（表16）。可以看出蜜蜂研究所在"Honey bees; Bees; Bee viruses"这个主题的发文最多，由此判断该研究所较为侧重这一领域的研究，在"Bee; Pollinator; Wild bee"主题的引文最多，表明在该领域文献的需求强度最高；该所在"Bees; Honey; Jelly RJ"这个主题的发文占该主题全球同期论文的 4.7%，说明其在全球范围内对该领域的研究有较为突出的贡献；该所参与的最受关注、发展势头最好的主题为"Bee; Pollinator; Wild bee"，主题显示度值为 99.814；而该所发文具有较高引文影响力的主题为"Electrocatalysts; Electrocatalysis; OER electrocatalysts"，发文 FWCI 值是同类论文的 7.4 倍。综上，通过主题分析的结果不仅从各个角度反映出蜜蜂研究所学科文献资源的精细化需求，同时也体现了研究所研究领域的分布态势，能够为其学科规划和发展提供参考。

表 16　蜜蜂研究所发文引文主要主题

主题	发文量	发文占主题同期论文比 (%)	引文量	主题显示度	FWCI 值
Honey bees; Bees; Bee viruses	21	3.09	533	96.897	1.01
Bee; Pollinator; Wild bee	17	0.69	547	99.814	2.26
Honey; Bees; Free acidity	16	1.53	316	99.092	1.50
Propolis; Bees; Green propolis	12	1.18	166	97.844	1.69
Royal Jelly; 10-hydroxy-2-decenoic acid; Hypopharyngeal glands	11	4.70	394	86.716	2.11
Drying; Solar dryers; Drying models	9	0.46	237	99.179	4.95
Bees; Honey; Bee gut	6	2.67	197	94.276	1.16
Bees; Apoidea; Bee bread	6	2.05	154	92.546	1.36
Varroa destructor; Apis mellifera; Varroa mite	5	1.27	126	90.628	0.56
Honey bees; *Apis mellifera; Mellifera mellifera*	4	1.61	86	83.647	0.44
Labor; Honey bees; Queen pheromones	4	1.56	176	86.983	1.41
Cytochrome P-450; Insecticide resistance; Detoxification enzymes	4	1.31	72	91.238	1.22
Drosophila; Peptidoglycan; Recognition proteins	4	0.73	106	96.270	0.51
Mycotoxins; Trichothecenes; DON exposure	4	0.65	119	97.690	1.61
Mycotoxins; Zearalenone; Deoxynivalenol DON	4	0.37	118	99.414	0.43

续表

主题	发文量	发文占主题同期论文比 (%)	引文量	主题显示度	FWCI 值
Genome, Mitochondrial; RNA, Transfer; T-rich region	4	0.26	57	93.662	0.47
Bombus; Apidae; Bumblebee species	3	4.11	51	71.581	0.14
Bombus; *Bombus terrestris*; *Crithidia bombi*	3	2.01	81	80.187	0.72
Bacillus thuringiensis; Genetically modified organisms; Non-target organisms	3	0.88	89	91.786	0.31
Logic gates; DNA; DNA Logic	3	0.76	68	97.770	1.48
Vitellogenins; Egg proteins; Fat body	2	2.33	30	69.492	0.24
Stilbenes; Dipterocarpaceae; Cell lines	2	1.01	15	84.307	0.97
Bees; Honey bees; Proboscis extension	2	0.67	66	87.275	1.48
Carbohydrate; Dietary carbohydrate; Dietary carbohydrates	2	0.67	5	91.478	1.68
DNA methylation; Bees; Social insect	2	0.66	90	93.409	1.29
Enantiomers; Enantioselectivity; Chiral pesticides	2	0.65	56	93.364	1.62
Odor compounds; Carrier proteins; Chemosensory proteins	2	0.49	83	93.839	0.34
Insecticides; Receptors, Nicotinic; Neonicotinoid insecticide	2	0.49	50	95.564	2.57
Gamma-Aminobutyric Acid; Glutamate decarboxylase; Lactobacillus brevis	2	0.48	82	93.772	0.27
Wines; Wine; Wine aroma	2	0.34	47	96.983	1.19
Plant immunity; Kinases; Receptors PRRs	2	0.28	26	98.829	0.87
Micrornas; Genes; Target prediction	2	0.13	53	99.336	0.72
RNA; MicroRNAs; Expression profile	2	0.08	53	99.861	0.44
Climate change; Models; Models SDMs	2	0.06	43	99.834	1.62
Electrocatalysts; Electrocatalysis; OER electrocatalysts	2	0.04	57	99.999	7.40
RNA, Long untranslated; Neoplasms; Proliferation migration	2	0.02	58	99.984	0.96

3. 需求期刊及保障情况

经引文分析得知蜜蜂研究所发文引用了 1 981 种外文期刊，与国家农业图书馆已订阅外文电子期刊品种进行比对，测算出其外文电子期刊全文保障率达到 90.54%，引文量前 40 的期刊见表 17。

表 17 蜜蜂研究所引文量前 40 期刊

编号	期刊名称	引用数量	是否保障
1	PLoS ONE	396	是
2	Journal of Agricultural and Food Chemistry	331	是
3	Food Chemistry	310	是
4	Apidologie	257	是
5	Proceedings of the National Academy of Sciences of the United States of America	252	是
6	Science	221	是
7	Nature	161	是
8	Journal of Apicultural Research	150	是
9	Nucleic Acids Research	143	是
10	Journal of Invertebrate Pathology	135	是
11	Journal of Proteome Research	132	是
12	Scientific Reports	132	是
13	Bioinformatics	101	是
14	Journal of Biological Chemistry	99	是
15	Journal of Chromatography A	96	是
16	BMC Genomics	94	是
17	Drying Technology	89	是
18	Journal of Insect Physiology	87	是
19	Analytica Chimica Acta	84	是
20	Applied and Environmental Microbiology	77	是
21	Food and Chemical Toxicology	74	是

续表

编号	期刊名称	引用数量	是否保障
22	Insect Biochemistry and Molecular Biology	74	是
23	Cell	73	是
24	Analytical Chemistry	70	是
25	Analytical and Bioanalytical Chemistry	69	是
26	Molecular Biology and Evolution	69	是
27	Insect Molecular Biology	68	是
28	Annual Review of Entomology	67	是
29	Aquatic Toxicology	65	是
30	Pest Management Science	61	是
31	Journal of Economic Entomology	59	是
32	Ecotoxicology and Environmental Safety	59	是
33	Chemosphere	58	是
34	Genome Biology	57	是
35	Environmental Pollution	53	是
36	Journal of Food Engineering	52	是
37	Journal of Experimental Biology	50	是
38	Environmental Science and Technology	50	是
39	Nature Communications	49	是
40	LWT - Food Science and Technology	49	是

4. 需求数据库分析

分析各直属研究所引用外文文献的来源数据库，从数据库层面把握各直属研究所需求，是外文全文数据库建设的重要依据，同时也为各直属研究所参与电子资源共建选择数据库提供参考。根据各直属研究所需求期刊分析结果，将其与国家农业图书馆订阅的27种外文全文数据库期刊目录进行比对，发现2017—2019年蜜蜂研究所引文主要来源数据库如图21所示，其中来源于ScienceDirect（39.26%）、Wiley（13.02%）和Springer（12.53%）的引用最多。

四　各直属研究所需求和保障分析

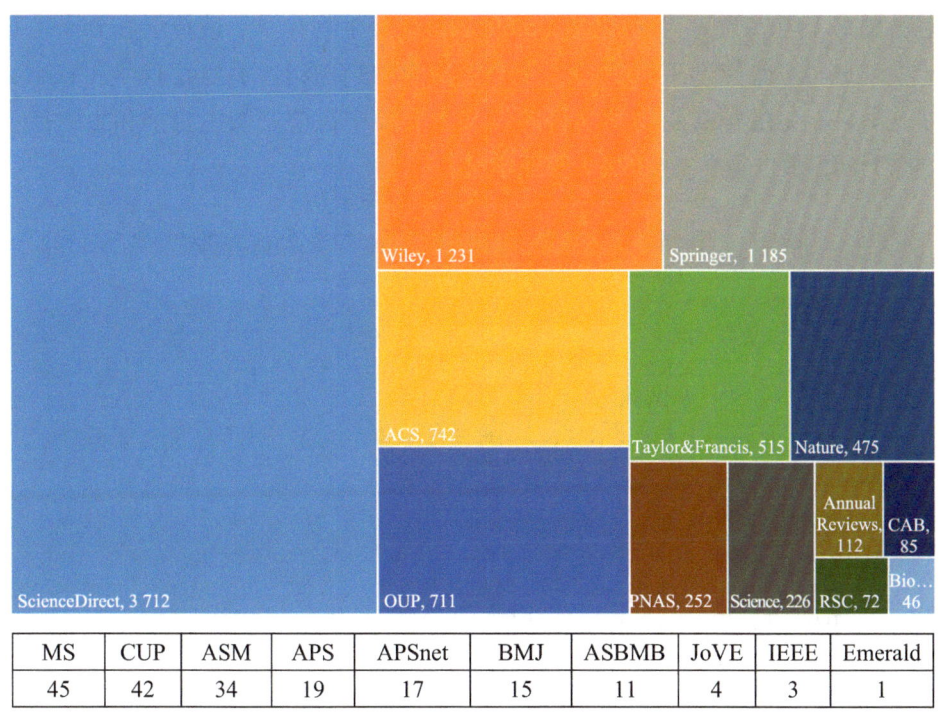

MS	CUP	ASM	APS	APSnet	BMJ	ASBMB	JoVE	IEEE	Emerald
45	42	34	19	17	15	11	4	3	1

图 21　蜜蜂研究所引文来源数据库分布

（七）饲料研究所

1. 需求学科分析

采集饲料研究所 2017—2019 年发表的外文期刊论文共计 277 篇，对其进行学科分析，可以看出该所发文主要集中在农业和生物科学（63.55%），生物化学、遗传学和分子生物学（30.43%），免疫与微生物学（16.72%）这三大学科（图 22）。除此之外，在环境科学、兽医学、医学、化学也有一定数量的发文，说明饲料研究所的研究在这些领域也有涉足。

对农业和生物科学，生物化学、遗传学和分子生物学和免疫与微生物学三大学科的亚学科进行分析，结果如图 22 所示，在农业和生物科学中，发文主要集中在动物科学与动物学（32.11%），食品科学（16.39%），综合农业和生物科学（11.71%），水产科学（8.70%），生态、进化、行为与系统学（3.34%）等亚学科中。生物化学、遗传学和分子生物学学科的发文主要集中在生物技术（10.70%），生物化学（5.69%），综合生物化学、遗传学和分子生物学（5.35%），遗传学（5.02%），分子生物学（3.68%），生物物理学（3.34%）等亚学科。免疫与微生物学学科的发文主要集中在应用微生物学和生物技术（11.71%），微生物学（4.35%）等亚学科。

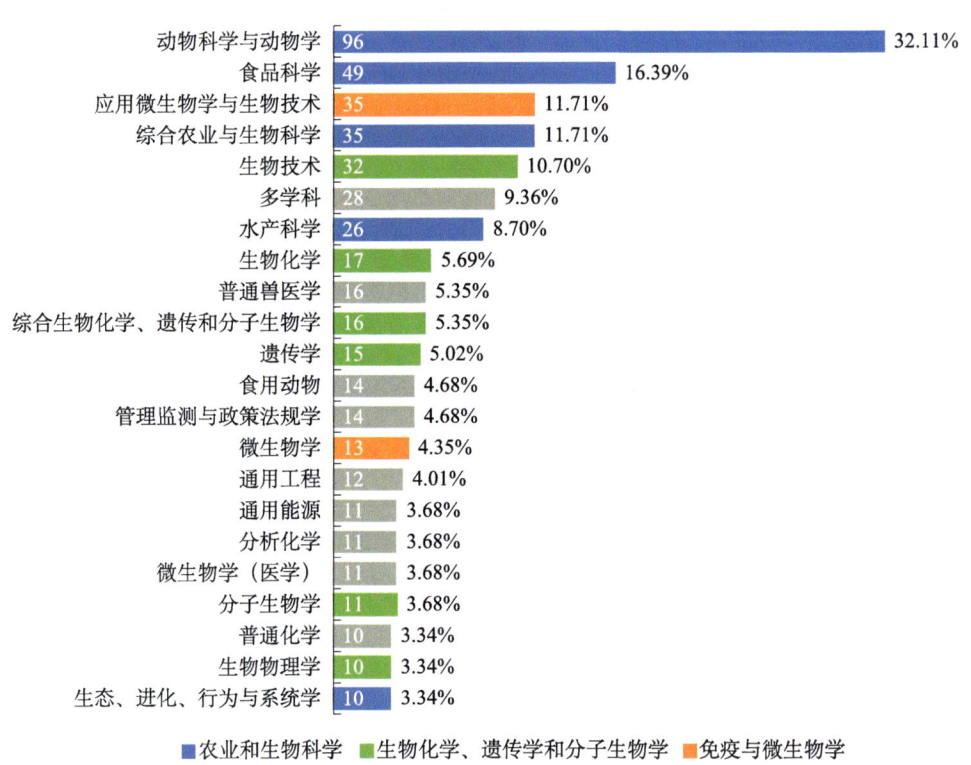

图22　饲料研究所2017—2019年发文学科分布

2. 发文和引文主题分析

将文献按照主题组织，进行更细粒度的需求分析，是为了解决单纯按照学科为单元进行分析，针对性不强，导致资源建设成本高、利用不充分的问题。2017—2019年饲料研究所发文共计涉及159个主题，通过相应的遴选指标，遴选出发文、引文涉及的主要主题（表18）。可以看出饲料研究所在"Calves; Dairies; Starter intake"这个主题的发文最多，由此判断该研究所较为侧重这一领域的研究，在"Probiotics; Digestive system; Immune parameters"主题的引文最多，表明在该领域文献的需求强度最高；该所在"Peptides; Pichia;

Methicillin-Resistant Staphylococcus aureus"这个主题的发文占该主题全球同期论文的 30.00%，说明其在全球范围内对该领域的研究有较为突出的贡献；该所参与的最受关注、发展势头最好的主题为"Probiotics; Digestive system; Immune parameters"，主题显示度值为 99.221；而该所发文具有较高引文影响力的主题为"Leptin; Receptors, Leptin; Leptin receptor"，发文 FWCI 值是同类论文的 2.78 倍。综上，通过主题分析的结果不仅从各个角度反映出饲料研究所学科文献资源的精细化需求，同时也体现了研究所研究领域的分布态势，能够为其学科规划和发展提供参考。

表 18 饲料研究所发文引文主要主题

主题	发文量	发文占主题同期论文比 (%)	引文量	主题显示度	FWCI 值
Calves; Dairies; Starter intake	14	3.20	207	90.803	0.52
Xylans; Endo-1,4-Beta Xylanases; Beechwood xylan	12	1.80	239	96.554	0.73
Saccharomyces cerevisiae; Rumen; Yeast culture	9	2.74	110	86.185	0.87
Probiotics; Digestive system; Immune parameters	8	0.51	525	99.221	2.53
Zinc; Copper; Mg Zn/Kg	7	1.87	131	89.157	0.52
6-Phytase; Phytases; Phytase production	7	1.06	172	94.892	0.84
Broiler chickens; Probiotics; Growth promoters	7	0.66	131	97.310	0.93
Fatty acid composition; Fish oils; Dietary lipid	7	0.53	211	97.857	0.83
Peptides; Pichia; Methicillin Resistant Staphylococcus aureus	6	30.00	126	51.832	0.68
Peptides; Antimicrobial cationic peptides; Potent antimicrobial	6	0.36	177	99.516	1.29
Egg quality; Laying hens; Hens fed	5	2.51	53	78.209	2.21
Broiler chickens; Lysine; Digestible lysine	5	1.78	96	82.344	1.65
Carbohydrate; Dietary carbohydrate; Dietary carbohydrates	5	1.68	76	91.478	0.33
Lignin; Peroxidases; Versatile peroxidase	5	1.44	90	95.400	0.80
Cellulase; Cellulose; Cellulose hydrolysis	5	1.19	130	95.184	0.91
Rumen; Metagenome; Rumen bacterial	5	0.90	164	97.609	0.56
Metagenome; Obesity; Microbial composition	5	0.06	172	99.985	1.67

续表

主题	发文量	发文占主题同期论文比(%)	引文量	主题显示度	FWCI值
Feedlots; Nellore; Metabolizable energy	4	2.12	46	69.413	0.61
Rumen fermentation; Methane production; Ruminal fermentation	4	1.18	70	86.443	2.22
Moringa oleifera; Moringa; Oleifera leaves	4	0.50	42	96.748	1.60
Nucleotides; Infant formula; Dietary nucleotides	3	2.97	35	79.343	2.15
Chickens; Egg shell; Eggshell membrane	3	1.61	55	84.133	1.66
Polygalacturonase; Pectins; Pectinase production	3	1.08	53	87.626	1.12
Clenbuterol; Food additives; Swine urine	3	0.88	31	95.281	0.37
Lactoferrin; Milk; Iron-binding glycoprotein	3	0.64	130	94.472	0.78
Cellulase; Trichoderma; Cellulase production	3	0.60	79	97.409	0.98
Mastitis; Milk; Dry cow	3	0.47	30	96.056	0.34
Methane; Methane production; Enteric methane	3	0.36	103	97.590	0.67
Acanthaceae; Apoptosis; S Crispus	2	12.50	3	42.000	0.16
Indoles; Mixed function oxygenases; Indole degradation	2	5.26	33	54.729	1.27
Endo-1,3(4)-Beta-Glucanase; Glucan 1,3-Beta-Glucosidase; Barley β-Glucan	2	2.38	53	73.398	0.45
Xylosidases; Xylans; Glycoside hydrolase	2	1.74	51	78.267	0.36
Leptin; Receptors, Leptin; Leptin receptor	2	1.24	61	85.759	2.78
Gossypol; Cottonseed oil; Free gossypol	2	1.23	21	76.240	0.83
Dairy cows; Methionine; Metabolizable protein	2	1.16	38	84.572	0.15
Broiler chickens; Light; Monochromatic light	2	1.14	16	76.180	1.56
Heifers; Calves; Holstein heifers	2	1.02	16	81.484	1.01

3. 需求期刊及保障情况

经引文分析得知饲料研究所发文引用了1 737种外文期刊，与国家农业图书馆已订阅外文电子期刊品种进行比对，测算出其外文电子期刊全文保障率达到 86.87%，引文量前 40 的期刊见表 19。

表 19　饲料研究所引文量前 40 期刊

编号	期刊名称	引用数量	是否保障
1	Journal of Dairy Science	455	是
2	Poultry Science	392	是
3	Journal of Animal Science	364	是
4	Aquaculture	310	是
5	Applied and Environmental Microbiology	276	是
6	Animal Feed Science and Technology	218	是
7	Applied Microbiology and Biotechnology	218	是
8	PLoS ONE	202	是
9	Journal of Biological Chemistry	167	是
10	Fish and Shellfish Immunology	148	是
11	Proceedings of the National Academy of Sciences of the United States of America	142	是
12	Antimicrobial Agents and Chemotherapy	132	是
13	Journal of Agricultural and Food Chemistry	123	是
14	Scientific Reports	113	是
15	Aquaculture Research	109	是
16	Journal of Nutrition	109	是
17	Food Chemistry	96	是
18	Nature	91	是
19	Bioresource Technology	88	是
20	Frontiers in Microbiology	86	是
21	British Poultry Science	85	是
22	British Journal of Nutrition	83	是
23	Livestock Science	83	是

续表

编号	期刊名称	引用数量	是否保障
24	Aquaculture Nutrition	82	是
25	Nucleic Acids Research	81	是
26	Asian-Australasian Journal of Animal Sciences	81	是
27	Small Ruminant Research	81	是
28	Journal of Applied Microbiology	71	是
29	Journal of Animal Physiology and Animal Nutrition	69	是
30	Science	69	是
31	Journal of the Science of Food and Agriculture	64	是
32	Biotechnology for Biofuels	60	是
33	Journal of Biotechnology	59	是
34	Meat Science	59	是
35	Biochemistry	57	是
36	Enzyme and Microbial Technology	56	是
37	American Journal of Physiology	53	是
38	Process Biochemistry	52	是
39	Biochemical and biophysical research communications	50	是
40	Biological Trace Element Research	49	是

4. 需求数据库分析

分析各直属研究所引用外文文献的来源数据库，从数据库层面把握各直属研究所需求，是外文全文数据库建设的重要依据，同时也为各直属研究所参与电子资源共建选择数据库提供参考。根据各直属研究所需求期刊分析结果，将其与国家农业图书馆订阅的27种外文全文数据库期刊目录进行比对，发现2017—2019年饲料研究所引文主要来源数据库如图23所示，其中来源于ScienceDirect（48.59%）、Wiley（12.62%）、Springer（11.11%）和OUP（10.57%）的引用最多。

四　各直属研究所需求和保障分析

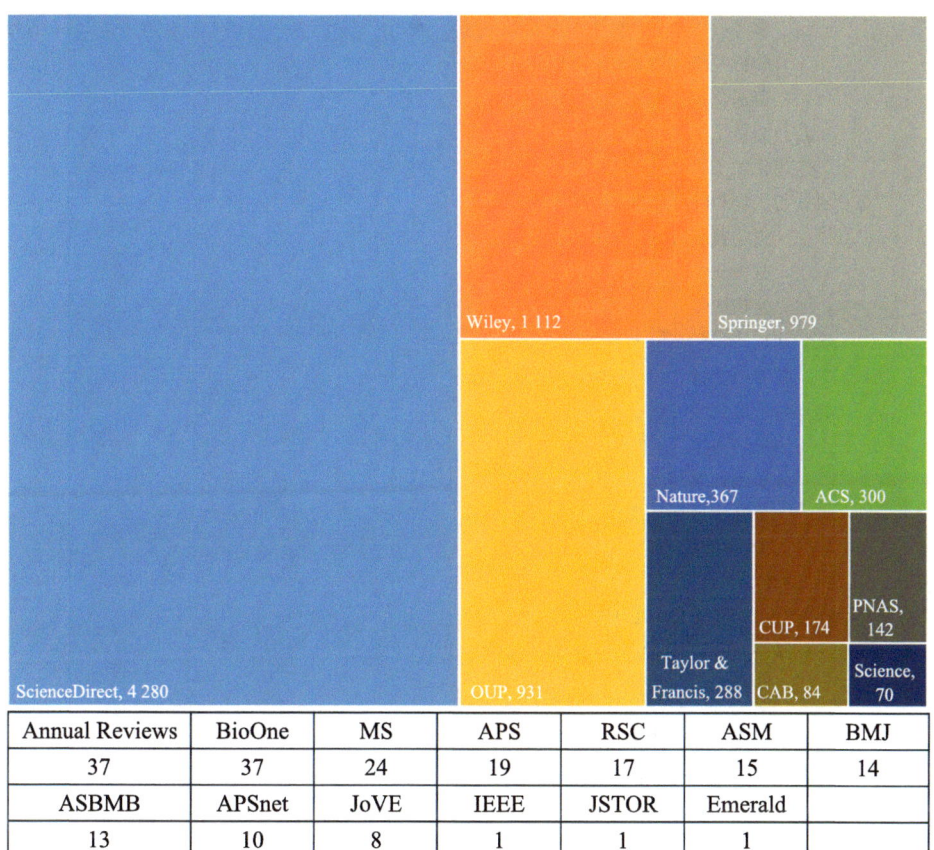

图23　饲料研究所引文来源数据库分布

（八）农产品加工研究所

1. 需求学科分析

采集农产品加工研究所（简称加工所）2017—2019年发表的外文期刊论文共计517篇，对其进行学科分析，可以看出该所发文主要集中在农业和生物科学（73.05%），化学（27.27%），生物化学、遗传学和分子生物学（19.78%）这三大学科（图24）。除此之外，在工程学，化学工程，药理学、毒理学和药剂学，免疫与微生物学也有一定数量的发文，说明加工所的研究在这些领域也有涉足。

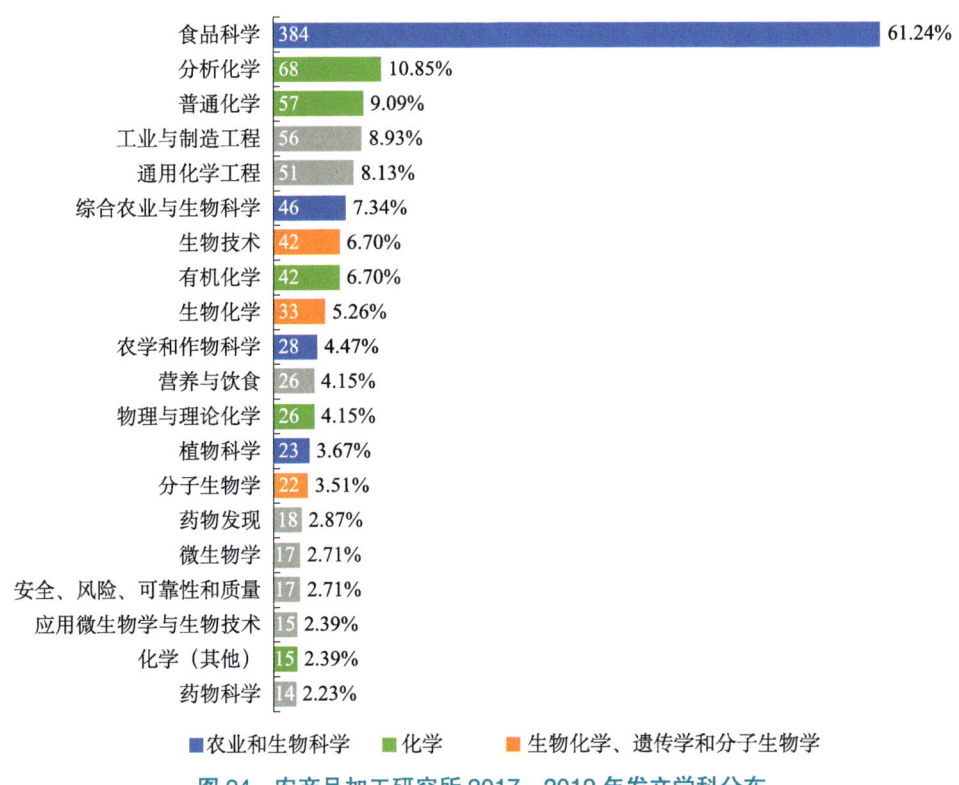

图 24　农产品加工研究所 2017—2019 年发文学科分布

对农业和生物科学，化学，生物化学、遗传学和分子生物学三大学科的亚学科进行分析，结果如图 24 所示，在农业和生物科学中，发文主要集中在食品科学（61.24%），综合农业和生物科学（7.34%），农学和作物科学（4.47%），植物科学（3.67%）等亚学科中。化学学科的发文主要集中在分析化学（10.85%），普通化学（9.09%），有机化学（6.70%），物理与理论化学（4.15%），化学（其他）（2.39%）等亚学科。生物化学、遗传学和分子生物学学科的发文主要集中在生物技术（6.70%），生物化学（5.26%），分子生物学（3.51%）等亚学科。

2. 发文和引文主题分析

将文献按照主题组织，进行更细粒度的需求分析，是为了解决单纯按照学科为单元进行分析，针对性不强，导致资源建设成本高、利用不充分的问题。2017—2019 年农产品加工研究所发文共计涉及 291 个主题，通过相应的遴选指标，遴选出发文、引文涉及的主要主题（表 20）。可以看出加工所在"Drying; Solar dryers; Drying models"这个主题的发文和引文最多，由此判断该研究所较为侧重这一领域的研究，在该领域文献的需求强度也最高；该所在"Dacarbazine; Explosions; Controlled pressure"这个主题的发文占该主题全球同期论文的 13.04%，说明其在全球范围内对该领域的研究有较为突出的贡献；该所参与的最受关注、发展势头最好的主题为"Drying; Solar dryers; Drying models"和"Pectins; Polysaccharides; Pectin yield"，主题显示度值分别为 99.024 和 99.179；而该所发文具有较高引文影响力的主题为"Verticillium; *Verticillium dahliae*; Dahliae isolates"和"Drying; Solar dryers; Drying models"，发文 FWCI 值是同类论文的 3.28 倍和 2.26 倍。综上，通过主题分析的结果不仅从各个角度反映出加工所学科文献资源的精细化需求，同时也体现了研究所研究领域的分布态势，能够为其学科规划和发展提供参考。

表 20 农产品加工研究所发文引文主要主题

主题	发文量	发文占主题同期论文比(%)	引文量	主题显示度	FWCI 值
Drying; Solar dryers; Drying models	26	1.33	513	99.179	2.01
Noodles; Pasta; Cooked noodles	25	4.24	218	93.754	0.67
Meat; Meat quality; Longissimus thoracis	22	4.39	377	94.648	1.09
Pectins; Polysaccharides; Pectin yield	12	1.51	193	99.024	2.26
Citrus; Flavonoids; Citrus fruits	12	1.40	206	97.463	1.37
Starch; Amylose; Digestible starch	10	0.42	374	99.536	2.02
Protein hydrolysates; Hydrolysates; Antioxidant peptides	9	0.68	159	98.583	1.06
Dehydration; Apples; Dehydration OD	9	1.88	151	94.573	0.63
Stable isotopes; Isotopes; Ratio mass	9	2.53	117	91.655	1.16
Metagenome; Obesity; Microbial composition	8	0.10	231	99.985	2.22
Extrusion; Snacks; Extruded snacks	8	1.30	140	95.485	0.56
Aspergillus flavus; Aflatoxins; Flavus strains	8	1.88	203	94.888	1.62
Soybean proteins; Soy protein; Isolate SPI	7	2.02	137	91.066	0.61
Gluten; Breads; Gluten-free breads	7	1.61	116	96.089	1.92
Oxidation; Pork; Carbonyl content	7	2.35	67	92.914	1.20
Glutenins; Triticum; Glutenin subunit	6	1.06	87	93.688	0.43
Peptides; Peptidyl-dipeptidase A; Inhibitory peptides	6	0.49	71	99.308	0.87

续表

主题	发文量	发文占主题同期论文比(%)	引文量	主题显示度	FWCI值
Verticillium; *Verticillium dahliae*; Dahliae isolates	6	1.84	228	93.518	3.28
Arabinoxylan; Dietary fiber; Arabinoxylan AX	6	1.92	95	93.671	0.47
Beef; Packaging; Retail display	6	2.76	126	89.565	0.66
Sourdough; Breads; Sourdough fermentation	6	1.38	69	95.618	0.88
Dacarbazine; Explosions; Controlled pressure	6	13.04	104	65.089	0.81
Breads; Bread; Frozen dough	5	1.44	107	91.94	0.33
Glass transition; Transition temperature; Water sorption	5	2.16	89	89.515	1.24
Emulsification; Emulsions; Lipid digestion	5	0.43	155	99.545	1.43
Gamma-aminobutyric acid; Glutamate decarboxylase; Lactobacillus Brevis	5	1.21	52	93.772	0.60
Ultrasonics; Sonication; Power ultrasound	5	0.61	85	98.887	0.57
Dietary fiber; Functional properties; Oil holding	5	1.14	112	93.126	1.36
High pressure treatment; Hydrostatic pressure; HHP treatment	5	6.58	86	85.121	0.84
Cooking; Meat; Cooking loss	5	3.50	62	77.873	0.77
Ginsenosides; Panax; Ginseng extract	4	0.25	45	98.544	1.99
Ochratoxins; Ochratoxin A; Fluorescence detection	4	0.66	203	97.927	1.13
AMP-activated protein kinases; Adenosine monophosphate; Monophosphate-activated protein	4	0.38	160	98.967	1.52
Aromatic amines; Amines; Amines HAAs	4	1.57	95	89.021	0.77
Beta-Glucans; Glucans; β-glucan content	4	0.93	74	94.743	0.76
Carotenoids; Vitamin A; Carotenoid bioaccessibility	4	0.98	78	96.760	1.29
Ipomoea batatas; Sweet potatoes; Potato leaves	4	2.40	90	83.213	1.30
Fungal proteins; Ganoderma; Fungal immunomodulatory	4	8.16	70	67.491	0.40

3. 需求期刊及保障情况

经引文分析得知农产品加工研究所发文引用了2 303种外文期刊，与国家农业图书馆已订阅外文电子期刊品种进行比对,测算出其外文电子期刊全文保障率达到 90.70%,引文量前 40 的期刊见表 21。

表 21 农产品加工研究所引文量前 40 期刊

编号	期刊名称	引用数量	是否保障
1	Food Chemistry	1 395	是
2	Journal of Agricultural and Food Chemistry	895	是
3	Journal of Food Engineering	580	是
4	Meat Science	501	是
5	Food Hydrocolloids	429	是
6	LWT - Food Science and Technology	426	是
7	Food Research International	388	是
8	Journal of Food Science	329	是
9	Carbohydrate Polymers	322	是
10	Drying Technology	253	是
11	Journal of Cereal Science	235	是
12	Journal of the Science of Food and Agriculture	230	是
13	Cereal Chemistry	214	是
14	International Journal of Food Science and Technology	211	是
15	Journal of Biological Chemistry	181	是
16	Food and Bioprocess Technology	170	是
17	Nature	167	是
18	International Journal of Food Microbiology	165	是
19	PLoS ONE	161	是
20	Innovative Food Science and Emerging Technologies	157	是
21	Food Control	150	是
22	Proceedings of the National Academy of Sciences of the United States of America	146	是
23	Postharvest Biology and Technology	135	是

续表

编号	期刊名称	引用数量	是否保障
24	Plant Cell	116	是
25	Trends in Food Science and Technology	115	是
26	Food and Chemical Toxicology	110	是
27	Journal of Dairy Science	109	是
28	Plant Physiology	109	是
29	Journal of Food Science and Technology	106	是
30	Journal of Functional Foods	105	是
31	Science	104	是
32	Applied and Environmental Microbiology	102	是
33	Critical Reviews in Food Science and Nutrition	100	是
34	Journal of Food Composition and Analysis	96	是
35	Journal of Animal Science	96	是
36	Molecular Nutrition and Food Research	92	是
37	Starch/Staerke	90	是
38	European Food Research and Technology	87	是
39	International Journal of Biological Macromolecules	77	是
40	Scientific Reports	76	是

4. 需求数据库分析

分析各直属研究所引用外文文献的来源数据库，从数据库层面把握各直属研究所需求，是外文全文数据库建设的重要依据，同时也为各直属研究所参与电子资源共建选择数据库提供参考。根据各直属研究所需求期刊分析结果，将其与国家农业图书馆订阅的27种外文全文数据库期刊目录进行比对，发现2017—2019年农产品加工研究所引文主要来源数据库如图25所示，其中来源于ScienceDirect（54.92%）、Wiley（14.13%）、ACS（7.77%）和Springer（7.49%）的引用最多。

四　各直属研究所需求和保障分析

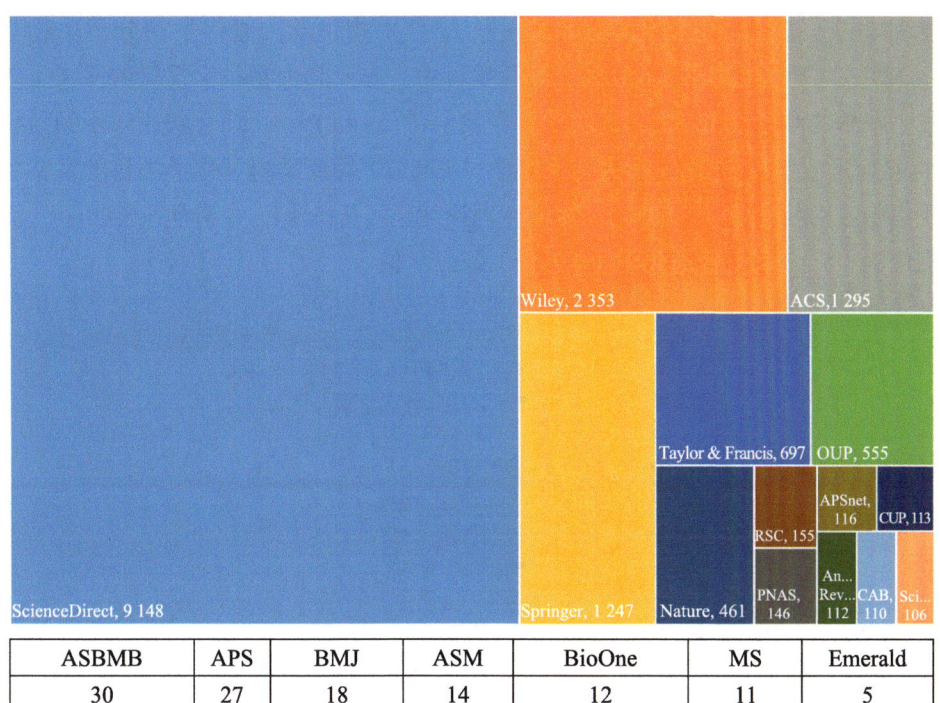

ASBMB	APS	BMJ	ASM	BioOne	MS	Emerald
30	27	18	14	12	11	5
IEEE	JoVE	ASME	ASCE			
4	4	2	1			

图 25　农产品加工研究所引文来源数据库分布

（九）生物技术研究所

1. 需求学科分析

采集生物技术研究所（简称生物所）2017—2019 年发表的外文期刊论文共计 280 篇，对其进行学科分析，可以看出该所发文主要集中在生物化学、遗传学和分子生物学（59.25%），农业和生物科学（53.42%），化学（15.41%）这三大学科（图 26）。除此之外，在免疫与微生物学、化学工程、医学、计算机科学也有一定数量的发文，说明生物所的研究在这些领域也有涉足。

对生物化学、遗传学和分子生物学，农业和生物科学，化学三大学科的亚学科进行分析，结果如图 26 所示，在生物化学、遗传学和分子生物学中，发文主要集中在遗传学（18.49%），分子生物学（17.12%），生物技术（9.93%），生理学（9.25%），生物化学（8.22%），综合生物化学、遗传学和分子生物学（8.22%），细胞生物学（6.16%）等亚学科中。农业和生物科学学科的发文主要集中在植物科学（32.53%），农学和作物科学（10.27%），综合农业和生物科学（9.93%），生态、进化、行为与系统学（5.48%）等亚学科。化学学科的发文主要集中在有机化学（7.53%），物理与理论化学（6.16%），光谱学（5.48%），无机化学（5.48%），普通化学（4.79%）等亚学科。

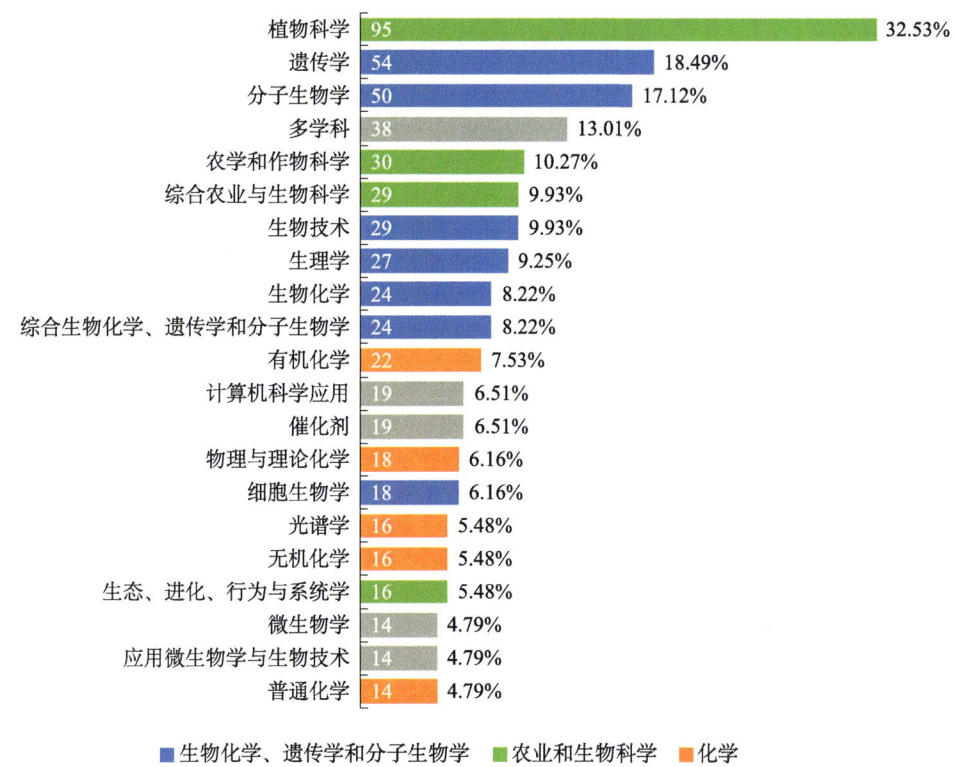

图 26　生物技术研究所 2017—2019 年发文学科分布

2. 发文和引文主题分析

将文献按照主题组织，进行更细粒度的需求分析，是为了解决单纯按照学科为单元进行分析，针对性不强，导致资源建设成本高、利用不充分的问题。2017—2019 年生物技术研究所发文共计涉及 180 个主题，通过相应的遴选指标，遴选出发文、引文涉及的主要主题（表 22）。可以看出生物所在"MicroRNAs; RNA; Degradome sequencing"这个主题的发文最多，由此判断该研究所较为侧重这一领域的研究,在"Droughts; Transcription factors; Freezing tolerance"主题的引文最多,表明在该领域文献的需求强度最高;该所在"DNA Methylation; Adenine; DNA modification"这个主题的发文占该主题全球同期论文的6.35%,说明其在全球范围内对该领域的研究有较为突出的贡献;该所参与的最受关注、发展势头最好的主题为"MicroRNAs; RNA; Degradome sequencing",主题显示度值为99.589;而该所发文具有较高引文影响力的主题为"DNA Methylation; Adenine; DNA modification",发文FWCI值是同类论文的6.51倍。综上,通过主题分析的结果不仅从各个角度反映出生物所学科文献资源的精细化需求,同时也体现了研究所研究领域的分布态势,能够为其学科规划和发展提供参考。

表22 生物技术研究所发文引文主要主题

主题	发文量	发文占主题同期论文比(%)	引文量	主题显示度	FWCI值
MicroRNAs; RNA; Degradome sequencing	8	0.38	237	99.589	0.92
Droughts; Transcription factors; Freezing tolerance	7	0.60	241	98.632	1.18
Folic acid; Vitamins; Total folate	6	2.21	136	90.693	0.61
Verticillium; Verticillium dahliae; Dahliae isolates	6	1.84	130	93.518	0.28
Ethylene; Ethylenes; Ethylene receptor	5	0.96	187	95.521	1.47
Arabidopsis; Histones; Imprinted genes	5	0.76	176	98.094	1.37
Rice; *Oryza sativa*; Cultivated rice	5	0.41	180	98.470	1.00
DNA Methylation; Adenine; DNA modification	4	6.35	66	83.261	6.51
Deinococcus; Radiation; Radiation resistance	4	1.53	79	90.729	0.10
Meristem; Leaves; Leaf primordia	4	1.11	92	92.031	1.28
Protein kinases; Calcium; CDPK Genes	4	1.10	79	94.126	0.78
Transcription factors; Genes; Factors TFs	4	0.76	67	95.156	0.80
Abscisic Acid; Arabidopsis; Guard cells	4	0.46	104	98.300	2.24
Ubiquitin; Ubiquitination; Enzymes DUBs	4	0.43	87	98.671	3.38
Anthocyanins; Transcription factors; Anthocyanin biosynthetic	4	0.26	79	98.997	2.53

续表

主题	发文量	发文占主题同期论文比(%)	引文量	主题显示度	FWCI值
Salinity; Salt tolerance; Salt tolerant	4	0.23	111	98.949	1.78
Genetically modified organisms; *Zea mays*; Modified maize	3	0.93	52	91.824	0.21
Organisms, Genetically modified; Genetically modified organisms; Organisms GMOs	3	0.81	53	91.612	0.85
Flowering; Rice; Long-day conditions	3	0.67	85	94.544	0.31
Codon; Genes; Mutation pressure	3	0.53	82	96.397	0.48
RNA; RNA, Small untranslated; mRNA targets	3	0.49	63	97.983	0
Corn; Hybrids; Plant densities	3	0.49	28	94.926	1.05
Phytochrome; Arabidopsis; Shade avoidance	3	0.47	166	98.457	2.12
Jasmonic acid; Oxylipins; Jasmonate signaling	3	0.45	120	98.285	1.96
Indoleacetic acids; Auxins; Auxin efflux	3	0.31	190	98.907	1.34
RNA; Methylation; Internal modification	3	0.25	144	99.771	1.98
Genome; Genes; Single guide	3	0.05	76	99.987	2.96
Gossypium hirsutum; Pollen tubes; Genetic transformation	2	5.41	26	17.257	0.17
Peptides; Genes; Disease virus	2	3.70	23	77.189	1.29
Helianthus annuus; Seed productivity; Head diameter	2	3.17	11	31.875	0.33
Setaria viridis; C4 Photosynthesis; Millets	2	2.13	34	69.904	0.63
Plants, Genetically modified; Genes; Transgenic tobacco	2	1.94	25	73.913	0.60
Inteins; Protein splicing; Proteins	2	1.53	15	83.857	0
Badnavirus; Viruses; Bacilliform virus	2	1.32	31	79.269	0.25
Silage; Corn silage; Corn	2	1.15	19	72.603	0.86
Chloroplasts; Plastids; Chloroplast gene	2	1.01	36	90.641	1.49

3. 需求期刊及保障情况

经引文分析得知生物技术研究所发文引用了1 492种外文期刊，与国家农业图书馆已订阅外文电子期刊品种进行比对，测算出其外文电子期刊全文保障率达到 91.70%，引文量前 40 的期刊见表 23。

表 23　生物技术研究所引文量前 40 期刊

编号	期刊名称	引用数量	是否保障
1	Plant Cell	634	是
2	Plant Physiology	536	是
3	Proceedings of the National Academy of Sciences of the United States of America	474	是
4	Plant Journal	436	是
5	PLoS ONE	317	是
6	Nature	271	是
7	Journal of Experimental Botany	254	是
8	Science	251	是
9	Nucleic Acids Research	236	是
10	Cell	196	是
11	Frontiers in Plant Science	191	是
12	Scientific Reports	146	是
13	Trends in Plant Science	135	是
14	Journal of Biological Chemistry	133	是
15	Plant Molecular Biology	132	是
16	Molecular Plant	127	是
17	Nature Genetics	125	是
18	Annual Review of Plant Biology	122	是
19	Journal of Physiology	121	是
20	Nature Biotechnology	120	是
21	Bioinformatics	117	是
22	PLoS Genetics	116	是
23	Plant and Cell Physiology	110	是

续表

编号	期刊名称	引用数量	是否保障
24	Applied and Environmental Microbiology	106	是
25	Current Opinion in Plant Biology	102	是
26	Plant Biotechnology Journal	101	是
27	Planta	95	是
28	BMC Genomics	90	是
29	BMC Plant Biology	88	是
30	Journal of Bacteriology	87	是
31	Theoretical and Applied Genetics	86	是
32	Nature Communications	84	是
33	Plant Cell Reports	82	是
34	Genetics	81	是
35	Journal of Agricultural and Food Chemistry	80	是
36	Crop Science	77	是
37	Applied Microbiology and Biotechnology	76	是
38	Plant, Cell and Environment	70	是
39	Genes and Development	67	是
40	Genome Biology	64	是

4. 需求数据库分析

分析各直属研究所引用外文文献的来源数据库，从数据库层面把握各直属研究所需求，是外文全文数据库建设的重要依据，同时也为各直属研究所参与电子资源共建选择数据库提供参考。根据各直属研究所需求期刊分析结果，将其与国家农业图书馆订阅的27种外文全文数据库期刊目录进行比对，发现2017—2019年生物技术研究所引文主要来源数据库如图27所示，其中来源于ScienceDirect（29.17%）、Wiley（15.94%）、Springer（14.22%）、OUP（11.49%）和Nature（10.21%）的引用最多。

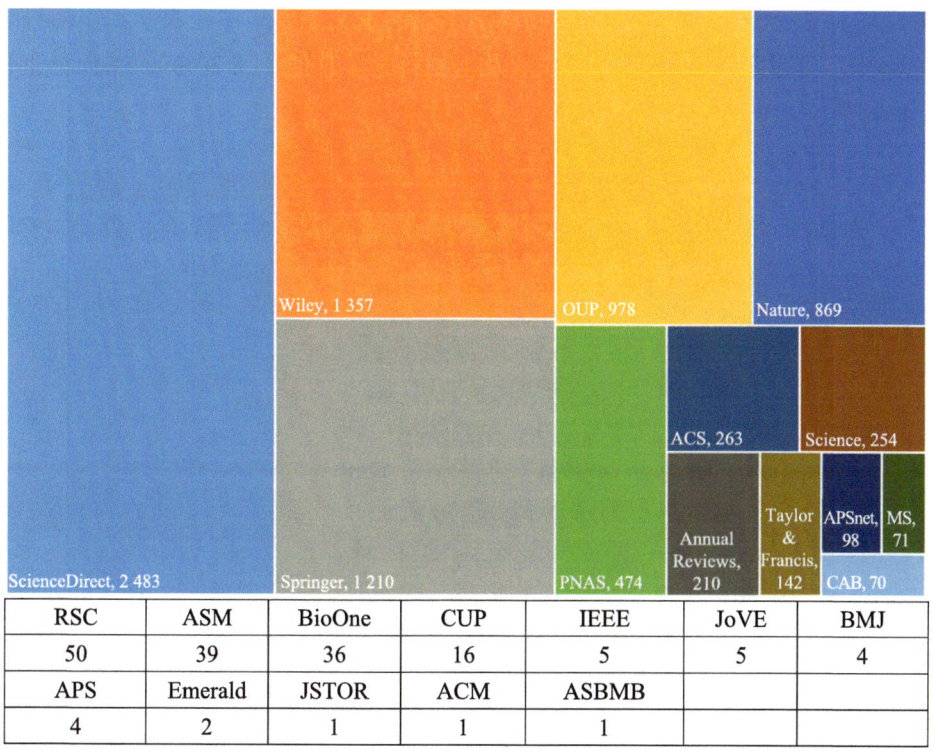

图 27 生物技术研究所引文来源数据库分布

（十）农业经济与发展研究所

1. 需求学科分析

采集农业经济与发展研究所（简称农经所）2017—2019 年发表的外文期刊论文共计 52 篇，对其进行学科分析，可以看出该所发文主要集中在环境科学（40.98%），农业和生物科学（37.70%），社会科学（26.23%）这三大学科（图 28）。除此之外，在能源，工程学，经济学、计量经济学和金融学也有一定数量的发文，说明农经所的研究在这些领域也有涉足。

在二级学科中占比最高的是社会科学中的地理、规划和发展，占总体的 19.67%。对环境科学，农业和生物科学两大学科的亚学科进行分析，结果如图 28 所示，在环境科学中，发文主要集中在管理监测与政策法规学（19.67%），环境化学（8.20%），综合环境科学（8.20%），土壤科学（6.56%），污染学

（6.56%）等亚学科中。农业和生物科学学科的发文主要集中在农学和作物科学（9.84%），植物科学（8.20%），农业及生物科学（其他）（8.20%），综合农业和生物科学（8.20%）等亚学科。

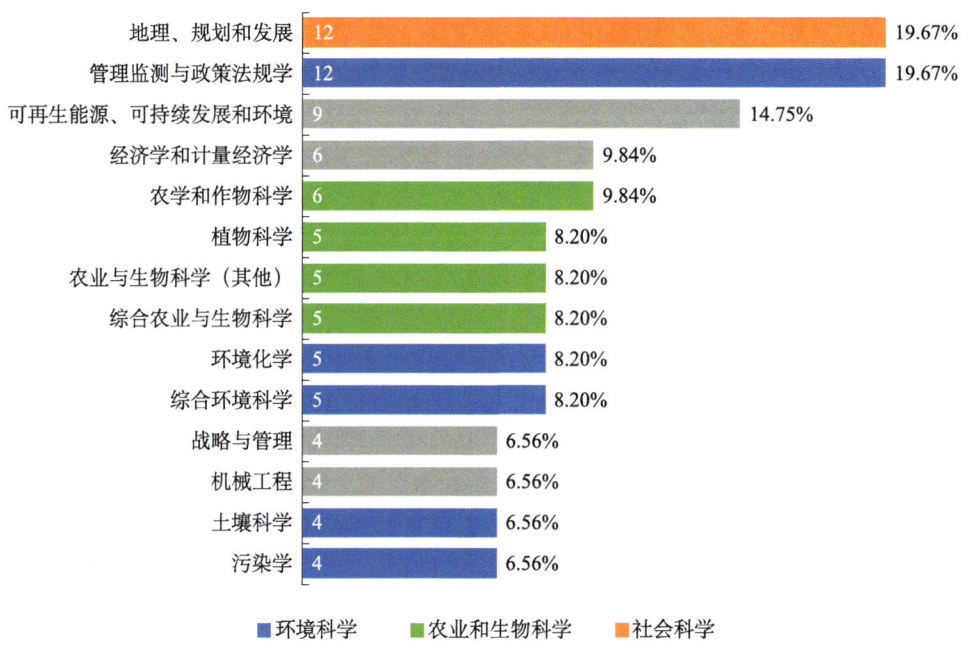

图 28　农业经济与发展研究所 2017—2019 年发文学科分布

2. 发文和引文主题分析

将文献按照主题组织，进行更细粒度的需求分析，是为了解决单纯按照学科为单元进行分析，针对性不强，导致资源建设成本高、利用不充分的问题。2017—2019 年农业经济与发展研究所发文共计涉及 51 个主题，通过相应的遴选指标，遴选出发文、引文涉及的主要主题（表24）。可以看出农经所在"Fertilizers; Carbon footprint; Energy inputs""International environmental agreements; Game theory; Coalitions"和"Terrace; Rice; Agricultural heritage"这 3 个主题的发文最多，由此判断该研究所较为侧重这些领域的研究，在"Glacier; Glacier mass balance; Debris cover"主题的引文最多，表明在该领域文献的需求强度最高；该所在"Avian influenza; Biosecurity; Farmers"这个主题的发文占该主题全球同期论文的 9.09%，说明其在全球范围内对该领域的研究有较为突出的贡献；该所参与的最受关注、发展势头最好的主题为"Climate change; Crop;

Crop models"和"Carbon footprint; Greenhouse gas emissions; Feed production",主题显示度值为 99.758 和 99.146;而该所发文具有较高引文影响力的主题为"Land; Land tenure; Land rental",发文 FWCI 值是同类论文的 2.92 倍。综上,通过主题分析的结果不仅从各个角度反映出农经所学科文献资源的精细化需求,同时也体现了研究所研究领域的分布态势,能够为其学科规划和发展提供参考。

表 24 农业经济与发展研究所发文引文主要主题

主题	发文量	发文占主题同期论文比(%)	引文量	主题显示度	FWCI 值
Fertilizers; Carbon footprint; Energy inputs	3	0.39	94	98.669	0.28
International environmental agreements; Game theory; Coalitions	3	0.78	61	89.456	0.31
Terrace; Rice; Agricultural heritage	3	6.25	21	70.947	1.16
Climate change; Crop; Crop models	2	0.08	84	99.758	0.73
Glacier; Glacier mass balance; Debris cover	2	0.14	113	99.146	1.38
Technical efficiency; Farms; Frontier production	2	0.18	21	96.590	0.41
Trade; Gravity model; Gravity equation	2	0.15	21	95.029	0.91
Crop insurance; Insurance; Index insurance	2	0.40	18	91.334	0.97
Food safety; HACCP; Food supply	2	0.47	20	90.698	1.28
China; Africa; Soft power	2	0.29	26	90.000	1.31
Avian influenza; Biosecurity; Farmers	2	9.09	8	52.184	0.24
Carbon footprint; Greenhouse gas emissions; Feed production	1	0.14	2	99.250	0.37
Ecosystem service; Conservation; PES Schemes	1	0.10	15	98.752	0
Sewage pumping plants; Wastewater treatment; Urban water	1	0.14	24	98.524	2.51
Additives; Manufacture; Traditional manufacturing	1	0.13	11	97.988	1.16
Nitrogen; Eutrophication; Nitrogen footprint	1	0.22	7	97.221	0
Supply chains; Food products; Product traceability	1	0.11	5	96.494	0

续表

主题	发文量	发文占主题同期论文比(%)	引文量	主题显示度	FWCI值
Urban sprawl; Urban growth; Urbanization	1	0.13	14	96.412	0
Food; Food, Genetically modified; Modified food	1	0.13	35	96.323	0
Poverty; Livelihood; Household survey	1	0.13	6	96.035	0
Cooling; Longwave radiation; Radiative cooling	1	0.25	30	95.835	0.76
Land; Land tenure; Land rental	1	0.13	12	95.119	2.92
Efficiency; Hospitals; Hospital efficiency	1	0.22	21	92.451	0
Rural areas; Land use; Rural residential	1	0.16	4	92.315	0
Bangladesh; Mangrove; Shrimp farming	1	0.35	0	90.930	2.84
Swine; Anti-bacterial agents; Antimicrobial usage	1	0.25	4	90.200	0
UNESCO; World; Heritage site	1	0.26	12	88.595	0
Consolidation; Fragmentation; Land fragmentation	1	0.40	2	88.373	2.06
Agriculture; Internet; Tech publications	1	0.79	1	83.300	1.52
Demand; Meat; Expenditure elasticities	1	0.33	8	82.708	0
Straw; Pelletizing; Moisture content	1	0.71	0	71.501	0
Manures; Livestock; Environmental pollution	1	0.87	0	62.944	0
Wine; Wheat; Political economy	1	1.28	1	57.752	1.14
Apiculture; Apoidea; Honey bees	1	2.38	0	56.675	0
Hayek; Coordination; Supply chain	1	9.09	0	42.308	0
Water; Energy; Carrying capacity	1	3.23	1	42.049	1.73
Telecommunication; Developing countries; Universal service	1	1.89	3	38.800	0.68
Technology; Disease outbreaks; Electrifying jaffa	1	8.33	1	35.568	1.21
Starch; Amylose; Resistant starch	1	8.33	0	28.384	0.25

3. 需求期刊及保障情况

经引文分析得知农业经济与发展研究所发文引用了557种外文期刊，与国家农业图书馆已订阅外文电子期刊品种进行比对,测算出其外文电子期刊全文保障率达到 84.44%,引文量前 40 的期刊见表 25。

表 25 农业经济与发展研究所引文量前 40 期刊

编号	期刊名称	引用数量	是否保障
1	American Journal of Agricultural Economics	36	是
2	Energy	35	是
3	Journal of Geophysical Research	30	是
4	Agricultural Economics	25	是
5	Journal of Glaciology	25	是
6	Journal of Cleaner Production	24	是
7	Renewable and Sustainable Energy Reviews	23	是
8	Land Use Policy	22	是
9	World Development	22	是
10	Journal of Environmental Economics and Management	21	是
11	Food Control	21	是
12	Food Policy	21	是
13	China Agricultural Economic Review	21	是
14	Ecological Economics	20	是
15	Science of the Total Environment	20	是
16	Proceedings of the National Academy of Sciences of the United States of America	19	是
17	American Economic Review	19	是
18	Science	18	是
19	China Economic Review	17	是
20	Environmental and Resource Economics	17	是
21	Sustainability	17	是
22	Cryosphere	16	是
23	Energy Policy	15	是
24	Applied Energy	15	是

续表

编号	期刊名称	引用数量	是否保障
25	Preventive Veterinary Medicine	14	是
26	Journal of Environmental Management	14	是
27	International Journal of Climatology	13	是
28	European Journal of Operational Research	13	是
29	Agricultural Systems	12	是
30	Nature Climate Change	12	是
31	Water Science and Technology	12	是
32	Journal of Economic Dynamics and Control	11	是
33	Journal of Development Economics	11	是
34	Journal of Integrative Agriculture	11	是
35	Agricultural and Forest Meteorology	11	是
36	Climate Dynamics	10	是
37	Field Crops Research	10	是
38	Journal of Agricultural Economics	10	是
39	Journal of Climate	9	是
40	Journal of Optimization Theory and Applications	9	是
41	Tourism Management	9	是

4. 需求数据库分析

分析各直属研究所引用外文文献的来源数据库，从数据库层面把握各直属研究所需求，是外文全文数据库建设的重要依据，同时也为各直属研究所参与电子资源共建选择数据库提供参考。根据各直属研究所需求期刊分析结果，将其与国家农业图书馆订阅的27种外文全文数据库期刊目录进行比对，发现2017—2019年农业经济与发展研究所引文主要来源数据库如图29所示，其中来源于ScienceDirect（54.13%）、Wiley（13.45%）、Springer（11.41%）和JSTOR（8.96%）的引用最多。

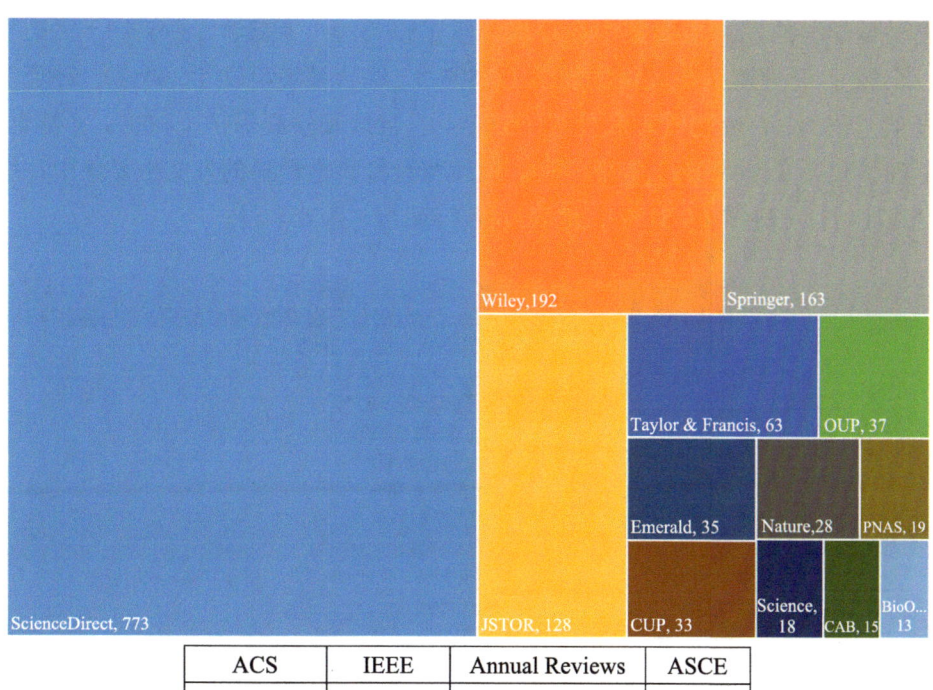

图29 农业经济与发展研究所引文来源数据库分布

（十一）农业资源与农业区划研究所

1. 需求学科分析

采集农业资源与农业区划研究所（简称资划所）2017—2019年发表的外文期刊论文共计986篇，对其进行学科分析，可以看出该所发文主要集中在农业和生物科学（53.85%），环境科学（33.44%），地球与行星科学（21.59%）这三大学科（图30）。除此之外，在生物化学、遗传学和分子生物学，免疫与微生物学，工程学，社会科学，计算机科学等也有一定数量的发文，说明资划所的研究在这些领域也有涉足。

对农业和生物科学，环境科学和地球与行星科学三大学科的亚学科进行分析，结果如图30所示，在农业和生物科学中，发文主要集中在土壤科学（23.55%），农学和作物科学（23.31%），植物科学（13.97%），综合农业和生物科学（11.30%），生态、进化、行为与系统学（9.18%）等亚学科中。环境科学学科的发文主要集中在环境化学（8.87%），生态学（8.48%），污染学（7.61%），管理监测与政策法规学（6.59%），综合环境科学（6.04%），环境工程学（5.65%），废物管理和处置（5.02%），自然和景观保护（4.00%），健康、毒理学和突变（4.00%）等亚学科。地球与行星科学学科的发文主要集中在综合地球与行星科学（9.81%），地表过程（5.81%）等亚学科。

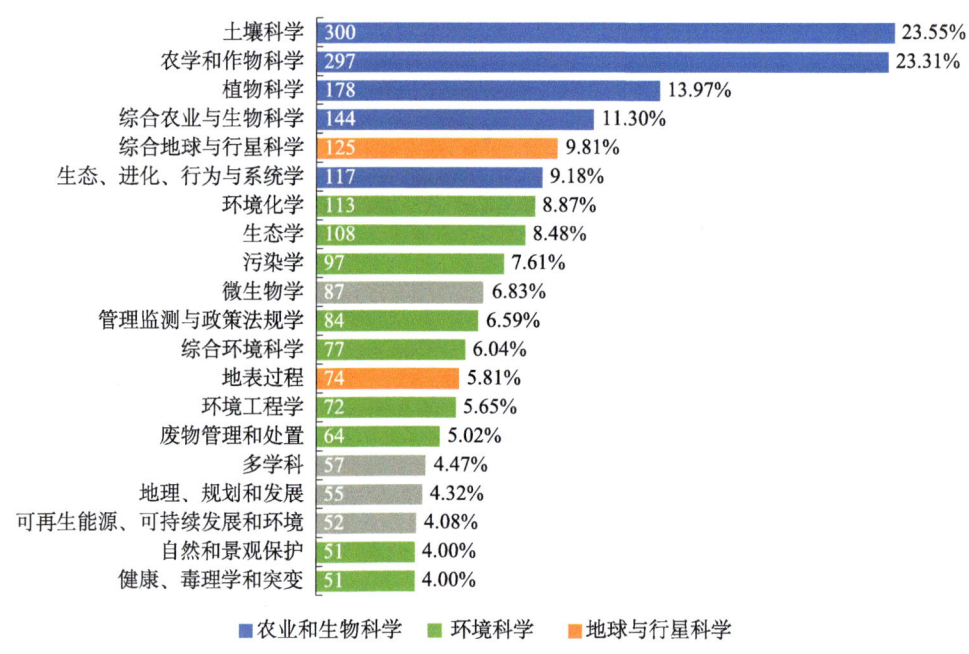

图30　农业资源与农业区划研究所2017—2019年发文学科分布

2. 发文和引文主题分析

将文献按照主题组织，进行更细粒度的需求分析，是为了解决单纯按照学科为单元进行分析，针对性不强，导致资源建设成本高、利用不充分的问题。2017—2019年农业资源与农业区划研究所发文共计涉及447个主题，通过相应的遴选指标，遴选出发文、引文涉及的主要主题（表26）。可以看出资化所在"Soil organic carbon; Organic carbon; Soil aggregation"这个主题的发文和引文最多，由此判断该研究所较为侧重这个领域的研究，在该领域文献的需求强度也最高；该所在"Alfalfa; China; Han dynasty"这个主题的发文占该主题全球同期论文的35.71%，说明其在全球范围内对该领域的研究有较为突出的贡献；该所参与的最受关注、发展势头最好的主题为"Landsat; Land cover;

Cover maps" 和 "Soil organic carbon; Organic carbon; Soil aggregation"，主题显示度值分别为 99.725 和 99.574；而该所发文具有较高引文影响力的主题为 "Antibiotic resistance; Drug resistance, Microbial; Antibiotic-resistant bacteria" 和 "Nanoparticles; Plants; Seedling growth"，发文 FWCI 值是同类论文的 4.86 倍和 4.37 倍。综上，通过主题分析的结果不仅从各个角度反映出资化所学科文献资源的精细化需求，同时也体现了研究所研究领域的分布态势，能够为其学科规划和发展提供参考。

表 26 农业资源与农业区划研究所发文引文主要主题

主题	发文量	发文占主题同期论文比(%)	引文量	主题显示度	FWCI 值
Soil organic carbon; Organic carbon; Soil aggregation	63	2.58	1 188	99.574	1.57
Landsat; Land cover; Cover maps	46	1.30	715	99.725	1.50
Land surface; Surface measurement; Emissivity separation	42	4.93	972	95.902	1.56
Nitrous oxide; Soil emission; Oxide emissions	30	2.12	579	99.321	1.41
Vitamin K 2; Bacterial typing techniques; Designated strain	27	1.11	424	99.020	0.56
Soil; Microbial community; Soil fungal	27	1.94	451	99.229	2.19
Pyrolysis; Soil amendment; Biochar amendment	23	0.42	650	99.968	2.93
Evapotranspiration; Energy balance; Evaporative fraction	23	2.48	593	98.195	1.12
Soil quality; Soil; Soil biological	19	1.71	371	98.369	1.62
Soil organic carbon; Soil carbon; Crop yield	19	10.16	155	76.673	1.07
Climate change; Crop; Crop models	16	0.65	380	99.758	1.20
Antibiotics; Oxytetracycline; Veterinary antibiotics	15	0.68	308	99.816	1.11
Soil moisture; Radiometers; Moisture retrievals	15	1.18	341	99.316	1.31
Remote sensing; Crops; Crop planting	15	11.81	102	68.298	0.54
Vegetation; Chlorophyll; Hyperspectral reflectance	14	0.71	341	99.410	1.18
Nitrogen; Eutrophication; Nitrogen footprint	14	3.04	252	97.221	2.17
Rice; Nutrient use efficiency; Grain yield	14	11.29	178	75.671	1.00

续表

主题	发文量	发文占主题同期论文比(%)	引文量	主题显示度	FWCI值
Phosphorus; Soil; Dissolved reactive	13	2.07	206	94.649	1.01
Phosphorus; Organic phosphorus; Moderately labile	13	2.43	252	96.670	0.76
Phosphorus; Phosphates; Phosphate starvation	11	1.39	265	97.851	2.91
Grazing; Grasslands; Grazing exclusion	11	2.22	169	96.414	1.18
Crops; MODIS; Yield prediction	11	2.79	311	91.601	2.11
Anaerobic digestion; Biogas; Methane yields	10	0.27	272	99.935	2.84
Alfalfa; China; Han dynasty	10	35.71	1	36.946	0.33
Ammonia; Archaea; Ammonia oxidizers	9	0.87	318	99.176	1.43
Soil; Soil organic carbon; Digital soil	9	0.77	113	98.999	0.98
Cadmium; Heavy metal; Hazard quotient	9	0.73	165	98.800	1.13
Paddy field; Nitrous oxide; Rice paddy	9	1.43	265	95.938	0.94
Microbial community; Soil microorganism; Acid PLFA	9	1.18	379	98.027	1.31
Soil respiration; Respiration; Heterotrophic respiration	8	0.86	189	96.825	0.81
Polysaccharides; Antioxidants; Polysaccharide fractions	8	0.39	138	99.661	1.34
Synthetic aperture radar; Soil moisture; Moisture retrieval	8	1.10	181	95.242	0.88
Nanoparticles; Plants; Seedling growth	8	0.48	310	99.695	4.37
Agricultural machinery; Tillage; Rotary tillage	8	2.04	34	85.928	0.74
Humic acids; Humic Substances; Substances HS	8	1.78	23	94.323	0.61
China; Food supply; Multiple cropping	8	3.32	69	88.777	0.49
Vegetable; Vegetables; Greenhouse vegetable	8	9.41	62	60.270	0.88
Functional diversity; Traits; Trait values	7	0.25	244	99.872	2.68
Antibiotic resistance; Drug resistance, Microbial; Antibiotic-resistant bacteria	7	0.33	234	99.881	4.86

3. 需求期刊及保障情况

经引文分析得知农业资源与农业区划研究所发文引用了 2 707 种外文期刊，与国家农业图书馆已订阅外文电子期刊品种进行比对，测算出其外文电子期刊全文保障率达到 91.41%，引文量前 40 的期刊见表 27。

表 27 农业资源与农业区划研究所引文量前 40 期刊

编号	期刊名称	引用数量	是否保障
1	Remote Sensing of Environment	1 609	是
2	Soil Biology and Biochemistry	1 355	是
3	Plant and Soil	728	是
4	International Journal of Remote Sensing	693	是
5	Agriculture, Ecosystems and Environment	633	是
6	Science of the Total Environment	617	是
7	Geoderma	607	是
8	Environmental Science and Technology	606	是
9	Global Change Biology	594	是
10	Nature	589	是
11	Proceedings of the National Academy of Sciences of the United States of America	579	是
12	International Journal of Systematic and Evolutionary Microbiology	572	是
13	IEEE Transactions on Geoscience and Remote Sensing	556	是
14	Remote Sensing	506	是
15	Field Crops Research	503	是
16	Science	497	是
17	Soil and Tillage Research	492	是
18	Soil Science Society of America Journal	492	是
19	Biology and Fertility of Soils	437	是
20	Journal of Geophysical Research	436	是
21	Bioresource Technology	427	是

续表

编号	期刊名称	引用数量	是否保障
22	Chemosphere	404	是
23	Applied and Environmental Microbiology	363	是
24	PLoS ONE	361	是
25	Agricultural and Forest Meteorology	349	是
26	Environmental Pollution	340	是
27	Journal of Hydrology	327	是
28	Nutrient Cycling in Agroecosystems	318	是
29	Agricultural Water Management	296	是
30	Applied Soil Ecology	294	是
31	Scientific Reports	270	是
32	Plant Physiology	260	是
33	Agronomy Journal	240	是
34	Journal of Physiology	240	是
35	Journal of Environmental Quality	227	是
36	Ecology	226	是
37	ITC Journal	218	是
38	ISME Journal	214	是
39	ISPRS Journal of Photogrammetry and Remote Sensing	212	是
40	European Journal of Soil Science	197	是

4. 需求数据库分析

分析各直属研究所引用外文文献的来源数据库，从数据库层面把握各直属研究所需求，是外文全文数据库建设的重要依据，同时也为各直属研究所参与电子资源共建选择数据库提供参考。根据各直属研究所需求期刊分析结果，将其与国家农业图书馆订阅的 27 种外文全文数据库期刊目录进行比对，发现 2017—2019 年农业资源与农业区划研究所引文主要来源数据库如图 31 所示，其中来源于 ScienceDirect（48.63%）、Springer（13.91%）和 Wiley（12.82%）的引用最多。

四 各直属研究所需求和保障分析

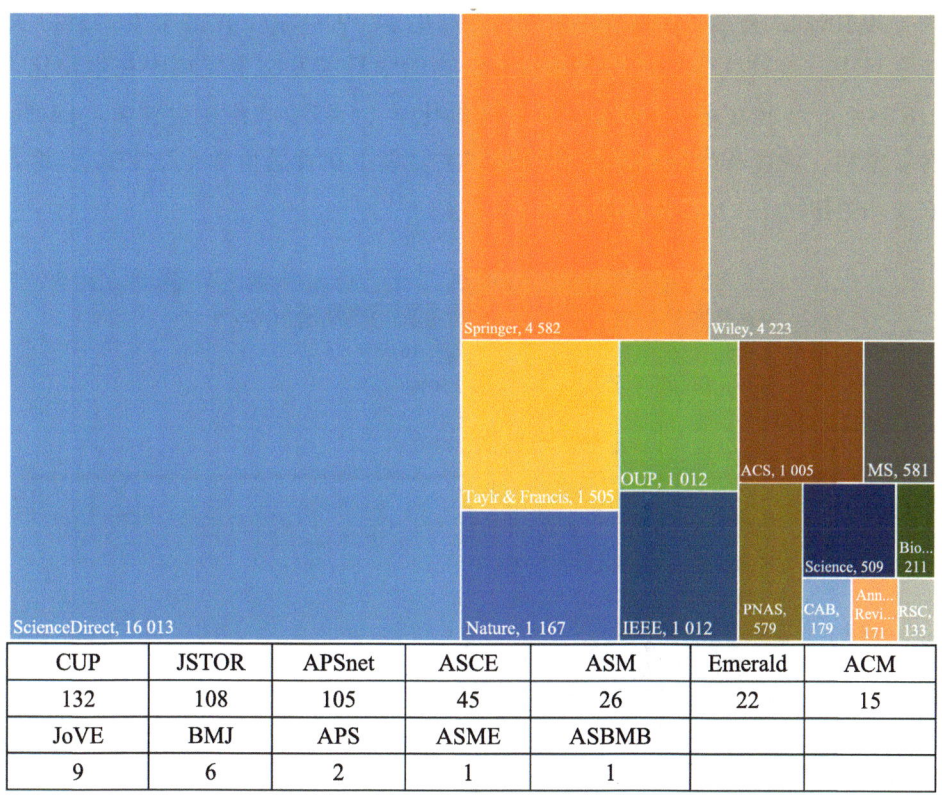

图 31 农业资源与农业区划研究所引文来源数据库分布

（十二）农业质量标准与检测技术研究所

1. 需求学科分析

采集农业质量标准与检测技术研究所（简称质标所）2017—2019 年发表的外文期刊论文共计 289 篇，对其进行学科分析，可以看出该所发文主要集中在化学（57.37%），农业和生物科学（33.97%），生物化学、遗传学和分子生物学（26.60%）这三大学科（图 32）。除此之外，在环境科学，工程学，药理学、毒理学和药剂学，化学工程等也有一定数量的发文，说明质标所的研究在这些领域也有涉足。

对化学，农业和生物科学，生物化学、遗传学和分子生物学三大学科的亚学科进行分析，结果如图 32 所示，在化学中，发文主要集中在分析化学（39.10%），普通化学（12.50%），有机化学（9.94%），光谱学（6.73%）等亚学科中。生物化学、遗传学和分子生物学学科的发文主要集中在生物化学（16.03%），生物技术（7.69%），临床生物化学（5.45%），细胞生物学（4.17%）等亚学科。农业和生物科学学科的发文主要集中在食品科学（25.32%），综合农业和生物科学（6.73%）等亚学科。

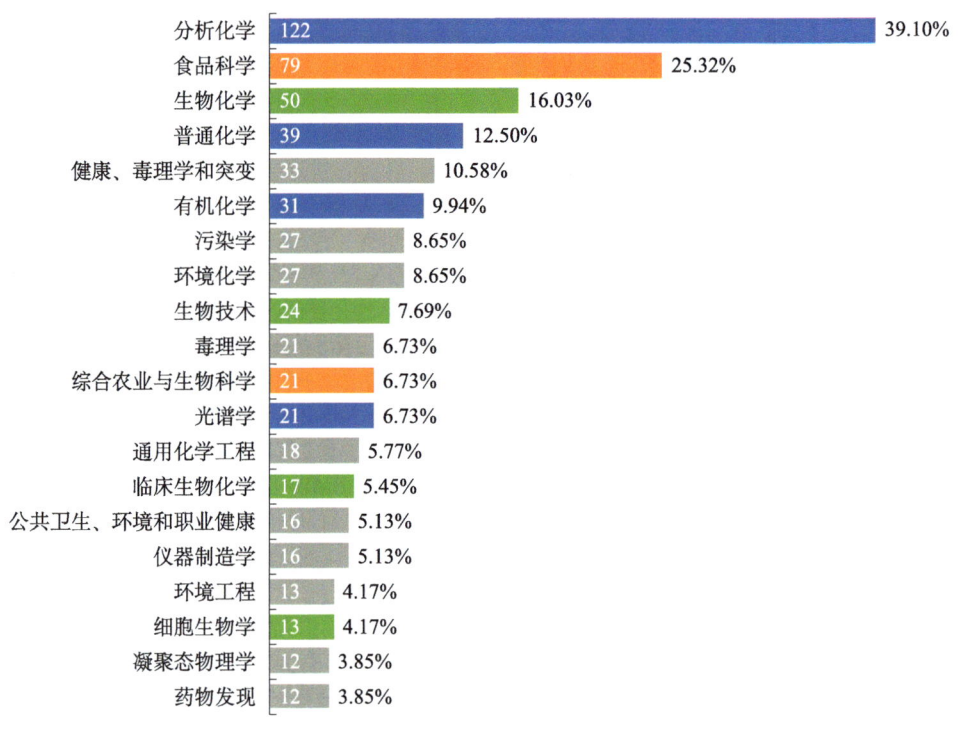

图 32　农业质量标准与检测技术研究所 2017—2019 年发文学科分布

2. 发文和引文主题分析

将文献按照主题组织，进行更细粒度的需求分析，是为了解决单纯按照学科为单元进行分析，针对性不强，导致资源建设成本高、利用不充分的问题。2017—2019 年农业质量标准与检测技术研究所发文共计涉及 176 个主题，通过相应的遴选指标，遴选出发文、引文涉及的主要主题（表 28）。可以看出质标所在"Polymers; Phase separation; Polymers MIPs"这个主题的发文最多，由此判断该研究所较为侧重这个领域的研究，在"Pesticides; Pesticide Residues;

Quick easy"主题的引文最多,表明在该领域文献的需求强度最高;该所在"Insecticides; Pesticides; Carbon electrode"这个主题的发文占该主题全球同期论文的 8.06%,说明其在全球范围内对该领域的研究有较为突出的贡献;该所参与的最受关注、发展势头最好的主题为"Polymers; Phase separation; Polymers MIPs"和"Pesticides; Pesticide Residues; Quick easy",主题显示度值分别为 99.843 和 99.141;而该所发文具有较高引文影响力的主题为"Ham; Volatile compounds; Dry-cured hams"和"Mycotoxins; Zearalenone; Deoxynivalenol DON",发文 FWCI 值是同类论文的 4.29 倍和 3.22 倍。综上,通过主题分析的结果不仅从各个角度反映出质标所学科文献资源的精细化需求,同时也体现了研究所研究领域的分布态势,能够为其学科规划和发展提供参考。

表 28 农业质量标准与检测技术研究所发文引文主要主题

主题	发文量	发文占主题同期论文比(%)	引文量	主题显示度	FWCI 值
Polymers; Phase separation; Polymers MIPs	21	0.87	312	99.843	1.28
Pesticides; Pesticide Residues; Quick easy	15	1.11	324	99.141	1.19
Clenbuterol; Food additives; Swine urine	10	2.92	199	95.281	1.40
Mycotoxins; Zearalenone; Deoxynivalenol DON	9	0.83	210	99.414	3.22
DNA; Amplification; Electrochemical aptasensor	7	0.29	145	99.911	1.23
Monoclonal antibodies; Haptens; Competitive enzyme-linked	6	3.41	117	88.664	1.12
Insecticides; Pesticides; Carbon electrode	5	8.06	56	78.207	1.21
Cattle; Cattle breeds; Cattle populations	5	1.55	52	86.404	0.47
Meat; Meat products; Meat species	5	0.94	51	95.799	1.20
Pesticides; Biosensors; Pesticides OPs	5	0.69	162	99.077	0.62
Dibutyl phthalate; Phthalic acids; Phthalate MEHP	5	0.30	119	99.572	1.38
Hydrides; Spectrometry; Photochemical vapor	4	1.75	88	92.605	0.43
Stable isotopes; Isotopes; Ratio mass	4	1.12	51	91.655	2.06
Ham; Volatile compounds; Dry-cured hams	4	0.81	71	91.560	4.29
Antibiotics; Fluoroquinolones; Drug Residues	4	0.72	76	96.870	0.98
Chitosan; Chitin; Weight chitosan	4	0.49	77	98.547	1.44

续表

主题	发文量	发文占主题同期论文比 (%)	引文量	主题显示度	FWCI值
Fluorocarbons; Alkanesulfonic Acids; Acids PFAAS	4	0.17	192	99.885	0.70
Mercury (metal); Atomic absorption spectrometry; Cold vapor	3	1.30	61	90.376	0.54
Enantiomers; Enantioselectivity; Chiral pesticides	3	0.97	63	93.364	1.27
Endocrine disruptors; Phenols; Nonylphenol NP	3	0.83	69	94.854	1.01
High pressure treatment; Hydrostatic pressure; High-pressure processing	3	0.55	28	96.430	0.35
Solid phase extraction; Nanomagnetics; Extraction MSPE	3	0.34	111	99.360	1.46
Gelation; Gels; Supramolecular gel	3	0.24	70	99.373	1.02
Amantadine; Memantine; Memantine hydrochloride	2	3.85	27	75.011	0.64
Chamomile; Matricaria; Medicinal plants	2	1.83	12	77.936	0.81
Endocrine disruptors; Steroids; H295R cells	2	1.61	19	86.237	0.71
Herbicides; Weed control; Sulfonylurea herbicide	2	1.44	29	81.675	0.81
Cholesterol; Phytosterols; Products cops	2	1.42	36	86.440	0.54
Myxococcales; Anti-Bacterial Agents; Gene cluster	2	1.35	19	89.623	0.22
Polychlorinated biphenyls; Dioxins; PCB Exposure	2	1.15	18	87.834	1.39
Halogenated diphenyl ethers; Hydroxylation; Ethers OH-PBDEs	2	1.14	54	90.287	1.47
Sulfonamides; High performance liquid chromatography; Simultaneous determination	2	0.85	34	91.836	0.90
Ochratoxins; Aptamers, Nucleotide; B1 AFB1	2	0.84	49	97.615	0.33
Chromophores; Nonlinear optics; Pm V-1	2	0.63	62	90.933	0.34
Toxicity; Drug combinations; Pharmaceutical preparations	2	0.61	51	94.878	1.70
Arsenic; Inductively coupled plasma mass spectrometry; Arsenic speciation	2	0.52	53	96.232	0.63
Fumonisins; Fusarium; B1 FB1	2	0.48	127	92.745	0.32
Halogenated diphenyl ethers; Flame retardants; Halogenated flame	2	0.11	110	99.675	1.33

3. 需求期刊及保障情况

经引文分析得知农业质量标准与检测技术研究所发文引用了 1 556 种外文期刊,与国家农业图书馆已订阅外文电子期刊品种进行比对,测算出其外文电子期刊全文保障率达到 92.52%,引文量前 40 的期刊见表 29。

表 29　农业质量标准与检测技术研究所引文量前 40 期刊

编号	期刊名称	引用数量	是否保障
1	Food Chemistry	544	是
2	Journal of Chromatography A	439	是
3	Journal of Agricultural and Food Chemistry	436	是
4	Analytical Chemistry	330	是
5	Biosensors and Bioelectronics	310	是
6	Analytica Chimica Acta	302	是
7	Talanta	268	是
8	Journal of the American Chemical Society	216	是
9	Environmental Science and Technology	196	是
10	Sensors and Actuators, B: Chemical	174	是
11	Food Control	172	是
12	Chemosphere	154	是
13	Analytical and Bioanalytical Chemistry	136	是
14	Mikrochimica Acta	126	是
15	Angewandte Chemie - International Edition	125	是
16	The Analyst	122	是
17	Science of the Total Environment	121	是
18	Journal of Chromatography B: Analytical Technologies in the Biomedical and Life Sciences	113	是
19	TrAC - Trends in Analytical Chemistry	111	是
20	Food and Chemical Toxicology	105	是
21	Chemical Communications	91	是
22	Chemical Society Reviews	87	是

续表

编号	期刊名称	引用数量	是否保障
23	Journal of Separation Science	85	是
24	Analytical Methods	84	是
25	RSC Advances	83	是
26	Food Additives and Contaminants - Part A Chemistry, Analysis, Control, Exposure and Risk Assessment	83	是
27	ACS Applied Materials and Interfaces	81	是
28	Science	80	是
29	Environmental Pollution	76	是
30	Environment International	74	是
31	Journal of Analytical Atomic Spectrometry	69	是
32	Food Analytical Methods	68	是
33	Environmental Health Perspectives	67	是
34	Chemical Reviews	64	是
35	Meat Science	62	是
36	Scientific Reports	62	是
37	Journal of AOAC International	61	是
38	Journal of Hazardous Materials	60	是
39	PLoS ONE	56	是
40	Nature	53	是

4. 需求数据库分析

分析各直属研究所引用外文文献的来源数据库，从数据库层面把握各直属研究所需求，是外文全文数据库建设的重要依据，同时也为各直属研究所参与电子资源共建选择数据库提供参考。根据各直属研究所需求期刊分析结果，将其与国家农业图书馆订阅的 27 种外文全文数据库期刊目录进行比对，发现 2017—2019 年农业质量标准与检测技术研究所引文主要来源数据库如图 33 所示，其中来源于 ScienceDirect（50.55%）、ACS（16.88%）和 Wiley（9.46%）的引用最多。

四　各直属研究所需求和保障分析

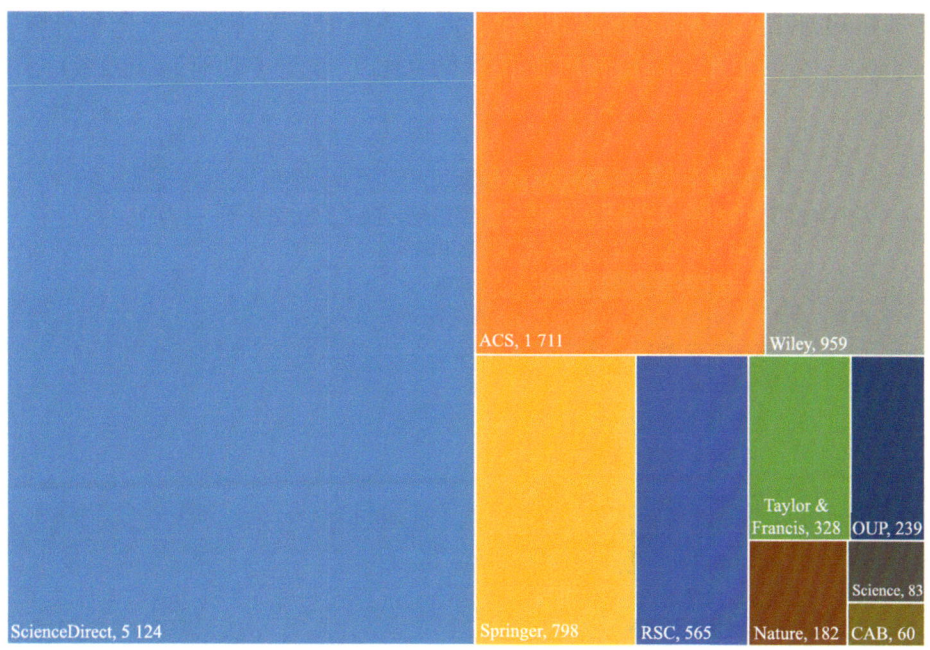

PNAS	CUP	Annual Reviews	APSnet	BioOne	ASBMB	IEEE
30	28	26	18	17	11	9
BMJ	APS	Emerald	ASM			
4	4	3	2			

图33　农业质量标准与检测技术研究所引文来源数据库分布

（十三）农业农村部食物与营养发展研究所

1. 需求学科分析

采集农业农村部食物与营养发展研究所（简称营养所）2017—2019年发表的外文期刊论文共计48篇，对其进行学科分析，可以看出该所发文主要集中在农业和生物科学（63.93%），医学（24.59%）这两大学科（图34）。除此之外，在环境科学，生物化学、遗传学和分子生物学，护理学，化学工程，化学，工程学等也有一定数量的发文，说明营养所的研究在这些领域也有涉足。

对农业和生物科学和医学这两大学科的亚学科进行分析，结果如图34所示，在农业和生物科学中，发文主要集中在食品科学（27.87%），综合农业和生物科学（21.31%），水产科学（8.20%），动物科学与动物学（4.92%），农学和作物科学（3.28%）等亚学科中。医学学科的发文主要集中在全科医学（6.56%），公共卫生、环境和职业卫生（4.92%），医学（其他）（4.92%）等亚学科。

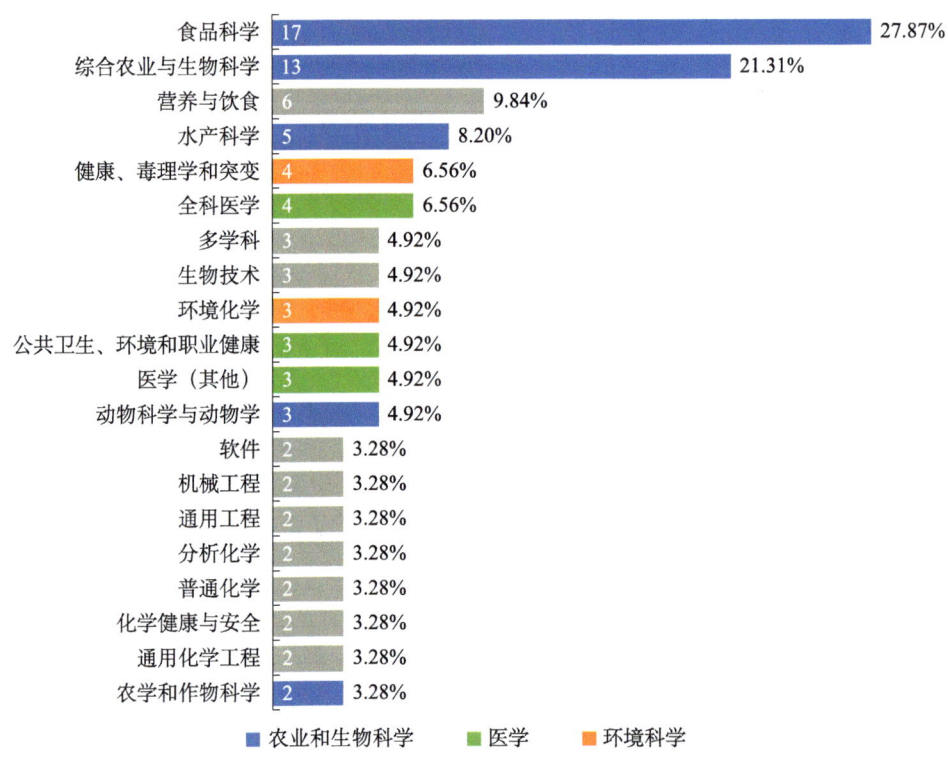

图34　农业农村部食物与营养发展研究所2017—2019年发文学科分布

2. 发文和引文主题分析

将文献按照主题组织，进行更细粒度的需求分析，是为了解决单纯按照学科为单元进行分析，针对性不强，导致资源建设成本高、利用不充分的问题。2017—2019年农业农村部食物与营养发展研究所发文共计涉及50个主题，通过相应的遴选指标，遴选出发文、引文涉及的主要主题（表30）。可以看出营养所在"Obesity; Overweight; Double burden""Antioxidants; Antioxidant activity; Phenolic acids"和"Child; Ethiopia; Diversity score"这3个主题的发文最多，由此判断该研究所较为侧重这些领域的研究，在"Fatty acid composition; Fish oils; Dietary lipid"主题的引文最多，表明在该领域文献的需求强度最高；该所在"Support vector machines; Near infrared spectroscopy; Buckwheat starch"

这个主题的发文占该主题全球同期论文的 16.67%，说明其在全球范围内对该领域的研究有较为突出的贡献；该所参与的最受关注、发展势头最好的主题为 "Food; Waste; Food wastage" 和 "NADPH Oxidase; Reactive Oxygen Species; Dinucleotide phosphate"，主题显示度值分别为 99.325 和 99.028；而该所发文具有较高引文影响力的主题为 "Blood Pressure; Cholesterol, LDL; Cooperative Behavior"，发文 FWCI 值是同类论文的 109.9 倍。综上，通过主题分析的结果不仅从各个角度反映出营养所学科文献资源的精细化需求，同时也体现了研究所研究领域的分布态势，能够为其学科规划和发展提供参考。

表 30　农业农村部食物与营养发展研究所发文引文主要主题

主题	发文量	发文占主题同期论文比(%)	引文量	主题显示度	FWCI 值
Antioxidants; Antioxidant activity; Phenolic acids	3	0.68	25	96.793	2.65
Child; Ethiopia; Diversity score	3	0.52	19	95.660	0
Obesity; Overweight; Double burden	3	0.44	16	97.601	75.90
Leptin; Receptors, Leptin; Leptin receptor	2	1.24	37	85.759	2.78
Dehydration; Drinking; Urine osmolality	2	0.46	33	90.448	1.12
Glutenins; Triticum; Glutenin subunit	2	0.35	25	93.688	1.05
Noodles; Pasta; Cooked noodles	2	0.34	30	93.754	0.68
Food; Waste; Food wastage	2	0.23	1	99.325	0
Proteins; Exercise; Protein ingestion	2	0.21	35	98.893	0.73
Fatty acid composition; Fish oils; Dietary lipid	2	0.15	62	97.857	0.96
Support vector machines; Near infrared spectroscopy; Buckwheat starch	1	16.67	1	23.750	1.18
Hypoxia; Mars; Atmospheric pressure	1	10.00	11	25.665	0
Blood pressure; Cholesterol, LDL; Cooperative behavior	1	3.13	3	86.444	109.90
Colitis; Dextran; Mouse brain	1	3.03	5	51.814	0.22
Swine; Finishing; Pigs fed	1	2.27	6	51.389	0.34
Telecommunication; Developing countries; Universal service	1	1.89	3	38.800	0.68

续表

主题	发文量	发文占主题同期论文比(%)	引文量	主题显示度	FWCI值
China; Mental health; Military personnel	1	1.59	1	67.336	0
Taurine; Fish meal; Dietary taurine	1	1.11	9	78.103	3.87
Drug therapy; Obesity; Obese patients	1	0.76	21	78.665	0.50
Siblings; Birth order; Educational attainment	1	0.70	2	79.425	0
Inositol; Polycystic ovary syndrome; Folic acid	1	0.41	8	87.841	1.05
Carbohydrate; Dietary carbohydrate; Dietary carbohydrates	1	0.34	25	91.478	0
Demand; Meat; Expenditure elasticities	1	0.33	3	82.708	0
Clenbuterol; Food additives; Swine urine	1	0.29	11	95.281	0.22
Stable isotopes; Isotopes; Ratio mass	1	0.28	7	91.655	0.25
Pesticides; Pesticide; Pesticide poisoning	1	0.26	4	92.146	10.70
Food safety; HACCP; Food supply	1	0.24	12	90.698	0.38
Linoleic acids, Conjugated; Milk; Trans-10 cis-12	1	0.20	3	94.460	1.21
Broiler chickens; Diet; Enzyme supplementation	1	0.18	4	90.920	0.61
Extrusion; Snacks; Extruded snacks	1	0.16	18	95.485	0
Yield curve; Term structure; Rate models	1	0.15	1	89.288	0.68
Oryza sativa; Rice bran; Pigmented rice	1	0.14	33	96.733	0.52
Food; Food labeling; Nutrition labelling	1	0.13	2	97.694	0
NADPH oxidase; Reactive oxygen species; Dinucleotide phosphate	1	0.12	5	99.028	0
Selenium; Selenites; Inorganic selenium	1	0.11	1	98.321	0
Anthocyanins; Blueberry plant; Beneficial effects	1	0.10	8	98.881	0
Genes; Gene expression; Stable genes	1	0.10	4	96.751	0

3. 需求期刊及保障情况

经引文分析得知农业农村部食物与营养发展研究所发文引用了777种外文

期刊，与国家农业图书馆已订阅外文电子期刊品种进行比对，测算出其外文电子期刊全文保障率达到83.42%，引文量前40的期刊见表31。

表31 农业农村部食物与营养发展研究所引文量前40期刊

编号	期刊名称	引用数量	是否保障
1	Aquaculture	69	是
2	Food Chemistry	55	是
3	Journal of Agricultural and Food Chemistry	40	是
4	Cereal Chemistry	36	是
5	The Lancet	34	是
6	American Journal of Clinical Nutrition	27	是
7	Animal Feed Science and Technology	24	是
8	Aquaculture Nutrition	22	是
9	Journal of Cereal Science	21	是
10	American Journal of Physiology	19	是
11	PLoS ONE	18	是
12	Food Control	18	是
13	General and Comparative Endocrinology	18	是
14	Aquaculture Research	17	是
15	Fish and Shellfish Immunology	16	是
16	Journal of Nutrition	16	是
17	Journal of the Science of Food and Agriculture	15	是
18	Appetite	15	是
19	Journal of Hypertension	15	否
20	Nature	15	是
21	Journal of Functional Foods	14	是
22	European Journal of Clinical Nutrition	13	是
23	Journal of Food Engineering	12	是
24	Journal of Food Science	11	是

续表

编号	期刊名称	引用数量	是否保障
25	Food Quality and Preference	11	是
26	British Journal of Nutrition	11	是
27	Obesity Reviews	11	是
28	Science of the Total Environment	11	是
29	Food Research International	10	是
30	Journal of the World Aquaculture Society	10	是
31	Circulation	10	否
32	Journal of Biological Chemistry	10	是
33	International Journal of Agricultural and Biological Engineering	10	是
34	LWT - Food Science and Technology	9	是
35	Journal of Food Science and Technology	9	是
36	British Food Journal	9	是
37	New England Journal of Medicine	9	是
38	Proceedings of the National Academy of Sciences of the United States of America	8	是
39	Public Health Nutrition	8	是
40	Science	8	是

4. 需求数据库分析

分析各直属研究所引用外文文献的来源数据库，从数据库层面把握各直属研究所需求，是外文全文数据库建设的重要依据，同时也为各直属研究所参与电子资源共建选择数据库提供参考。根据各直属研究所需求期刊分析结果，将其与国家农业图书馆订阅的 27 种外文全文数据库期刊目录进行比对，发现 2017—2019 年农业农村部食物与营养发展研究所引文主要来源数据库如图 35 所示，其中来源于 ScienceDirect（52.29%）、Wiley（16.81%）、Springer（7.59%）和 OUP（6.90%）的引用最多。

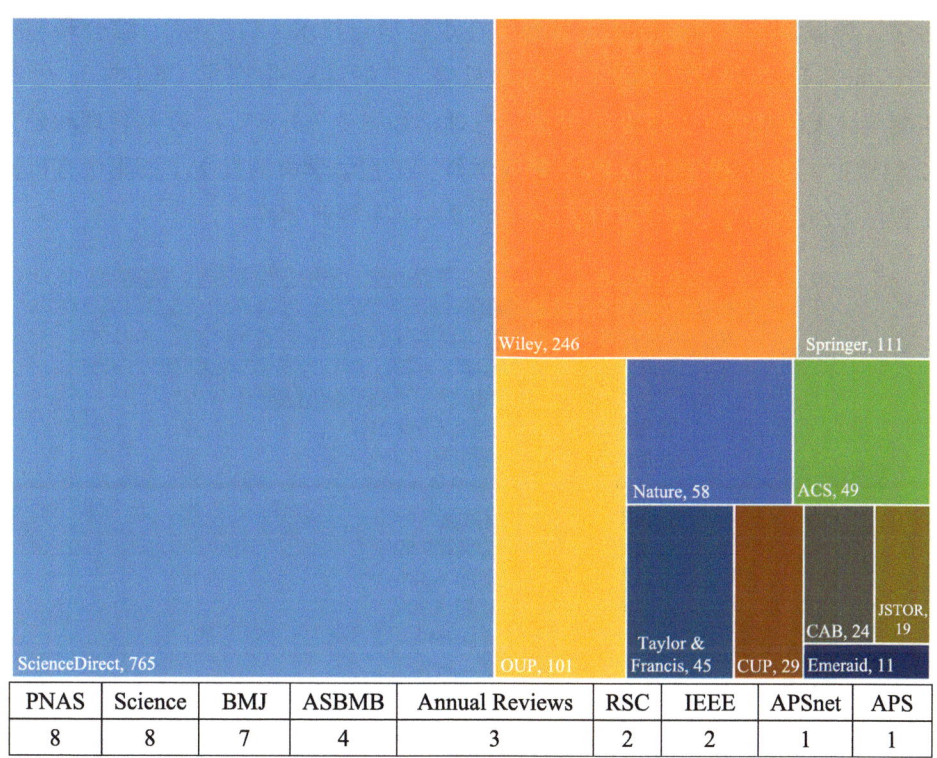

图35　农业农村部食物与营养发展研究所引文来源数据库分布

（十四）农田灌溉研究所

1. 需求学科分析

采集农田灌溉研究所（简称灌溉所）2017—2019年发表的外文期刊论文共计84篇，对其进行学科分析，可以看出该所发文主要集中在农业和生物科学（65.96%），环境科学（39.72%），工程学（29.79%）这三大学科（图36）。除此之外，在生物化学、遗传学和分子生物学，地球与行星科学，社会科学等也有一定数量的发文，说明灌溉所的研究在这些领域也有涉足。

对农业和生物科学，环境科学和工程学这三大学科的亚学科进行分析，结果如图36所示，在农业和生物科学中，发文主要集中在综合农业和生物科学（24.82%），农学和作物科学（22.70%），土壤科学（21.99%），植物科学（8.51%），生态、进化、行为与系统学（4.96%），水产科学（4.96%）等亚学科中。环境科学学科的发文主要集中在水科学与技术（17.73%），综合环境科学（7.80%），污染学（7.09%），环境化学（7.09%），生态学（6.38%），管理监测与政策法规学（3.55%），健康、毒理学和突变（3.55%），废物管理和处置（2.84%），环境工程学（2.84%）等亚学科。工程学学科的发文主要集中在机械工程学（25.53%），土木与结构工程学（2.84%）等亚学科。

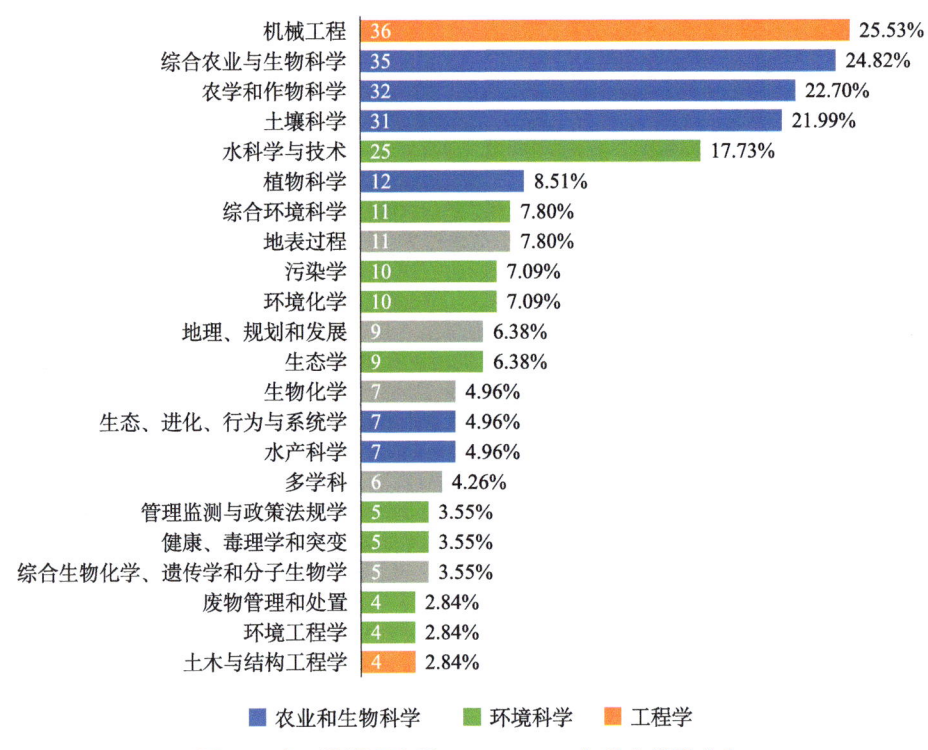

图36　农田灌溉研究所2017—2019年发文学科分布

2. 发文和引文主题分析

将文献按照主题组织，进行更细粒度的需求分析，是为了解决单纯按照学科为单元进行分析，针对性不强，导致资源建设成本高、利用不充分的问题。2017—2019年农田灌溉研究所发文共计涉及88个主题，通过相应的遴选指标，遴选出发文、引文涉及的主要主题（表32）。可以看出灌溉所在"Winter wheat; Irrigation; Jointing stage"这个主题的发文最多，由此判断该研究所较为侧重这一领域的研究，在"Pyrolysis; Soil amendment; Biochar amendment"主题的引文最多，表明在该领域文献的需求强度最高；该所在"Soil water; China; Soil moisture"这个主题的发文占该主题全球同期论文的14.29%，说明其在全球范围内对该领域的研究有较为突出的贡献;该所参与的最受关注、发展势头最好的主题为"Pyrolysis; Soil amendment; Biochar amendment",主题显示度值为99.968;而该所发文具有较高引文影响力的主题为"Evapotranspiration; Penman-Monteith equation; Evapotranspiration ET0",发文 FWCI 值是同类论文的 3.71 倍。综上,通过主题分析的结果不仅从各个角度反映出灌溉所学科文献资源的精细化需求,同时也体现了研究所研究领域的分布态势,能够为其学科规划和发展提供参考。

表 32 农田灌溉研究所发文引文主要主题

主题	发文数	发文占主题同期论文比 (%)	引文量	主题显示度	FWCI 值
Winter wheat; Irrigation; Jointing stage	8	2.60	74	83.480	1.44
Irrigation; Deficit irrigation; Root-zone drying	7	2.33	76	90.822	0.21
Pyrolysis; Soil amendment; Biochar amendment	5	0.09	91	99.968	1.54
Cotton; Microirrigation; Seed cotton	4	8.51	9	60.505	0.29
Microirrigation; Irrigation; Emitter clogging	4	1.10	1	83.369	0.35
Irrigation; Heavy metal; Water irrigation	3	8.57	15	58.801	0.24
Nitrogen; Nutrition; Dilution curve	3	3.09	67	80.054	1.76
China; Corn; Accumulated temperature	3	1.53	5	76.899	0.10
Irrigation; Sprinklers; Center pivot	3	1.04	6	85.920	0.59
Microirrigation; Irrigation; Subsurface drip	3	0.90	38	86.403	0
Deficit irrigation; Irrigation; Regulated deficit	3	0.42	77	96.521	0.98
Soil; Microbial community; Soil fungal	3	0.22	35	99.229	0.25
Vegetation; Chlorophyll; Hyperspectral reflectance	3	0.15	44	99.410	2.14
Evapotranspiration; Eddy covariance; Canopy resistance	2	3.33	34	70.578	2.10
Gorge; Reservoir; Algal bloom	2	1.65	2	71.634	0.59
Saline water; Microirrigation; Salt accumulation	2	0.77	38	82.397	0.16
Flood control; Floods; Joint return	2	0.54	5	92.441	0.41
Rice; *Oryza sativa*; Super rice	2	0.51	16	88.148	0.31

续表

主题	发文数	发文占主题同期论文比 (%)	引文量	主题显示度	FWCI 值
Agricultural machinery; Tillage; Rotary tillage	2	0.51	6	85.928	1.35
Cotton; Gossypium hirsutum; Seed cotton	2	0.50	48	89.739	0.62
Rice; Drought; Lowland rice	2	0.34	16	95.657	0.28
Mulching; Plastic film; Residual plastic	2	0.33	25	94.587	0.89
Evapotranspiration; Penman-Monteith equation; Evapotranspiration ET0	2	0.28	59	95.416	3.71
Microbial community; Soil microorganism; Acid PLFA	2	0.26	18	98.027	0.13
Evapotranspiration; Energy balance; Evaporative fraction	2	0.22	22	98.195	0.28
Trend analysis; Rainfall; Slope estimator	2	0.18	3	97.803	0
Centrifugal pumps; Pumps; Impeller inlet	2	0.16	17	93.759	0.08
Nitrous oxide; Soil emission; Oxide emissions	2	0.14	89	99.321	1.39
Antibiotic resistance; Drug resistance, Microbial; Antibiotic-resistant bacteria	2	0.09	61	99.881	1.54
Soil water; China; Soil moisture	1	14.29	0	26.333	0.51
Accident prevention; Accidents; Soil-based control	1	9.09	0	13.309	0.33
Tobacco; Irrigation; Flue-cured tobacco	1	7.69	2	35.750	0.86
Artificial neural network; Land reclamation; Saline soil	1	3.03	2	56.643	0.38
Rice; Leaves; Leaf rolling	1	2.70	3	45.195	0
Flooded conditions; Cotton; Summer maize	1	1.85	14	74.749	1.54
Acid sulfate soils; Rice; Acid sulfate soil	1	1.82	5	58.426	0
Valves (mechanical); Seals; Butterfly valves	1	1.49	1	59.550	0

3. 需求期刊及保障情况

经引文分析得知农田灌溉研究所发文引用了 723 种外文期刊，与国家农业图书馆已订阅外文电子期刊品种进行比对，测算出其外文电子期刊全文保障率达到 91.83%，引文量前 40 的期刊见表 33。

表 33 农田灌溉研究所引文量前 40 期刊

编号	期刊名称	引用数量	是否保障
1	Agricultural Water Management	310	是
2	Field Crops Research	133	是
3	Plant and Soil	109	是
4	Soil Biology and Biochemistry	98	是
5	Irrigation Science	71	是
6	Water Resources Research	63	是
7	Environmental Science and Technology	60	是
8	Agricultural and Forest Meteorology	53	是
9	Agronomy Journal	50	是
10	Journal of Hydrology	47	是
11	Science of the Total Environment	46	是
12	Global Change Biology	44	是
13	Journal of Experimental Botany	41	是
14	Nature	38	是
15	Chemosphere	37	是
16	Agriculture, Ecosystems and Environment	37	是
17	Environmental Science and Pollution Research	35	是
18	Geoderma	34	是
19	Environmental Pollution	34	是
20	Soil Science Society of America Journal	34	是
21	Soil and Tillage Research	31	是
22	PLoS ONE	30	是
23	Biology and Fertility of Soils	30	是
24	Scientific Reports	29	是

续表

编号	期刊名称	引用数量	是否保障
25	Proceedings of the National Academy of Sciences of the United States of America	29	是
26	European Journal of Agronomy	27	是
27	Applied and Environmental Microbiology	25	是
28	Journal of Plant Nutrition	24	是
29	Journal of Hazardous Materials	23	是
30	Water Research	23	是
31	Science	22	是
32	Plant Physiology	22	是
33	Remote Sensing of Environment	21	是
34	Journal of Physiology	21	是
35	Journal of Soils and Sediments	21	是
36	Ecology	21	是
37	Environmental and Experimental Botany	20	是
38	Water (Switzerland)	20	是
39	Advances in Water Resources	20	是
40	Scientia Horticulturae	20	是

4. 需求数据库分析

分析各直属研究所引用外文文献的来源数据库，从数据库层面把握各直属研究所需求，是外文全文数据库建设的重要依据，同时也为各直属研究所参与电子资源共建选择数据库提供参考。根据各直属研究所需求期刊分析结果，将其与国家农业图书馆订阅的27种外文全文数据库期刊目录进行比对，发现2017—2019年农田灌溉研究所引文主要来源数据库如图37所示，其中来源于ScienceDirect（52.68%）、Springer（19.03%）和Wiley（12.57%）的引用最多。

四 各直属研究所需求和保障分析

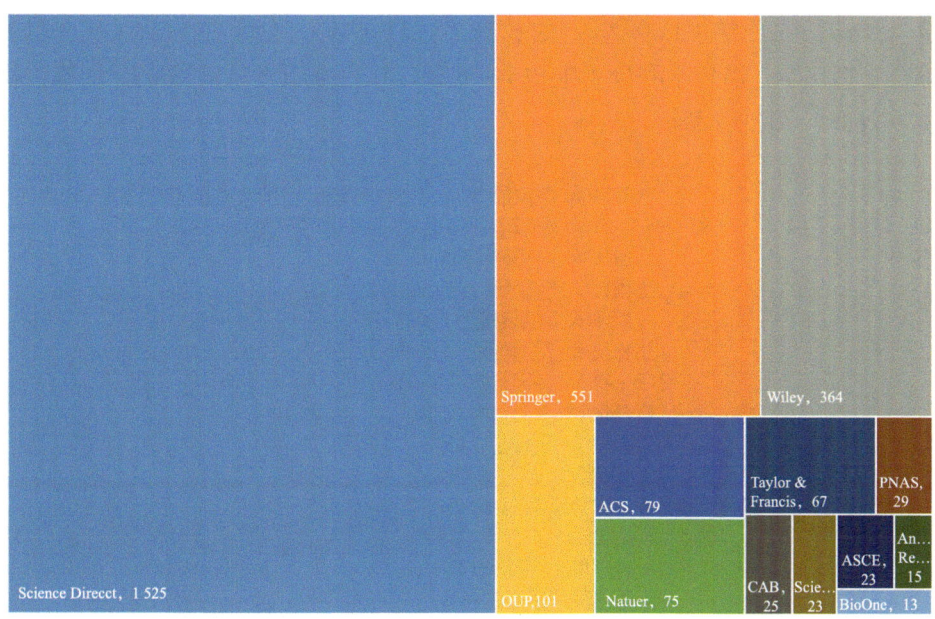

CUP	RSC	IEEE	JSTOR	ASME	MS	APSnet	Emerald
13	11	6	2	2	1	1	1

图37 农田灌溉研究所引文来源数据库分布

(十五) 水稻研究所

1. 需求学科分析

采集水稻研究所2017—2019年发表的外文期刊论文共计446篇，对其进行学科分析，可以看出该所发文主要集中在农业和生物科学（74.19%），生物化学、遗传学和分子生物学（48.18%）这两大学科（图38）。除此之外，在化学、化学工程、环境科学、计算机科学、免疫与微生物学等也有一定数量的发文，说明水稻研究所的研究在这些领域也有涉足。

对农业和生物科学，生物化学、遗传学和分子生物学这两大学科的亚学科进行分析，结果如图38所示，在农业和生物科学中，发文主要集中在植物科学（52.01%），农学和作物科学（38.81%），土壤科学（12.81%），综合农业和生物科学（7.65%），生态、进化、行为与系统学（5.93%），食品科学（3.63%）等亚学科中。生物化学、遗传学和分子生物学学科的发文主要集中在遗传学

（13.58%），生理学（11.09%），生物技术（11.09%），分子生物学（10.90%），综合生物化学、遗传学和分子生物学（6.50%），生物化学（4.78%），细胞生物学（3.63%）等亚学科。

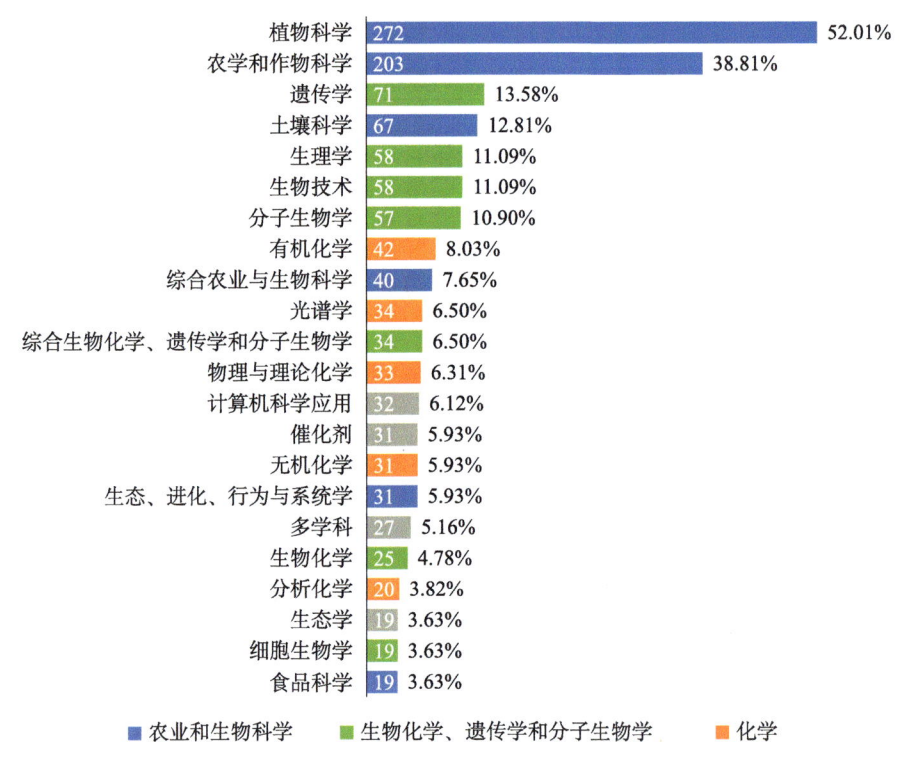

图 38 水稻研究所 2017—2019 年发文学科分布

2. 发文和引文主题分析

将文献按照主题组织，进行更细粒度的需求分析，是为了解决单纯按照学科为单元进行分析，针对性不强，导致资源建设成本高、利用不充分的问题。2017—2019 年水稻研究所发文共计涉及 213 个主题，通过相应的遴选指标，遴选出发文、引文涉及的主要主题（表 34）。可以看出水稻所在 "Rice; *Oryza sativa*; Cultivated rice" 这个主题的发文和引文最多，由此判断该研究所较为侧重这一领域的研究，在该领域文献的需求强度也最高；该所在 "Mutants; Rice; Mimic mutant" 这个主题的发文占该主题全球同期论文的 20.93%，说明其在全球范围内对该领域的研究有较为突出的贡献；该所参与的最受关注、发展势头最好的主题为 "Genome; Genes; Single guide"，主题显示度值为 99.987；

而该所发文具有较高引文影响力的主题为"Arsenic; *Oryza sativa*; Arsenic accumulation",发文 FWCI 值是同类论文的 5.13 倍。综上,通过主题分析的结果不仅从各个角度反映出水稻研究所学科文献资源的精细化需求,同时也体现了研究所研究领域的分布态势,能够为其学科规划和发展提供参考。

表 34　水稻研究所发文引文主要主题

主题	发文量	发文占主题同期论文比(%)	引文量	主题显示度	FWCI 值
Rice; *Oryza sativa*; Cultivated rice	54	4.38	1 318	98.470	1.25
Rice; *Oryza sativa*; Super rice	21	5.38	318	88.148	0.69
Genome; Genes; Single guide	21	0.33	333	99.987	3.51
Phytoremediation; Cadmium; Pot experiment	13	1.06	264	98.956	1.93
Chloroplasts; Plastids; Chloroplast gene	10	5.05	210	90.641	1.12
Rice; Temperature; Night temperature	10	3.62	235	89.540	1.17
Mutants; Rice; Mimic mutant	9	20.93	177	66.837	0.59
Aluminum; Toxicity; Aluminum tolerance	9	1.70	260	95.234	1.48
Salinity; Salt tolerance; Salt tolerant	9	0.51	244	98.949	1.18
Rice; *Oryza sativa*; Cooked rice	8	3.83	176	83.339	0.39
Starch; Endosperm; Starch biosynthetic	8	1.78	244	94.777	2.73
Senescence; Transcription factors; Leaf senescence	8	1.27	185	96.753	1.02
Rice; *Oryza sativa*; Oryzae isolates	7	1.74	119	91.841	2.31
Flowering; Rice; Long-day conditions	7	1.57	274	94.544	1.61
Paddy field; Nitrous oxide; Rice paddy	7	1.11	140	95.938	1.09
Flowers; Genes; Organ identity	7	0.92	234	96.989	1.33
Mutants; Rice; Recessive nuclear	6	6.82	104	71.256	0.74
Organic nitrogen; Nitrogen; Soil nitrogen	6	3.26	150	86.620	1.02
Photosynthesis; Leaves; Mesophyll conductance	6	0.90	108	97.772	2.87
Rice; *Oryza sativa*; Genic male	5	9.09	47	48.791	0.43
Pollen; Anthers; Tapetal cells	5	1.25	224	94.342	1.52

续表

主题	发文量	发文占主题同期论文比 (%)	引文量	主题显示度	FWCI值
RNA editing; Genome, Mitochondrial; Editing factors	5	0.95	172	96.083	0.76
Flooded conditions; Submergence; Aerenchyma formation	5	0.61	160	96.747	1.16
Rice; Leaves; Leaf rolling	4	10.81	68	45.195	0.73
Rice; Cold tolerance; Booting stage	4	4.65	85	77.420	1.76
C4 photosynthesis; Photosynthesis; Bundle sheath	4	1.28	65	94.110	0.70
Nucleopolyhedrovirus; Baculoviridae; Budded virus	4	1.22	56	88.362	0.38
Magnaporthe; *Oryza sativa*; Plant infection	4	0.90	124	93.250	0.73
Electronic tongues; Tongue; Taste	4	0.87	100	93.831	0.63
Nitrates; Nitrogen; Nitrate transporters	4	0.77	179	97.199	0.93
Rice; Drought; Lowland rice	4	0.68	89	95.657	1.14
Oryza sativa; Rice bran; Pigmented rice	4	0.55	86	96.733	4.64
Acetylation; Lysine; Acetylated proteins	4	0.47	76	99.261	0.48
Arsenic; *Oryza sativa*; Arsenic accumulation	4	0.36	117	99.216	5.13
Nitrogen; *Oryza sativa*; Dry matter	3	17.65	36	31.216	1.65
Eye color; Culicidae; Pteridines	3	6.82	52	61.054	0.95
Rice; Burkholderia; B glumae	3	5.00	18	64.406	0.27
Rice; Blight; Rice sheath	3	3.61	58	65.645	0.89
Rice; *Oryza sativa*; Rice populations	3	2.80	29	79.406	1.73

3. 需求期刊及保障情况

经引文分析得知水稻研究所发文引用了1 452种外文期刊，与国家农业图书馆已订阅外文电子期刊品种进行比对，测算出其外文电子期刊全文保障率达到93.58%，引文量前40的期刊见表35。

表 35 水稻研究所引文量前 40 期刊

编号	期刊名称	引用数量	是否保障
1	Plant Physiology	1 083	是
2	Plant Cell	726	是
3	Journal of Experimental Botany	721	是
4	Plant Journal	666	是
5	Proceedings of the National Academy of Sciences of the United States of America	578	是
6	Theoretical and Applied Genetics	395	是
7	PLoS ONE	377	是
8	Frontiers in Plant Science	347	是
9	Nature Genetics	342	是
10	Field Crops Research	316	是
11	Plant Molecular Biology	283	是
12	Plant and Cell Physiology	283	是
13	Journal of Physiology	281	是
14	Molecular Plant	274	是
15	Plant, Cell and Environment	266	是
16	Nature	261	是
17	Planta	229	是
18	Science	224	是
19	Plant and Soil	223	是
20	Trends in Plant Science	207	是
21	Journal of Integrative Plant Biology	201	是
22	Annual Review of Plant Biology	184	是
23	Scientific Reports	180	是
24	Plant Science	175	是

续表

编号	期刊名称	引用数量	是否保障
25	Current Opinion in Plant Biology	167	是
26	Annals of Botany	154	是
27	Rice	150	是
28	Nucleic Acids Research	150	是
29	Plant Biotechnology Journal	142	是
30	Plant Growth Regulation	141	是
31	Journal of Agricultural and Food Chemistry	137	是
32	Food Chemistry	135	是
33	Genetics	133	是
34	BMC Plant Biology	131	是
35	Bioinformatics	127	是
36	Journal of Plant Physiology	126	是
37	Journal of Biological Chemistry	126	是
38	Physiologia Plantarum	123	是
39	Environmental and Experimental Botany	119	是
40	Nature Communications	118	是

4. 需求数据库分析

分析各直属研究所引用外文文献的来源数据库，从数据库层面把握各直属研究所需求，是外文全文数据库建设的重要依据，同时也为各直属研究所参与电子资源共建选择数据库提供参考。根据各直属研究所需求期刊分析结果，将其与国家农业图书馆订阅的27种外文全文数据库期刊目录进行比对，发现2017—2019年水稻研究所引文主要来源数据库如图39所示，其中来源于ScienceDirect（31.25%）、Springer（18.75%）、Wiley（17.20%）和OUP（11.88%）的引用最多。

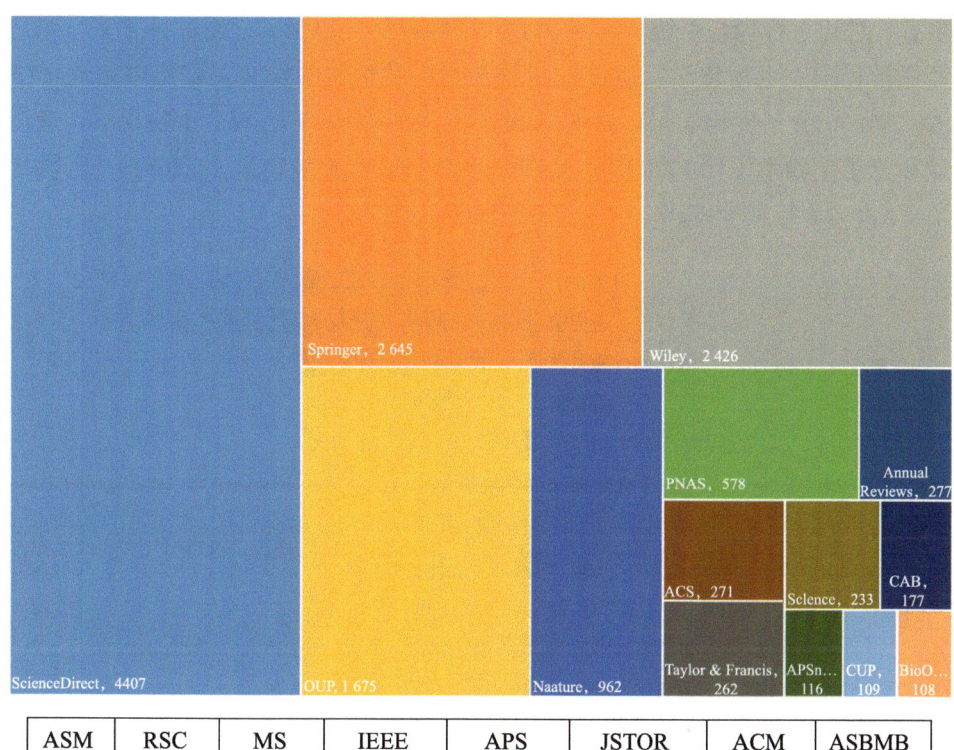

图 39　水稻研究所引文来源数据库分布

（十六）棉花研究所

1. 需求学科分析

采集棉花研究所 2017—2019 年发表的外文期刊论文共计 351 篇，对其进行学科分析，可以看出该所发文主要集中在农业和生物科学（63.56%），生物化学、遗传学和分子生物学（57.18%）这两大学科（图 40）。除此之外，在化学、计算机科学、环境科学等也有一定数量的发文，说明棉花研究所的研究在这些领域也有涉足。

对农业和生物科学，生物化学、遗传学和分子生物学这两大学科的亚学科进行分析，结果如图 40 所示，在农业和生物科学中，发文主要集中在植物科学（34.57%），农学和作物科学（21.28%），综合农业和生物科学（13.56%），生态、进化、行为与系统学（4.79%），土壤科学（2.93%），昆虫科学（2.66%）等亚学科中。生物化学、遗传学和分子生物学学科的发文主要集中在遗传学（29.79%），分子生物学（13.83%），生物技术（12.77%），综合生物化学、遗传学和分子生物学（10.37%），生理学（5.59%），细胞生物学（2.66%），生物化学（2.66%）等亚学科。

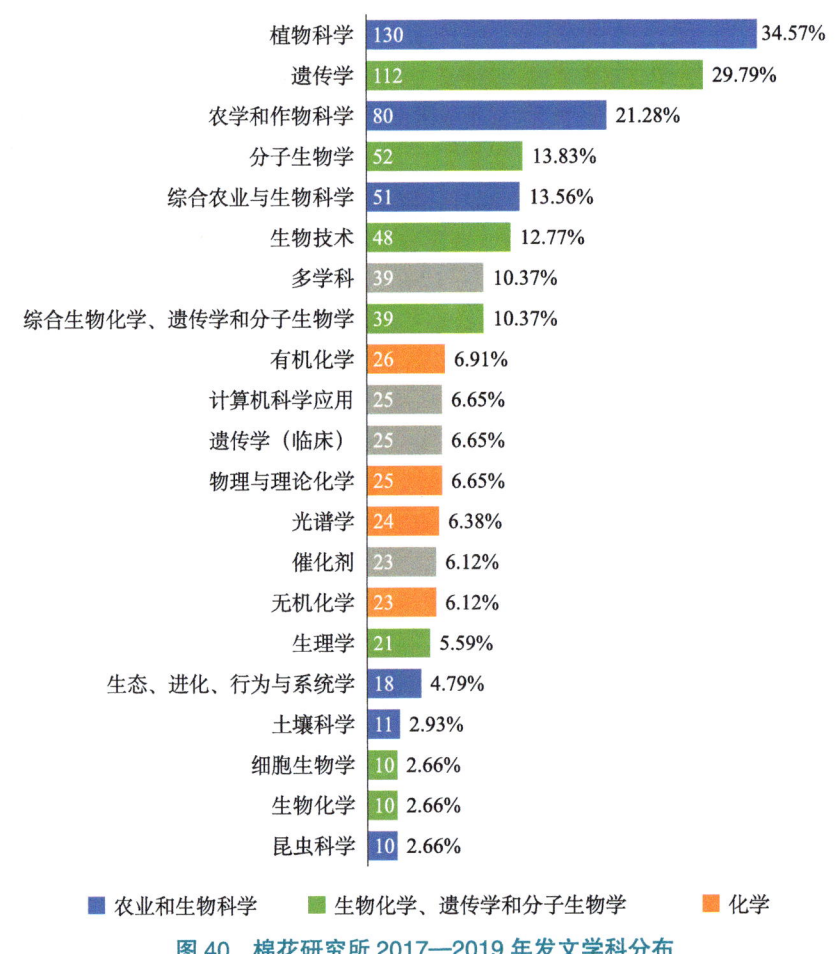

图 40　棉花研究所 2017—2019 年发文学科分布

2. 发文和引文主题分析

将文献按照主题组织，进行更细粒度的需求分析，是为了解决单纯按照学科为单元进行分析，针对性不强，导致资源建设成本高、利用不充分的问题。2017—2019 年棉花研究所发文共计涉及 157 个主题，通过相应的遴选指标，遴选出发文、引文涉及的主要主题（表 36）。可以看出棉花研究所在"Gossypium; *Gossypium hirsutum*; Fiber elongation"这个主题的发文和引文最多，由此判断该研究所较为侧重这一领域的研究，在该领域文献的需求强度最高，并且该主题的发文占该主题全球同期论文的 17.95%，说明其在全球范围内对该领域的研究有较为突出的贡献；该所参与的最受关注、发展势头最好的主题分别为"MicroRNAs; RNA; Degradome sequencing"和"DNA methylation; Epigenetics; Methylation RdDM"，主题显示度值分别为 99.589 和 99.098；而该所发文具有较高引文影响力的主题为"Genome; Genes; Single guide"，发文 FWCI 值是同类论文的 4.43 倍。综上，通过主题分析的结果不仅从各个角度反映出棉花研究所学科文献资源的精细化需求，同时也体现了研究所研究领域的分布态势，能够为其学科规划和发展提供参考。

表 36 棉花研究所发文引文主要主题

主题	发文量	发文占主题同期论文比(%)	引文量	主题显示度	FWCI 值
Gossypium; *Gossypium hirsutum*; Fiber elongation	93	17.95	2 735	93.294	1.29
Verticillium; *Verticillium dahliae*; Dahliae isolates	16	4.91	308	93.518	1.46
Cotton; *Gossypium hirsutum*; Seed cotton	15	3.73	175	89.739	0.39
Senescence; Transcription factors; Leaf senescence	9	1.42	273	96.753	1.45
Salinity; Salt tolerance; Salt tolerant	8	0.46	223	98.949	1.55
Bacillus thuringiensis; Genetically modified organisms; Non-target organisms	8	2.35	166	91.786	0.76
MicroRNAs; RNA; Degradome sequencing	5	0.24	333	99.589	1.04
DNA Methylation; Epigenetics; Methylation RdDm	5	0.50	168	99.098	0.62
Indoleacetic acids; Auxins; Auxin efflux	5	0.52	233	98.907	2.02
Transcription factors; Genes; Factors TFs	5	0.95	222	95.156	1.21
Rice; *Oryza sativa*; Cultivated rice	4	0.32	263	98.470	2.86
Abscisic acid; Arabidopsis; Guard cells	4	0.46	170	98.300	2.42
Brassinosteroids; Arabidopsis; BR Biosynthesis	4	0.52	202	97.909	0.41
Diacylglycerol O-Acyltransferase; Seeds; Oil biosynthesis	4	0.78	81	96.332	0.90

续表

主题	发文量	发文占主题同期论文比 (%)	引文量	主题显示度	FWCI 值
Genome; Genes; Single guide	3	0.05	109	99.987	4.43
Wolbachia; Symbionts; Cytoplasmic incompatibility	3	0.23	72	99.267	0.52
Arabidopsis; Meristem; Shoot apical	3	0.44	112	98.863	3.75
Droughts; Transcription factors; Freezing tolerance	3	0.26	349	98.632	2.43
Polyploidy; Allopolyploidy; Diploid progenitors	3	0.49	114	97.489	0.93
Gibberellins; Plant growth regulators; Gibberellic acid	3	0.58	118	95.769	0
Flowering; Rice; Long-day conditions	3	0.67	109	94.544	1.86
Pollen; Anthers; Tapetal cells	3	0.75	101	94.342	0.99
Protein kinases; Calcium; CDPK genes	3	0.83	132	94.126	3.63
Odor compounds; Carrier proteins; Chemosensory proteins	3	0.73	76	93.839	0.21
Meristem; Leaves; Leaf primordia	3	0.83	120	92.031	1.14
Polygalacturonase; Botrytis; Plant cell	3	3.61	93	80.473	1.30
Cotton; Microirrigation; Seed cotton	3	6.38	28	60.505	1.63
RNA, Long Untranslated; Neoplasms; Proliferation migration	2	0.02	135	99.984	0.34
Climate change; Crop; Crop models	2	0.08	42	99.758	0.72
Herbivores; Herbivory; Volatiles HIPVs	2	0.21	29	98.624	0.09
Lignin; Cell walls; Lignin biosynthesis	2	0.23	105	98.238	0.55
Wheat; Triticum; Adult plant	2	0.24	69	97.364	0
Flowers; Genes; Organ identity	2	0.26	157	96.989	1.28
Genes; Gene expression; Stable genes	2	0.19	183	96.751	0.33
RNA editing; Genome, Mitochondrial; Editing factors	2	0.38	114	96.083	1.01
Genes; Gene Regulatory Networks; Co-expression networks	2	0.62	52	94.255	1.14
Arabidopsis; Plants; Vacuolar trafficking	2	0.63	48	94.049	1.37
Retroelements; DNA transposable elements; Inverted-repeat transposable	2	0.55	97	92.375	0.38
Genes; Transcription factors; Genome	2	4.65	56	64.494	2.71

3. 需求期刊及保障情况

经引文分析得知棉花研究所发文引用了 1 427 种外文期刊,与国家农业图书馆已订阅外文电子期刊品种进行比对,测算出其外文电子期刊全文保障率达到 92.85%,引文量前 40 的期刊见表 37。

表 37 棉花研究所引文量前 40 期刊

编号	期刊名称	引用数量	是否保障
1	Plant Physiology	808	是
2	Plant Cell	724	是
3	PLoS ONE	668	是
4	Plant Journal	546	是
5	Proceedings of the National Academy of Sciences of the United States of America	451	是
6	Nucleic Acids Research	437	是
7	Nature Genetics	433	是
8	BMC Genomics	398	是
9	Frontiers in Plant Science	388	是
10	Journal of Experimental Botany	357	是
11	Nature Biotechnology	352	是
12	Theoretical and Applied Genetics	340	是
13	Nature	301	是
14	BMC Plant Biology	289	是
15	Scientific Reports	283	是
16	Bioinformatics	278	是
17	Plant Molecular Biology	259	是
18	Euphytica	232	是
19	Science	225	是
20	Journal of Physiology	218	是
21	Crop Science	197	是
22	Plant Biotechnology Journal	185	是

续表

编号	期刊名称	引用数量	是否保障
23	Field Crops Research	179	是
24	Molecular Genetics and Genomics	178	是
25	Plant and Cell Physiology	178	是
26	Trends in Plant Science	173	是
27	Molecular Biology and Evolution	165	是
28	Planta	157	是
29	Genetics	155	是
30	Current Opinion in Plant Biology	154	是
31	Plant Science	154	是
32	Annual Review of Plant Biology	148	是
33	PCR Methods and Applications	148	是
34	Cell	146	是
35	Plant Cell Reports	146	是
36	Molecular Breeding	135	是
37	Journal of Biological Chemistry	133	是
38	Genome Biology	132	是
39	Journal of Integrative Plant Biology	123	是
40	Molecular Plant	113	是

4. 需求数据库分析

分析各直属研究所引用外文文献的来源数据库，从数据库层面把握各直属研究所需求，是外文全文数据库建设的重要依据，同时也为各直属研究所参与电子资源共建选择数据库提供参考。根据各直属研究所需求期刊分析结果，将其与国家农业图书馆订阅的27种外文全文数据库期刊目录进行比对，发现2017—2019年棉花研究所引文主要来源数据库如图41所示，其中来源于ScienceDirect（25.95%）、Springer（21.01%）、Wiley（14.85%）、OUP（14.67%）和Nature（11.27%）的引用最多。

四　各直属研究所需求和保障分析　117

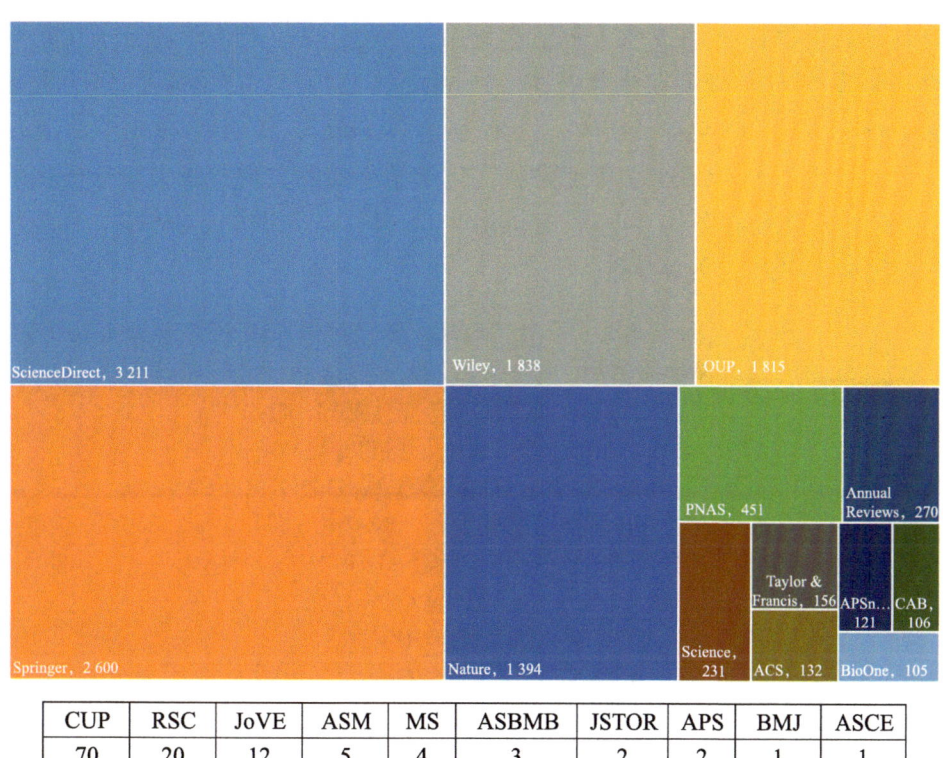

图41　棉花研究所引文来源数据库分布

（十七）油料作物研究所

1. 需求学科分析

采集油料作物研究所（简称油料所）2017—2019年发表的外文期刊论文共计399篇，对其进行学科分析，可以看出该所发文主要集中在农业和生物科学（57.44%），生物化学、遗传学和分子生物学（44.42%）和化学（23.95%）这三大学科（图42）。除此之外，在化学工程，环境科学，免疫与微生物学，药理学、毒理学和药剂学，医学，工程学，计算机科学等也有一定数量的发文，说明油料所的研究在这些领域也有涉足。

对农业和生物科学，生物化学、遗传学和分子生物学和化学这三大学科的亚学科进行分析，结果如图42所示，在农业和生物科学中，发文主要集中在植物科学（31.16%），农学和作物科学（16.51%），食品科学（13.95%），综合农业和生物科学（9.77%）等亚学科中。生物化学、遗传学和分子生物学学科的发文主要集中在生物技术（15.58%），遗传学（15.35%），分子生物学（8.60%），生物化学（6.74%），生理学（4.88%），综合生物化学、遗传学和分子生物学（4.65%）等亚学科。化学学科的发文主要集中在分析化学（10.47%），普通化学（7.44%），有机化学（6.51%），光谱学（4.65%），物理与理论化学（4.19%）等亚学科。

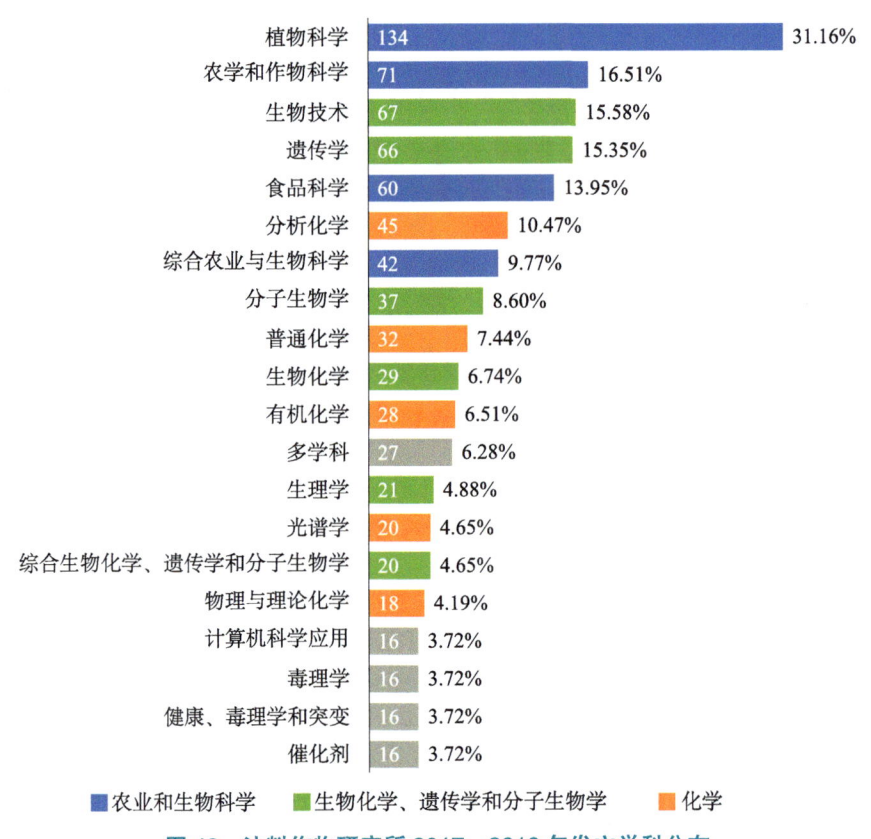

图 42　油料作物研究所 2017—2019 年发文学科分布

2. 发文和引文主题分析

将文献按照主题组织，进行更细粒度的需求分析，是为了解决单纯按照学科为单元进行分析，针对性不强，导致资源建设成本高、利用不充分的问题。2017—2019 年油料作物研究所发文共计涉及 208 个主题，通过相应的遴选指标，遴选出发文、引文涉及的主要主题（表 38）。可以看出油料所在"*Arachis hypogaea*; Peanuts; Cultivated peanut"这个主题的发文最多，由此判断该研究所较为侧重这个领域的研究，在"*Brassica napus*; *Brassica rapa*; Linkage map"主题的引文最多，表明在该领域文献的需求强度最高；该所在"*Sesamum indicum*; Sesamum; Sesame accessions"这个主题的发文占该主题全球同期论文的 7.43%，说明其在全球范围内对该领域的研究有较为突出的贡献；该所参与的最受关注、发展势头最好的主题为"Mycotoxins; Zearalenone; Deoxynivalenol DON"，主题显示度值为 99.414；而该所发文具有较高引文影响力的主题为"Genome; Genes; Single guide"，发文 FWCI 值是同类论文的 3.08 倍。综上，通过主题分析的结果不仅从各个角度反映出油料所学科文献资源的精细化需求，同时也体现了研究所研究领域的分布态势，能够为其学科规划和发展提供参考。

表 38 油料作物研究所发文引文主要主题

主题	发文量	发文占主题同期论文比(%)	引文量	主题显示度	FWCI 值
Arachis hypogaea; Peanuts; Cultivated peanut	23	7.19	470	87.210	2.59
Brassica napus; *Brassica rapa*; Linkage map	21	4.94	512	94.999	1.58
Mycotoxins; Zearalenone; Deoxynivalenol DON	14	1.30	304	99.414	1.24
Brassica rapa; Rapeseed oil; Rapeseed oils	12	7.06	146	85.043	0.49
Sesamum indicum; Sesamum; Sesame accessions	11	7.43	247	73.899	1.01
Organisms, Genetically modified; Genetically modified organisms; Organisms GMOs	10	2.70	155	91.612	0.66
Diacylglycerol O-Acyltransferase; Seeds; Oil biosynthesis	9	1.76	247	96.332	0.33
Lipids; Mass spectrometry; Shotgun lipidomics	7	0.81	152	99.023	0.80
Genome; Genes; Single guide	6	0.10	295	99.987	3.08
Droughts; Transcription factors; Freezing tolerance	6	0.51	280	98.632	1.48
Monoclonal antibodies; Haptens; Competitive enzyme-linked	6	3.41	68	88.664	1.39
Phosphorus; Phosphates; Phosphate starvation	5	0.63	88	97.851	1.36
Abscisic acid; Arabidopsis; Guard cells	5	0.57	232	98.300	0.62
Sclerotinia sclerotiorum; Sclerotinia; Sclerotiorum isolates	5	1.60	105	89.291	1.08

续表

主题	发文量	发文占主题同期论文比(%)	引文量	主题显示度	FWCI值
Oils and fats; Oils; Oil adulteration	5	0.77	89	96.798	0.74
Phytoplasma; Witches' broom; Aster yellows	4	0.51	27	91.367	0.83
Salinity; Salt tolerance; Salt tolerant	4	0.23	112	98.949	2.77
Selenium; Selenites; Inorganic selenium	4	0.42	135	98.321	1.10
Anthocyanins; Transcription factors; Anthocyanin biosynthetic	4	0.26	149	98.997	0.74
Flowers; Genes; Organ identity	4	0.53	112	96.989	0.45
Phytosterols; Cholesterol; Plant stanol	4	0.85	117	95.697	1.83
Agglomeration; Fluorescence; Aggregation-caused quenching	4	0.14	75	99.941	2.01
Lipases; Oils and fats; Enzymatic interesterification	4	1.02	77	93.982	0.56
Enzyme immobilization; Lipases; Cross-linked enzyme	4	0.26	89	99.728	1.67
Aspergillus flavus; Aflatoxins; Flavus strains	4	0.94	137	94.888	1.24
Olea; Olive oil; Olive paste	3	0.19	87	99.626	0.44
DNA; Amplification; Electrochemical aptasensor	3	0.13	66	99.911	1.17
Flooded conditions; Submergence; Aerenchyma formation	3	0.37	83	96.747	0.78
Cadmium; Phytochelatins; Cadmium stress	3	0.25	64	98.655	1.21
Glucosinolates; Brassica; Glucosinolate biosynthesis	3	0.35	74	97.826	0.42
Melatonin; Antioxidants; Exogenous melatonin	3	0.24	80	99.537	2.17
Carbon nitride; Photocatalysts; Photocatalysis	3	0.05	90	99.996	1.21
Polyploidy; Allopolyploidy; Diploid progenitors	3	0.49	134	97.489	0.92
Triglycerides; Glycerol; Triacylglycerols TAGs	3	2.16	74	87.138	0.07
Sesamum; Sesame oil; Sesame seeds	3	1.18	85	89.396	1.52
Proteomics; Droughts; Protein spots	3	0.83	49	90.931	1.38

3. 需求期刊及保障情况

经引文分析得知油料作物研究所发文引用了 1 941 种外文期刊，与国家农业图书馆已订阅外文电子期刊品种进行比对，测算出其外文电子期刊全文保障率达到 92.61%，引文量前 40 的期刊见表 39。

表 39　油料作物研究所引文量前 40 期刊

编号	期刊名称	引用数量	是否保障
1	Plant Physiology	588	是
2	Plant Cell	519	是
3	PLoS ONE	480	是
4	Plant Journal	479	是
5	Proceedings of the National Academy of Sciences of the United States of America	389	是
6	Frontiers in Plant Science	383	是
7	Journal of Agricultural and Food Chemistry	371	是
8	Theoretical and Applied Genetics	354	是
9	Food Chemistry	354	是
10	Journal of Experimental Botany	319	是
11	Nucleic Acids Research	308	是
12	BMC Plant Biology	253	是
13	Analytical Chemistry	245	是
14	Science	243	是
15	Scientific Reports	236	是
16	BMC Genomics	225	是
17	Nature	223	是
18	Bioinformatics	204	是
19	Plant Biotechnology Journal	182	是
20	Nature Genetics	177	是
21	Biosensors and Bioelectronics	171	是
22	Journal of Physiology	169	是

续表

编号	期刊名称	引用数量	是否保障
23	Trends in Plant Science	161	是
24	Plant and Cell Physiology	153	是
25	Plant Molecular Biology	151	是
26	JAOCS, Journal of the American Oil Chemists' Society	150	是
27	Genetics	145	是
28	Analytica Chimica Acta	143	是
29	Current Opinion in Plant Biology	131	是
30	Annual Review of Plant Biology	130	是
31	Nature Biotechnology	122	是
32	Genome Biology	120	是
33	Euphytica	116	是
34	Cell	115	是
35	Plant Cell Reports	110	是
36	Plant Physiology and Biochemistry	109	是
37	Journal of Chromatography A	109	是
38	Nature Communications	109	是
39	Plant Science	108	是
40	Journal of Biological Chemistry	107	是

4. 需求数据库分析

分析各直属研究所引用外文文献的来源数据库，从数据库层面把握各直属研究所需求，是外文全文数据库建设的重要依据，同时也为各直属研究所参与电子资源共建选择数据库提供参考。根据各直属研究所需求期刊分析结果，将其与国家农业图书馆订阅的27种外文全文数据库期刊目录进行比对，发现2017—2019年油料作物研究所引文主要来源数据库如图43所示，其中来源于ScienceDirect（34.51%）、Springer（15.63%）、Wiley（14.45%）和OUP（10.53%）的引用最多。

四 各直属研究所需求和保障分析

图 43 油料作物研究所引文来源数据库分布

（十八）麻类研究所

1. 需求学科分析

采集麻类研究所2017—2019年发表的外文期刊论文共计189篇，对其进行学科分析，可以看出该所发文主要集中在生物化学、遗传学和分子生物学（35.00%），农业和生物科学（34.50%），化学（19.50%）和环境科学（19.00%）这四大学科（图44）。除此之外，在药理学、毒理学和药剂学，化学工程，材料科学，医学，工程学等也有一定数量的发文，说明麻类研究所的研究在这些领域也有涉足。

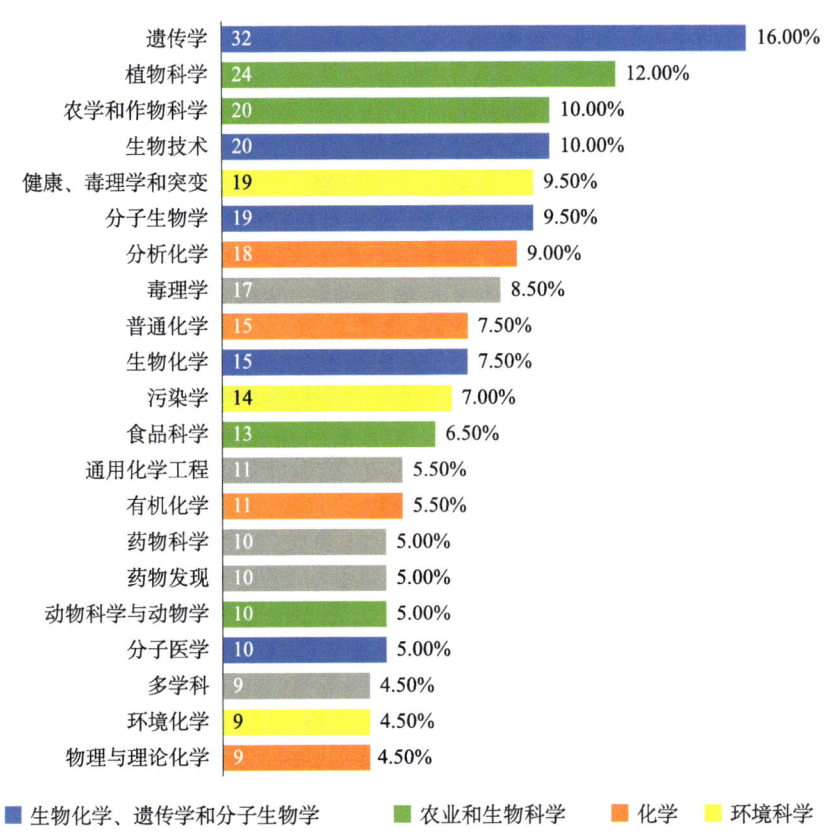

图 44　麻类研究所 2017—2019 年发文学科分布

对生物化学、遗传学和分子生物学，农业和生物科学，化学和环境科学这四大学科的亚学科进行分析，结果如图 44 所示，在生物化学、遗传学和分子生物学中，发文主要集中在遗传学（16.00%），生物技术（10.00%），分子生物学（9.50%），生物化学（7.50%），分子医学（5.00%）等亚学科中。农业和生物科学学科发文主要集中在植物科学（12.00%），农学和作物科学（10.00%），食品科学（6.50%），动物科学与动物学（5.00%）等亚学科中。化学学科的发文主要集中在分析化学（9.00%），普通化学（7.50%），有机化学（5.50%），物理与理论化学（4.50%）等亚学科。环境科学学科发文主要集中在健康、毒理学和突变（9.50%），污染学（7.00%），环境化学（4.50%）等亚学科。

2. 发文和引文主题分析

将文献按照主题组织，进行更细粒度的需求分析，是为了解决单纯按照学科为单元进行分析，针对性不强，导致资源建设成本高、利用不充分的问题。2017—2019年麻类研究所发文共计涉及126个主题，通过相应的遴选指标，遴选出发文、引文涉及的主要主题（表40）。可以看出麻类研究所在"Zinc Oxide; Nanoparticles; Oxide nanoparticles"这个主题的发文和引文最多，由此判断该研究所较为侧重这一领域的研究，在该领域文献的需求强度也最高；该所在"Degumming; Hemp; Ramie fiber"这个主题的发文占该主题全球同期论文的25.00%，说明其在全球范围内对该领域的研究有较为突出的贡献；该所参与的最受关注、发展势头最好的主题为"Eutectics; Solvents; Chloride ChCl"和"Zinc Oxide; Nanoparticles; Oxide nanoparticles"，主题显示度值分别为99.755和99.198；而该所发文具有较高引文影响力的主题为"Autophagy; Nanoparticles; Reactive oxygen"，发文FWCI值是同类论文的3.34倍。综上，通过主题分析的结果不仅从各个角度反映出麻类所学科文献资源的精细化需求，同时也体现了研究所研究领域的分布态势，能够为其学科规划和发展提供参考。

表40　麻类研究所发文引文主要主题

主题	发文量	发文占主题同期论文比(%)	引文量	主题显示度	FWCI值
Zinc oxide; Nanoparticles; Oxide nanoparticles	11	0.88	221	99.198	2.18
Boehmeria; Ramie; Genetic diversity	9	20.00	102	65.227	1.09
Genome, Chloroplast; Genome, Mitochondrial; Copy SSC	6	0.41	38	81.962	0.06
Kenaf; *Hibiscus cannabinus*; Panty liner	5	8.47	45	52.831	0.18
Polygalacturonase; Pectins; Pectinase production	5	1.80	54	87.626	1.03
Degumming; Hemp; Ramie fiber	4	25.00	26	36.387	0.65
Enantiomers; Membranes; Imprinted membranes	4	2.70	61	88.283	1.49
Apocynum; Flavonoids; Venetum L	3	9.38	23	45.047	0.14
Corchorus olitorius; Jute fibers; Farmers right	3	6.12	45	71.878	0.13
Alpha-Glucosidases; Ultrafiltration; Liquid chromatography	3	4.48	19	76.238	0.28
Nilaparvata lugens; *Bacillus thuringiensis*; Transgenics	3	3.70	38	67.220	0.42
Cadmium; Beetles; Metal pollution	3	2.61	32	79.212	0.64
Autophagy; Nanoparticles; Reactive oxygen	3	2.21	30	90.925	3.34

续表

主题	发文量	发文占主题同期论文比(%)	引文量	主题显示度	FWCI值
Electric fields; Food products; Microbial inactivation	3	0.50	82	97.613	2.67
Solvent extraction; Ionic liquids; Binodal curves	3	0.41	98	97.709	1.25
Eutectics; Solvents; Chloride ChCl	3	0.20	100	99.755	1.82
Polyphenols; Flavonoids; Dietary polyphenols	2	10.00	46	71.732	0.61
Peptides, Cyclic; Flax; Cyclic peptides	2	8.00	18	62.912	0.96
Antioxidant activity; Phytochemicals; Adinandra nitida	2	2.90	25	81.984	1.68
Flax; *Linum usitatissimum*; Genetic diversity	2	2.44	40	61.828	0.80
Coprinopsis cinerea; Fruiting bodies; Pheromone receptors	2	1.40	27	80.811	1.33
Apomixis; Asteraceae; Seed formation	2	1.17	60	87.148	0.16
Allium; Onions; Molecular markers	2	1.09	13	73.904	0.51
DNA; Thymus gland; Minor groove	2	0.72	24	92.296	1.23
Microsatellite repeats; Genome; Repeat motifs	2	0.57	16	88.113	0
Lipopeptides; Bacillus; Amyloliquefaciens strain	2	0.26	8	97.454	0.61
Ionic liquids; Toxicity; Chiral Ionic	2	0.24	83	99.133	2.51
Graphene; Adsorption; Adsorption kinetics	2	0.16	81	99.624	1.05
Cadmium; Phytochelatins; Cadmium stress	2	0.16	29	98.655	0.87
Rice; *Oryza sativa*; Cultivated rice	2	0.16	73	98.470	0.38
Serum Albumin; Serum Albumin, Bovine; Static quenching	2	0.12	53	99.370	1.07
RNA; Transcriptome; Novo Transcriptome	2	0.11	93	99.440	0.49
Vitamin K 2; Bacterial typing techniques; Designated strain	2	0.08	24	99.020	0
Adsorption; Dyes; Intraparticle diffusion	2	0.04	35	99.912	1.75
Metagenome; Obesity; Microbial composition	2	0.02	37	99.985	0.24

3. 需求期刊及保障情况

经引文分析得知麻类研究所发文引用了 1 492 种外文期刊,与国家农业图书馆已订阅外文电子期刊品种进行比对,测算出其外文电子期刊全文保障率达到 90.12%,引文量前 40 的期刊见表 41。

表 41 麻类研究所引文量前 40 期刊

编号	期刊名称	引用数量	是否保障
1	PLoS ONE	160	是
2	Food Chemistry	103	是
3	Bioinformatics	102	是
4	Journal of Agricultural and Food Chemistry	91	是
5	Nucleic Acids Research	86	是
6	Journal of Hazardous Materials	82	是
7	Industrial Crops and Products	80	是
8	Proceedings of the National Academy of Sciences of the United States of America	76	是
9	BMC Genomics	68	是
10	Separation and Purification Technology	66	是
11	Plant Physiology	64	是
12	Scientific Reports	62	是
13	Nature	61	是
14	Chemical Engineering Journal	59	是
15	Environmental Toxicology and Pharmacology	52	是
16	Journal of Chromatography A	51	是
17	Applied and Environmental Microbiology	51	是
18	Molecules	50	是
19	International Journal of Molecular Sciences	50	是
20	Bioresource Technology	49	是
21	Plant Journal	48	是
22	Plant Cell	46	是

续表

编号	期刊名称	引用数量	是否保障
23	Theoretical and Applied Genetics	45	是
24	Nanotoxicology	44	是
25	Environmental Science and Technology	44	是
26	Journal of Colloid and Interface Science	44	是
27	Molecular Breeding	43	是
28	Carbohydrate Polymers	43	是
29	Frontiers in Plant Science	41	是
30	Science	41	是
31	RSC Advances	39	是
32	Ecotoxicology and Environmental Safety	39	是
33	Chemosphere	38	是
34	Food and Chemical Toxicology	37	是
35	Gene	36	是
36	Nature Biotechnology	36	是
37	Green Chemistry	35	是
38	Genetics	34	是
39	Nature Genetics	34	是
40	Plant Molecular Biology	34	是

4. 需求数据库分析

分析各直属研究所引用外文文献的来源数据库，从数据库层面把握各直属研究所需求，是外文全文数据库建设的重要依据，同时也为各直属研究所参与电子资源共建选择数据库提供参考。根据各直属研究所需求期刊分析结果，将其与国家农业图书馆订阅的 27 种外文全文数据库期刊目录进行比对，发现 2017—2019 年麻类研究所引文主要来源数据库如图 45 所示，其中来源于 ScienceDirect（44.08%）、Springer（14.48%）、Wiley（10.51%）和 OUP（8.10%）的引用最多。

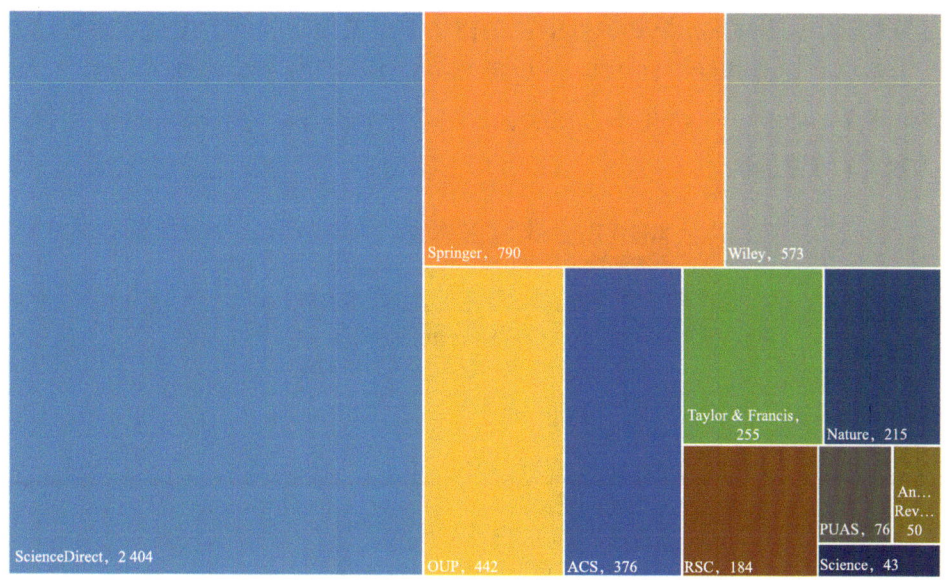

图 45 麻类研究所引文来源数据库分布

（十九）果树研究所

1. 需求学科分析

采集果树研究所 2017—2019 年发表的外文期刊论文共计 90 篇，对其进行学科分析，可以看出该所发文主要集中在农业和生物科学（79.10%），生物化学、遗传学和分子生物学（25.37%）这两大学科（图 46）。除此之外，在化学，环境科学，化学工程等也有一定数量的发文，说明果树研究所的研究在这些领域也有涉足。

对农业和生物科学，生物化学、遗传学和分子生物学这两大学科的亚学科进行分析，结果如图 46 所示，在农业和生物科学中，发文主要集中在植物科学（38.81%），园艺学（23.13%），农学和作物科学（20.15%），综合农业和生物科学（20.15%），食品科学（5.22%），土壤科学（4.48%），生态、进化、行为与系统学（4.48%）等亚学科中。生物化学、遗传学和分子生物学学科的发文主要集中在遗传学（11.94%），生理学（5.22%），分子生物学（4.48%），生物技术（4.48%），生物化学（2.99%），综合生物化学、遗传学和分子生物学（2.99%）等亚学科。

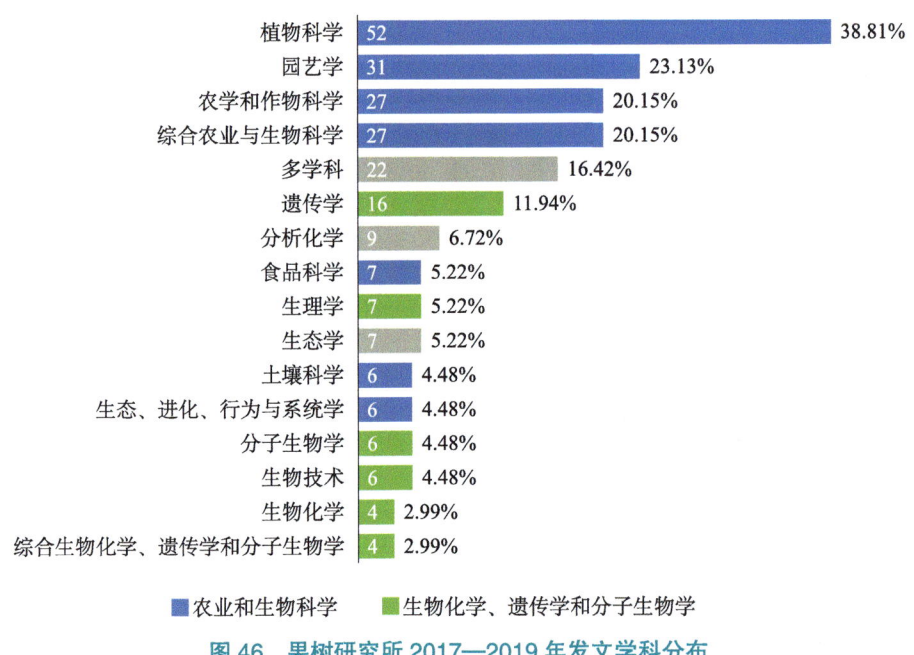

图46　果树研究所2017—2019年发文学科分布

2. 发文和引文主题分析

将文献按照主题组织，进行更细粒度的需求分析，是为了解决单纯按照学科为单元进行分析，针对性不强，导致资源建设成本高、利用不充分的问题。2017—2019年果树研究所发文共计涉及92个主题，通过相应的遴选指标，遴选出发文、引文涉及的主要主题（表42）。可以看出果树研究所在"Viruses; Apple stem grooving virus; Virus ACLSV"这个主题的发文最多，由此判断该研究所较为侧重这一领域的研究，在"Polymers; Phase separation; Polymers MIPs"主题的引文最多，表明在该领域文献的需求强度最高；该所在"Semiconductor quantum dots; Grapes; Odors"这个主题的发文占该主题全球同期论文的20.00%，说明其在全球范围内对该领域的研究有较为突出的贡献；该所参与的最受关注、发展势头最好的主题为"Polymers; Phase separation; Polymers MIPs"，主题显示度值为99.834；而该所发文具有较高引文影响力的主题分别为"Trehalose;

Arabidopsis; Abscisic acid"和"Expansins; Cell wall; Expansin gene",发文 FWCI 值是同类论文的 2.95 倍和 2.49 倍。综上,通过主题分析的结果不仅从各个角度反映出果树研究所学科文献资源的精细化需求,同时也体现了研究所研究领域的分布态势,能够为其学科规划和发展提供参考。

表 42　果树研究所发文引文主要主题

主题	发文量	发文占主题同期论文比(%)	引文量	主题显示度	FWCI 值
Viruses; Apple stem grooving virus; Virus ACLSV	10	3.95	107	84.048	0.51
Viruses; Grapevine leafroll-associated virus; *Vitis vinifera*	8	2.47	83	92.849	0.50
Pears; Pyrus; Pear cultivars	4	4.08	43	64.788	0.58
Apples; Malus; Apple germplasm	4	1.32	47	90.962	1.57
Polymers; Phase separation; Polymers MIPs	4	0.17	116	99.843	1.69
Apples; Nutrition; Fragrant pear	3	7.89	0	56.378	0.13
Expansins; Cell wall; Expansin gene	3	2.86	52	72.535	2.49
Enantiomers; Enantioselectivity; Chiral pesticides	3	0.97	41	93.364	1.01
Senescence; Transcription factors; Leaf senescence	3	0.47	2	96.753	0.17
Anthocyanins; Transcription factors; Anthocyanin biosynthetic	3	0.19	91	98.997	1.13
Semiconductor quantum dots; Grapes; Odors	2	20.00	2	21.335	0.43
Physics; Competition; Dimensions relating	2	13.33	5	32.523	0.20
Fungicides, Industrial; Maneb; Liquid chromatography	2	2.25	9	77.576	0.11
Grapes; Brazil; Titratable acidity	2	2.20	0	54.396	0
Trehalose; Arabidopsis; Abscisic acid	2	0.64	53	93.303	2.95
Odor compounds; Carrier proteins; Chemosensory proteins	2	0.49	59	93.839	0.94
Malus; Apples; Apple peel	2	0.47	36	94.154	0
Transcription factors; Genes; Factors TFs	2	0.38	46	95.156	1.87
Phosphorus; Organic phosphorus; Moderately labile	2	0.37	20	96.670	0

续表

主题	发文量	发文占主题同期论文比(%)	引文量	主题显示度	FWCI值
Wines; Wine; Wine aroma	2	0.34	9	96.983	0.33
Postharvest diseases; *Penicillium digitatum*; Control postharvest	2	0.28	29	96.724	1.67
Fruits; Harvesting; Fruit detection	2	0.22	26	96.026	0
Mycotoxins; Zearalenone; Deoxynivalenol DON	2	0.19	18	99.414	2.06
Vitis vinifera; Small fruits; Grape composition	2	0.17	1	98.393	0
Metagenome; Metagenomics; Amplicon sequencing	2	0.09	14	99.817	2.56
Transcription Factor 3; Cells; Peptides	1	5.26	6	11.808	0.17
Thiourea; Nutrient uptake; Foliar spray	1	2.38	23	31.911	0.72
Viruses; Pepper; Vein yellows	1	2.27	1	44.685	2.12
Bags; Fruit quality; Fruit bagging	1	2.27	11	42.167	0
Apples; Rootstocks; Fruit weight	1	1.82	2	56.618	0
Venturia inaequalis; Fungicides; Apple scab	1	1.67	2	65.364	0
Soybeans; *Phytophthora sojae*; Rot PRR	1	1.59	24	70.519	0.60
Viruses; Nepovirus; Virus GFLV	1	1.39	5	71.625	0.26
Eriobotrya japonica; Cultivars; Loquat fruit	1	1.37	4	63.778	0
Rootstocks; Grapes; Salt tolerance	1	1.33	1	59.985	0
Organic acids and salts; Fruit; Malic acid	1	1.18	17	71.273	0.68
Alternaria alternata; Alternaria; Brown spot	1	1.10	8	77.180	0
Polylysine; Lysine; E-PL production	1	1.04	13	72.054	1.02

3. 需求期刊及保障情况

经引文分析得知果树研究所发文引用了695种外文期刊，与国家农业图书馆已订阅外文电子期刊品种进行比对，测算出其外文电子期刊全文保障率达到91.42%，引文量前40的期刊见表43。

表43 果树研究所引文量前40期刊

编号	期刊名称	引用数量	是否保障
1	Plant Cell	95	是
2	Plant Physiology	79	是
3	Food Chemistry	73	是
4	Plant Journal	70	是
5	PLoS ONE	69	是
6	Journal of Agricultural and Food Chemistry	63	是
7	Scientia Horticulturae	55	是
8	Proceedings of the National Academy of Sciences of the United States of America	52	是
9	Nucleic Acids Research	52	是
10	Journal of Experimental Botany	46	是
11	Postharvest Biology and Technology	46	是
12	Food Control	43	是
13	Plant Disease	40	是
14	Nature	38	是
15	Bioinformatics	38	是
16	Journal of Chromatography A	34	是
17	Journal of Separation Science	34	是
18	Trends in Plant Science	34	是
19	Archives of Virology	33	是
20	Frontiers in Plant Science	31	是
21	Phytopathology	31	是
22	Science	28	是
23	Plant and Cell Physiology	27	是
24	Planta	27	是

续表

编号	期刊名称	引用数量	是否保障
25	Analytical and Bioanalytical Chemistry	25	是
26	Scientific Reports	24	是
27	BMC Plant Biology	24	是
28	Soil Biology and Biochemistry	24	是
29	Current Opinion in Plant Biology	23	是
30	Food and Chemical Toxicology	22	是
31	Acta Horticulturae	22	是
32	Analytica Chimica Acta	21	是
33	Physiologia Plantarum	21	是
34	Molecular Biology and Evolution	21	是
35	Plant Molecular Biology	21	是
36	Plant Science	20	是
37	Theoretical and Applied Genetics	20	是
38	BMC Genomics	20	是
39	Annual Review of Plant Biology	19	是
40	Nature Genetics	18	是

4. 需求数据库分析

分析各直属研究所引用外文文献的来源数据库，从数据库层面把握各直属研究所需求，是外文全文数据库建设的重要依据，同时也为各直属研究所参与电子资源共建选择数据库提供参考。根据各直属研究所需求期刊分析结果，将其与国家农业图书馆订阅的 27 种外文全文数据库期刊目录进行比对，发现 2017—2019 年果树研究所引文主要来源数据库如图 47 所示，其中来源于 ScienceDirect（37.69%）、Springer（16.75%）、Wiley（13.96%）和 OUP（9.77%）的引用最多。

四　各直属研究所需求和保障分析

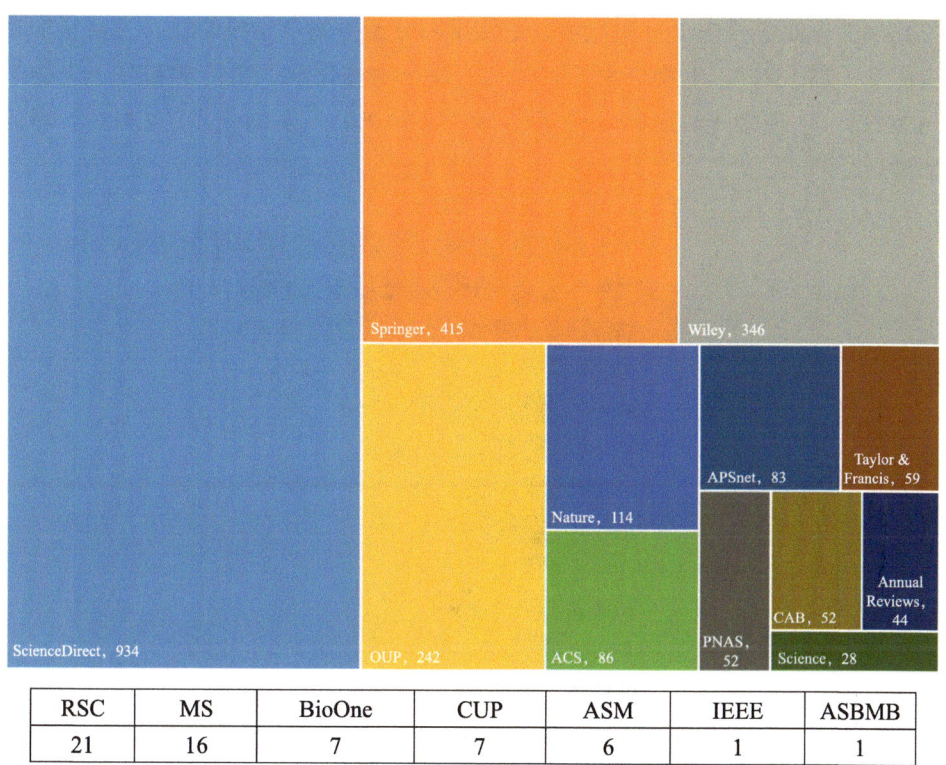

图47　果树研究所引文来源数据库分布

（二十）郑州果树研究所

1. 需求学科分析

采集郑州果树研究所（简称郑果所）2017—2019年发表的外文期刊论文共计128篇，对其进行学科分析，可以看出该所发文主要集中在农业和生物科学（78.03%），生物化学、遗传学和分子生物学（36.99%）这两大学科（图48）。除此之外，在免疫与微生物学、化学等也有一定数量的发文，说明郑果所的研究在这些领域也有涉足。

对农业和生物科学，生物化学、遗传学和分子生物学这两大学科的亚学科进行分析，结果如图48所示，在农业和生物科学中，发文主要集中在园艺学（39.31%），植物科学（29.48%），综合农业和生物科学（12.72%），农学和作物科学（10.40%），食品科学（6.94%），生态、进化、行为与系统学

（2.89%）等亚学科中。生物化学、遗传学和分子生物学学科的发文主要集中在遗传学（23.12%），生物技术（9.25%），综合生物化学、遗传学和分子生物学（6.36%），生理学（4.05%），分子生物学（2.89%），生物化学（2.31%）等亚学科。

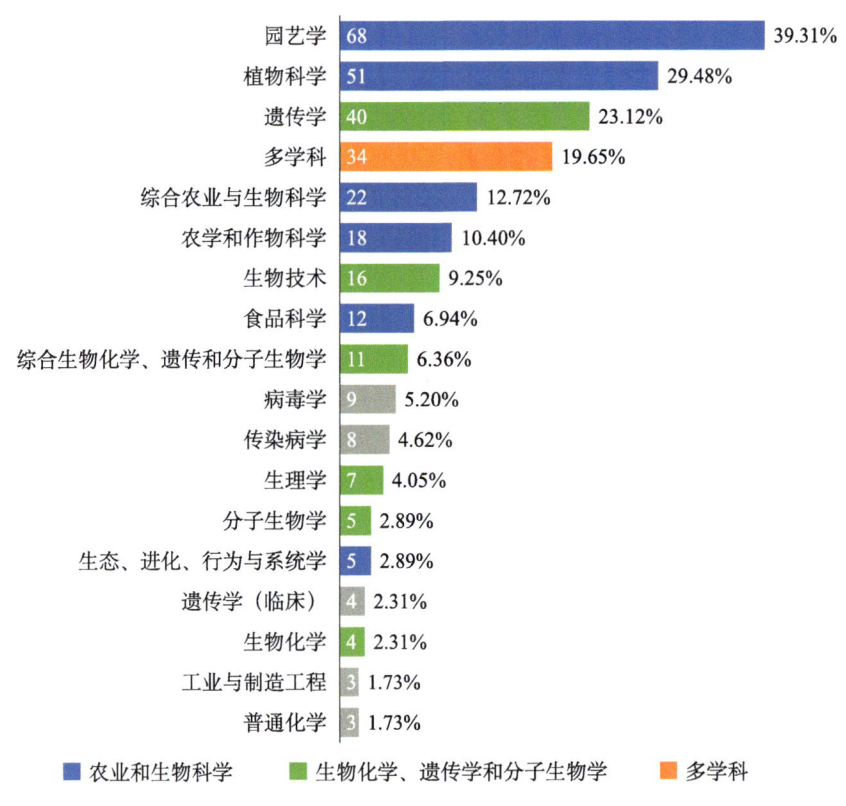

图 48　郑州果树研究所 2017—2019 年发文学科分布

2. 发文和引文主题分析

将文献按照主题组织，进行更细粒度的需求分析，是为了解决单纯按照学科为单元进行分析，针对性不强，导致资源建设成本高、利用不充分的问题。2017—2019 年郑州果树研究所发文共计涉及 92 个主题，通过相应的遴选指标，遴选出发文、引文涉及的主要主题（表 44）。可以看出郑果所在"Vitis; *Vitis vinifera*; Grapevine varieties"和"Peaches; Cultivars; Pox virus"这 2 个主题的发文最多，由此判断该研究所较为侧重这 2 个领域的研究，在"Anthocyanins; Transcription factors; Anthocyanin biosynthetic"主题的引文最多，表明在该领域文献的需求强度最高；该所在"Genes; Seeds; Fruit growth"这个主题的发文占该主题全球同期论文的 22.22%，说明其在全球范围内对该领域的研究有较为突出的贡献；该所参与的最受关注、发展势头最好的主题为"Genome; Algorithms; Novo genome"和"Anthocyanins; Transcription factors; Anthocyanin biosynthetic"，主题显示度值为 99.448 和 98.997；而该所发文具有较高引文影响力的主题为"Genome; Algorithms; Novo genome"，发文 FWCI 值是同类论文的 6.02 倍。综上，通过主题分析的结果不仅从各个角度反映出郑果所学科文献资源的精细化需求，同时也体现了研究所研究领域的分布态势，能够为其学科规划和发展提供参考。

表 44　郑州果树研究所发文引文主要主题

主题	发文量	发文占主题同期论文比(%)	引文量	主题显示度	FWCI 值
Vitis; *Vitis vinifera*; Grapevine varieties	12	2.89	187	91.256	1.32
Peaches; Cultivars; Pox virus	12	2.71	182	85.679	0.78
Anthocyanins; Transcription factors; Anthocyanin biosynthetic	10	0.64	236	98.997	1.44
Watermelons; *Citrullus lanatus*; Watermelon cultivars	7	5.30	78	72.537	1.63
Kiwifruit; Actinidia; Kiwi Fruit	6	1.89	66	87.186	0.41
Ethylene; Ethylenes; Ethylene receptor	6	1.15	92	95.521	1.06
Pears; Pyrus; Pear cultivars	4	4.08	21	64.788	0.44
Mosaic Viruses; Tobamovirus; Virus CGMMV	4	3.77	24	76.532	0.40
Melons; *Cucumis melo*; Melon accessions	4	1.80	92	84.275	0.95
Wines; Wine; Wine color	4	0.49	56	98.061	0.32
Cultivars; Pollen; Gametophytic self-incompatibility	3	1.44	10	83.299	0.17
Citrus tristeza virus; Citrus; Viruses	3	1.24	47	82.836	0.96
Apples; Malus; Apple germplasm	3	0.99	59	90.962	0.94
Lignin; Cell walls; Lignin biosynthesis	3	0.35	55	98.238	0.60
Genome, Chloroplast; Chloroplasts; Cp Genomes	3	0.30	23	97.696	0.61
Genes; Seeds; Fruit growth	2	22.22	10	12.104	0.77

续表

主题	发文量	发文占主题同期论文比 (%)	引文量	主题显示度	FWCI值
Organic acids and salts; Fruit; Malic acid	2	2.35	14	71.273	1.55
Viruses; Luteoviridae; Yellow dwarf	2	0.82	24	88.723	0
Tomatoes; *Lycopersicon esculentum*; Tomato varieties	2	0.59	48	95.701	0.33
Tylenchoidea; Nematoda; Cyst nematodes	2	0.53	18	94.738	0.60
Brassica napus; *Brassica rapa*; Linkage map	2	0.47	25	94.999	2.98
Dietary fiber; Functional properties; Oil holding	2	0.46	22	93.126	0.88
Potyvirus; Mosaic viruses; Virus PPV	2	0.43	32	91.703	1.28
Transcription factors; Genes; Factors TFs	2	0.38	23	95.156	0.45
Carotenoids; Carotenes; Cleavage dioxygenase	2	0.33	54	97.061	0.10
Flowers; Genes; Organ identity	2	0.26	43	96.989	0.83
Indoleacetic acids; Auxins; Auxin efflux	2	0.21	49	98.907	0.28
Salinity; Salt tolerance; Salt tolerant	2	0.11	27	98.949	0.24
Micrornas; RNA; Degradome sequencing	2	0.10	55	99.589	0.62
Genome; Algorithms; Novo genome	2	0.10	36	99.448	6.02
Phyllonorycter; Gracillariidae; Sex pheromone	1	12.50	4	12.976	1.57
Broad bean wilt virus 2; China; Pepper	1	3.57	5	35.859	0
Grapes; Cultivars; Embryo rescue	1	3.23	2	27.242	0
Haploidy; Cucumbers; Haploid plants	1	1.96	11	56.544	0
Pectins; Pectinesterase; Methylesterases PMEs	1	1.47	30	82.402	0.40
Mutants; Rice; Recessive nuclear	1	1.14	1	71.256	0
Agrobacterium; Roots; Rol genes	1	1.01	4	80.368	0
Punica granatum; Cultivars; Fruit weight	1	1.00	26	68.436	0

3. 需求期刊及保障情况

经引文分析得知郑州果树研究所发文引用了 654 种外文期刊，与国家农业图书馆已订阅外文电子期刊品种进行比对，测算出其外文电子期刊全文保障率达到 90.62%，引文量前 40 的期刊见表 45。

表 45　郑州果树研究所引文量前 40 期刊

编号	期刊名称	引用数量	是否保障
1	Plant Physiology	180	是
2	Journal of Experimental Botany	169	是
3	PLoS ONE	161	是
4	Plant Journal	143	是
5	Theoretical and Applied Genetics	132	是
6	Plant Cell	117	是
7	Bioinformatics	110	是
8	Proceedings of the National Academy of Sciences of the United States of America	108	是
9	Nature Genetics	103	是
10	Nucleic Acids Research	99	是
11	Scientia Horticulturae	94	是
12	BMC Plant Biology	93	是
13	Food Chemistry	88	是
14	BMC Genomics	81	是
15	Journal of Agricultural and Food Chemistry	75	是
16	Frontiers in Plant Science	72	是
17	Tree Genetics and Genomes	62	是
18	Science	59	是
19	Journal of the American Society for Horticultural Science	57	是
20	Plant Science	54	是
21	Planta	53	是
22	Trends in Plant Science	53	是
23	Scientific Reports	53	是

续表

编号	期刊名称	引用数量	是否保障
24	Current Opinion in Plant Biology	53	是
25	Journal of Physiology	51	是
26	Nature	50	是
27	Genetics	48	是
28	Genome Biology	48	是
29	PCR Methods and Applications	41	是
30	Plant Physiology and Biochemistry	38	是
31	Nature Biotechnology	37	是
32	Plant Molecular Biology	36	是
33	Plant and Cell Physiology	35	是
34	Molecular Breeding	35	是
35	Molecular Biology and Evolution	33	是
36	Plant Disease	33	是
37	Annual Review of Plant Biology	33	是
38	Hortscience	32	是
39	Nature Methods	32	是
40	Physiologia Plantarum	31	是

4. 需求数据库分析

分析各直属研究所引用外文文献的来源数据库，从数据库层面把握各直属研究所需求，是外文全文数据库建设的重要依据，同时也为各直属研究所参与电子资源共建选择数据库提供参考。根据各直属研究所需求期刊分析结果，将其与国家农业图书馆订阅的27种外文全文数据库期刊目录进行比对，发现2017—2019年郑州果树研究所引文主要来源数据库如图49所示，其中来源于 ScienceDirect（27.86%）、Springer（19.50%）、OUP（15.50%）和 Wiley（14.93%）的引用最多。

四 各直属研究所需求和保障分析

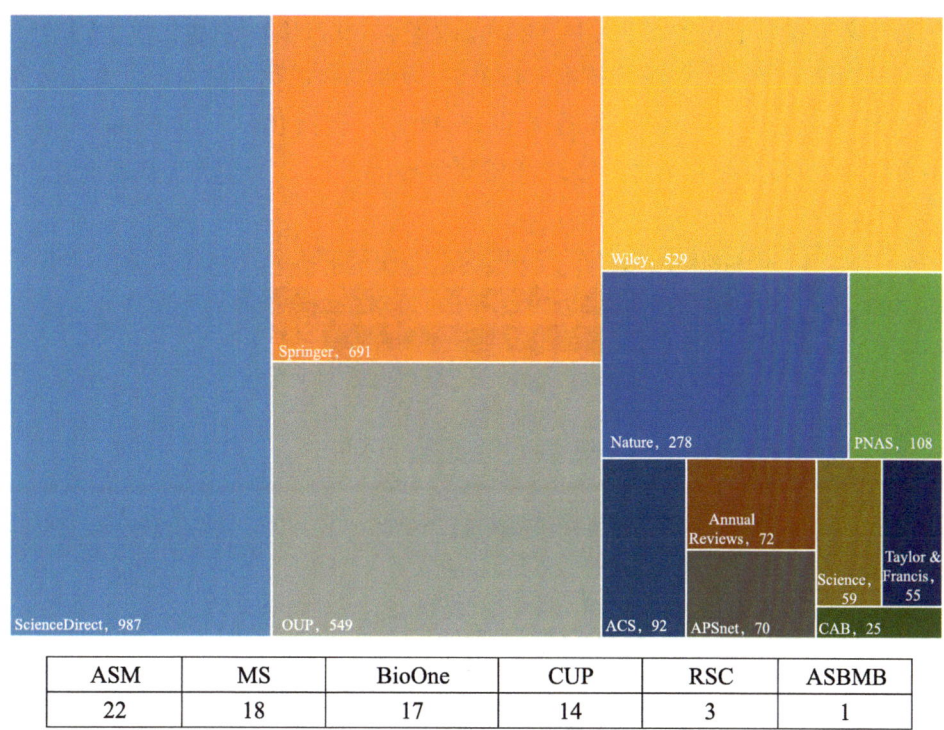

ASM	MS	BioOne	CUP	RSC	ASBMB
22	18	17	14	3	1

图49 郑州果树研究所引文来源数据库分布

（二十一）茶叶研究所

1. 需求学科分析

采集茶叶研究所2017—2019年发表的外文期刊论文共计281篇，对其进行学科分析，可以看出该所发文主要集中在农业和生物科学（72.82%），生物化学、遗传学和分子生物学（33.98%）和化学（24.27%）这三大学科（图50）。除此之外，在环境科学，医学，工程学，药理学、毒理学和药剂学，化学工程等也有一定数量的发文，说明茶叶研究所的研究在这些领域也有涉足。

对农业和生物科学，生物化学、遗传学和分子生物学和化学这三大学科的亚学科进行分析，结果如图50所示，在农业和生物科学中，发文主要集中在植物科学（24.27%），食品科学（20.71%），农学和作物科学（14.56%），综合农业和生物科学（10.68%），昆虫科学（9.71%），园艺学（6.80%），生态、进化、行为与系统学（3.88%）等亚学科中。生物化学、遗传学和分子生物学学科的发文主要集中在生理学（11.33%），遗传学（9.71%），生物化学（6.15%），分子生物学（5.50%），生物技术（4.53%）等亚学科。化学学科的发文主要集中在分析化学（13.59%），普通化学（7.44%），有机化学（7.12%），光谱学（4.85%），物理与理论化学（4.53%）等亚学科。

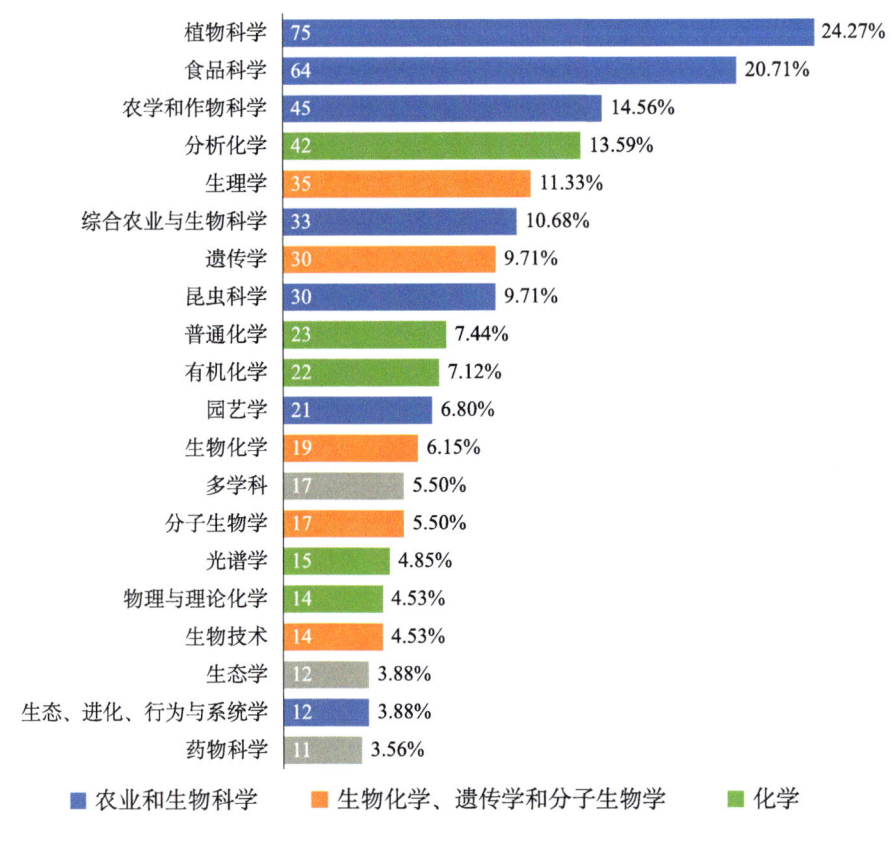

图 50　茶叶研究所 2017—2019 年发文学科分布

2. 发文和引文主题分析

将文献按照主题组织，进行更细粒度的需求分析，是为了解决单纯按照学科为单元进行分析，针对性不强，导致资源建设成本高、利用不充分的问题。2017—2019 年茶叶研究所发文共计涉及 130 个主题，通过相应的遴选指标，遴选出发文、引文涉及的主要主题（表 46）。可以看出茶叶所在 "Tea; Black tea; Oolong tea" 这个主题的发文最多，由此判断该研究所较为侧重这一领域的研究，并且该主题的发文占该主题全球同期论文的 12.3%，说明其在全球范围内对该领域的研究有较为突出的贡献；在"Odor compounds; Carrier proteins; Chemosensory proteins"主题的引文最多，表明在该领域文献的需求强度最高；该所参与的最受关注、发展势头最好的主题为"Image analysis; Meats; Optimal wavelengths"和"Pesticides; Pesticide Residues; Quick easy"，主题显示度值分别为 99.123 和 99.141；而该所发文具有较高引文影响力的主题为"Image analysis; Meats; Optimal wavelengths"，发文 FWCI 值是同类论文的 6.83 倍。综上，通过主题分析的结果不仅从各个角度反映出茶叶研究所学科文献资源的精细化需求，同时也体现了研究所研究领域的分布态势，能够为其学科规划和发展提供参考。

表 46 茶叶研究所发文引文主要主题

主题	发文量	发文占主题同期论文比 (%)	引文量	主题显示度	FWCI 值
Tea; Black tea; Oolong tea	47	12.30	666	93.770	1.44
Odor compounds; Carrier proteins; Chemosensory proteins	24	5.83	758	93.839	1.12
Tea; *Camellia Sinensis*; Tea leaves	11	6.08	257	88.345	1.79
Herbivores; Herbivory; Volatiles HIPVs	9	0.93	233	98.624	1.94
Tea; Catechin; White tea	8	0.76	271	98.621	2.60
Droughts; Transcription factors; Freezing tolerance	8	0.68	180	98.632	3.10
Anthocyanins; Transcription factors; Anthocyanin biosynthetic	7	0.45	231	98.997	2.08
Pesticides; Pesticide Residues; Quick easy	6	0.44	175	99.141	1.64
Tea; *Camellia sinensis*; Tea cultivars	6	5.50	126	71.779	1.35
Sex pheromones; Sex attractants; Pheromones	6	10.53	79	58.850	1.32
Nitric oxide; Plants; Nitroprusside SNP	4	0.50	46	96.774	3.56
Nitrates; Nitrogen; Nitrate transporters	4	0.77	79	97.199	1.70
Jasmonic acid; Oxylipins; Jasmonate signaling	4	0.60	80	98.285	1.23
Sex attractants; Sex pheromones; Activating neuropeptide	4	4.76	96	68.181	0.16
Pesticide Residues; Pesticides; Residue levels	4	1.65	80	84.835	1.69
Tea; *Camellia sinensis*; Tea samples	4	1.67	115	90.278	0.93

续表

主题	发文量	发文占主题同期论文比 (%)	引文量	主题显示度	FWCI 值
Tea; *Camellia sinensis*; Pu-erh Tea	4	2.23	105	85.379	1.39
Carbon dioxide; Photosynthesis; Elevated atmospheric	3	0.47	56	96.619	2.48
Aluminum; Toxicity; Aluminum tolerance	3	0.57	98	95.234	1.96
Spectrometry; Ions; Ion mobility-mass	3	0.35	35	98.911	1.41
Indoleacetic acids; Auxins; Auxin efflux	3	0.31	76	98.907	1.54
Near infrared spectroscopy; Near-infrared spectroscopy; Content SSC	3	0.32	29	97.035	1.36
Tea; Catechin; Tea catechins	3	0.69	88	96.640	1.77
Terpenes; Diterpenes; Diterpene synthases	3	0.55	40	97.712	2.10
Enantiomers; Enantioselectivity; Chiral pesticides	3	0.97	66	93.364	2.17
Protonation; Electrospray ionization; Ionization of gases	3	5.36	33	61.037	0.31
Fipronil; Insecticides; Fipronil sulfone	3	1.39	38	88.426	2.25
Transcription factors; Genes; Factors TFs	3	0.57	59	95.156	1.73
Odors; Chemical sensors; Nose E-nose	2	0.19	33	97.972	1.23
Image analysis; Meats; Optimal wavelengths	2	0.12	35	99.123	6.83
Transporters; Phloem; Sucrose transporter	2	0.54	39	95.515	1.79
Glutamate-Ammonia Ligase; Nitrogen; Glutamate synthase	2	1.31	25	85.506	0.28
Volatilization; Urea; Urease inhibitors	2	0.59	41	92.679	1.74
Stable isotopes; Isotopes; Ratio mass	2	0.56	17	91.655	2.16
Tephritidae; Fruit flies; Parasitoid species	2	1.27	19	72.461	0.98
Miridae; Hemiptera; Tarnished plant	2	2.08	68	66.959	0.72
Basic-Leucine Zipper Transcription Factors; Transcription factors; Leucine zipper	2	1.22	33	86.652	1.82

3. 需求期刊及保障情况

经引文分析得知茶叶研究所发文引用了 1 414 种外文期刊，与国家农业图书馆已订阅外文电子期刊品种进行比对，测算出其外文电子期刊全文保障率达到 93.32%，引文量前 40 的期刊见表 47。

表 47　茶叶研究所引文量前 40 期刊

编号	期刊名称	引用数量	是否保障
1	Food Chemistry	502	是
2	Journal of Agricultural and Food Chemistry	481	是
3	Plant Physiology	318	是
4	PLoS ONE	300	是
5	Proceedings of the National Academy of Sciences of the United States of America	214	是
6	Journal of Chemical Ecology	199	是
7	Plant Journal	184	是
8	Frontiers in Plant Science	170	是
9	Plant Cell	168	是
10	Scientific Reports	145	是
11	Journal of Experimental Botany	145	是
12	Journal of Chromatography A	138	是
13	Food Research International	136	是
14	Insect Biochemistry and Molecular Biology	119	是
15	Insect Molecular Biology	112	是
16	Journal of the Science of Food and Agriculture	112	是
17	Trends in Plant Science	112	是
18	Plant Physiology and Biochemistry	110	是
19	BMC Genomics	107	是
20	Journal of Physiology	105	是
21	Science	100	是
22	Nature	99	是

续表

编号	期刊名称	引用数量	是否保障
23	Plant, Cell and Environment	87	是
24	Planta	87	是
25	Plant Molecular Biology	87	是
26	Phytochemistry	87	是
27	Journal of Insect Physiology	83	是
28	BMC Plant Biology	77	是
29	Journal of Biological Chemistry	73	是
30	Bioinformatics	72	是
31	Nucleic Acids Research	71	是
32	Plant and Cell Physiology	71	是
33	Current Opinion in Plant Biology	66	是
34	Journal of Plant Physiology	65	是
35	Molecular Plant	63	是
36	Annual Review of Plant Biology	62	是
37	International Journal of Molecular Sciences	61	是
38	Annual Review of Entomology	60	是
39	Analytical Chemistry	59	是
40	Talanta	58	是

4. 需求数据库分析

分析各直属研究所引用外文文献的来源数据库，从数据库层面把握各直属研究所需求，是外文全文数据库建设的重要依据，同时也为各直属研究所参与电子资源共建选择数据库提供参考。根据各直属研究所需求期刊分析结果，将其与国家农业图书馆订阅的27种外文全文数据库期刊目录进行比对，发现2017—2019年茶叶研究所引文主要来源数据库如图51所示，其中来源于ScienceDirect（40.40%）、Springer（15.52%）和Wiley（15.30%）的引用最多。

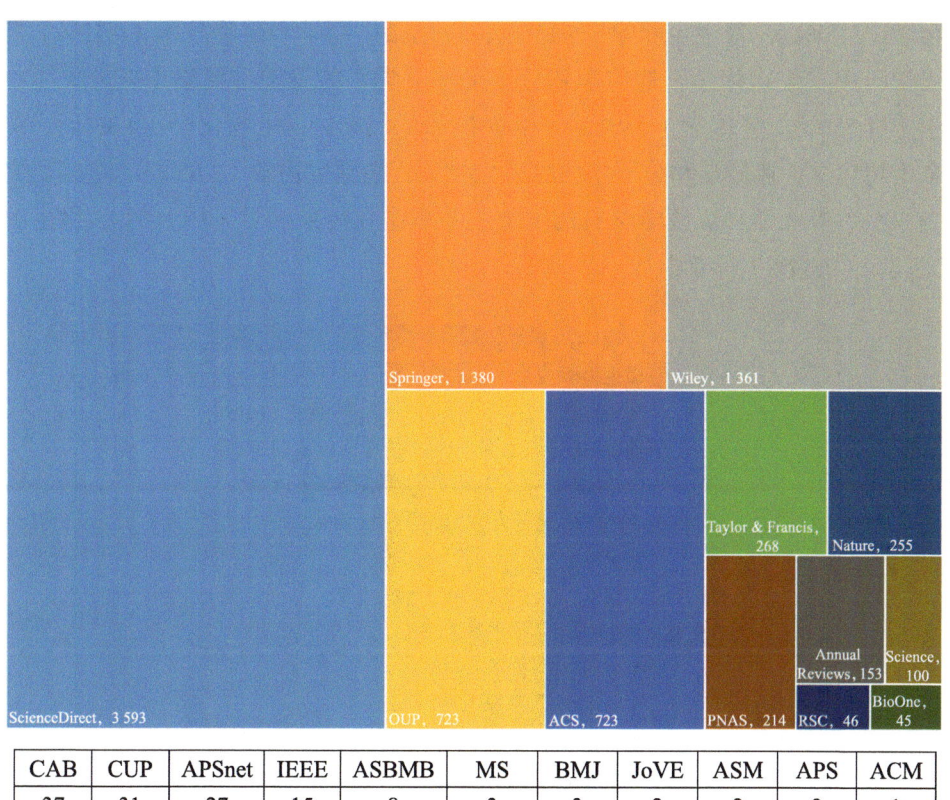

图 51　茶叶研究所引文来源数据库分布

（二十二）哈尔滨兽医研究所

1. 需求学科分析

采集哈尔滨兽医研究所 2017—2019 年发表的外文期刊论文共计 473 篇，对其进行学科分析，可以看出该所发文主要集中在免疫与微生物学（64.74%），医学（28.87%），生物化学、遗传学和分子生物学（27.42%）这三大学科（图 52）。此外，除兽医学外，农业和生物科学，药理学、毒理学和药剂学等也有一定数量的发文，说明哈尔滨兽医研究所的研究在这些领域也有涉足。

对免疫与微生物学，医学，生物化学、遗传学和分子生物学这三大学科的亚学科进行分析，结果如图 52 所示，在免疫与微生物学中，发文主要集中在病毒学（31.55%），微生物学（27.01%），免疫学（18.14%），综合免疫和微生物学（5.77%），寄生生物学（5.15%），应用微生物学和生物技术（4.12%）等亚学科中。生物化学、遗传学和分子生物学学科的发文主要集中在分子生物学（11.75%），遗传学（4.95%），生物技术（4.74%），生物化学（4.33%），综合生物化学、遗传学和分子生物学（4.33%），细胞生物学（3.92%），癌症研究（3.30%）等亚学科。医学学科的发文主要集中在传染病学（19.18%），微生物（医学）（7.84%）等亚学科。

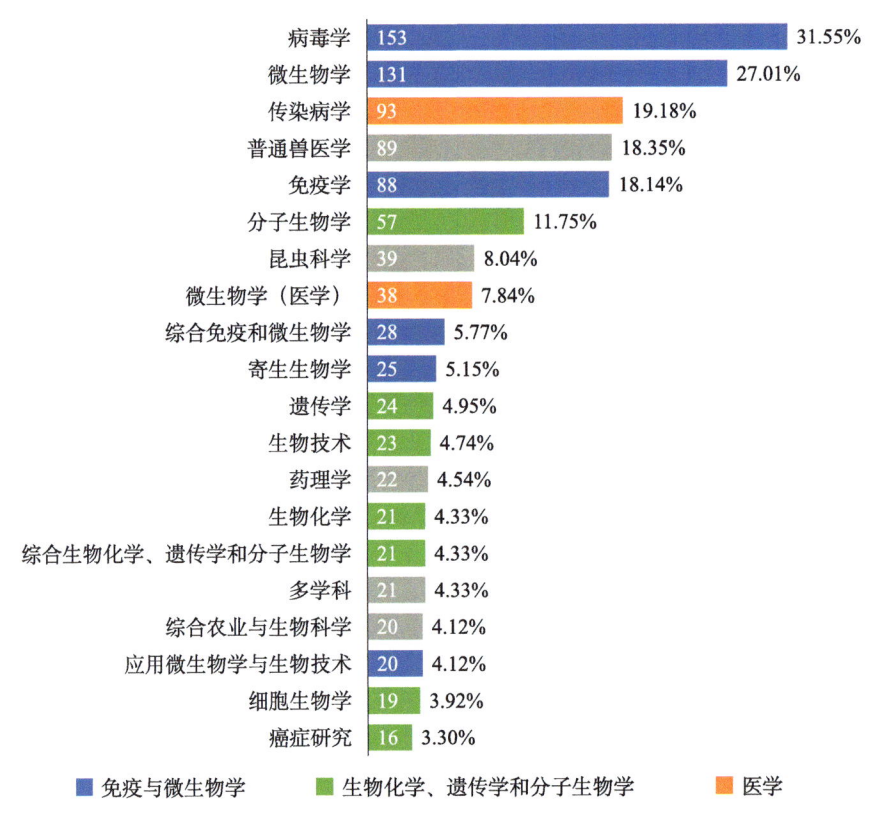

图 52　哈尔滨兽医研究所 2017—2019 年发文学科分布

2. 发文和引文主题分析

将文献按照主题组织，进行更细粒度的需求分析，是为了解决单纯按照学科为单元进行分析，针对性不强，导致资源建设成本高、利用不充分的问题。2017—2019 年哈尔滨兽医研究所发文共计涉及 215 个主题，通过相应的遴选指标，遴选出发文、引文涉及的主要主题（表 48）。可以看出哈尔滨兽医研究所在"Porcine respiratory and reproductive syndrome virus; Porcine Reproductive and

Respiratory Syndrome; Pathogenic porcine"这个主题的发文和引文最多,由此判断该研究所较为侧重这一领域的研究,并且对该领域文献的需求强度也最高;该所在"Classical swine fever virus; Classical Swine Fever; CSFV infection"这个主题的发文占该主题全球同期论文的6.62%,说明其在全球范围内对该领域的研究有较为突出的贡献;该所参与的最受关注、发展势头最好的主题有"Ebolavirus; Hemorrhagic Fever, Ebola; Ebola virus"和"Antiviral Agents; Interferons; Acid-inducible gene",主题显示度值分别为99.792和99.756;而该所发文具有较高引文影响力的主题有"African Swine Fever; African Swine Fever Virus; ASFV infection"和"Circovirus; Swine; PCV2 DNA",发文FWCI值分别是同类论文的6.04倍和4.60倍。综上,通过主题分析的结果不仅从各个角度反映出哈尔滨兽医研究所学科文献资源的精细化需求,同时也体现了研究所研究领域的分布态势,能够为其学科规划和发展提供参考。

表48 哈尔滨兽医研究所发文引文主要主题

主题	发文量	发文占主题同期论文比(%)	引文量	主题显示度	FWCI值
Porcine respiratory and reproductive syndrome virus; Porcine Reproductive and Respiratory Syndrome; Pathogenic porcine	28	3.48	748	96.354	1.19
Porcine epidemic diarrhea virus; Swine; Deltacoronavirus PDCoV	21	3.28	384	94.518	1.19
Classical swine fever virus; Classical Swine Fever; CSFV infection	19	6.62	364	87.631	1.37
Orthomyxoviridae; Influenza In birds; Swine influenza	18	1.87	455	97.672	2.70
Infectious bronchitis virus; Chickens; Bronchitis IB	14	4.14	427	88.526	2.27
Circovirus; Swine; PEV2 DNA	13	2.39	343	96.508	4.60
Marek disease; Viruses; Disease MD	10	5.13	275	78.736	0.38
African Swine Fever; African Swine Fever Virus; ASFV infection	10	2.42	143	94.934	6.04
Antiviral agents; Interferons; Acid-inducible Gene	10	0.60	380	99.756	1.78
Avian lLeukosis virus; Chickens; Virus ALV	8	3.62	186	78.328	0.88
Herpesvirus 1, Suid; Pseudorabies; Pseudorabies virus	7	3.41	154	84.856	0.47

续表

主题	发文量	发文占主题同期论文比(%)	引文量	主题显示度	FWCI值
Infectious bursal disease virus; Chickens; IBDV infection	7	3.03	209	83.825	1.96
Newcastle disease virus; Newcastle disease; Avian paramyxovirus	7	1.28	164	93.141	0.81
Adenoviridae; Aviadenovirus; Body hepatitis	6	2.83	123	84.106	2.22
Acetaminophen; Liver; APAP-induced hepatotoxicity	6	0.94	50	96.336	0.48
Foot-and-mouth disease virus; Foot-and-Mouth Disease; Cloven-hoofed animals	6	0.85	147	94.562	1.77
Influenza in birds; Orthomyxoviridae; Domestic poultry	6	0.53	208	98.607	1.48
Viruses; Metagenomics; Viral genomes	5	1.12	32	95.398	0.23
Influenza A Virus; Orthomyxoviridae; IAV infection	5	0.88	164	97.178	0.64
Autophagy; Infection; Antigen presentation	5	0.65	116	98.462	1.32
Middle East; Coronavirus; East respiratory	5	0.35	129	98.208	1.20
Peptides; Antimicrobial Cationic Peptides; Potent antimicrobial	5	0.30	140	99.516	0.34
Ebolavirus; Hemorrhagic Fever, Ebola; Ebola virus	5	0.19	100	99.792	0.47
Infectious Anemia Virus, Equine; Equine Infectious Anemia; EIAV infection	4	6.67	98	63.781	0.95
Hepatitis Virus, Duck; Hepatitis A virus; Virus DHAV	4	5.80	48	69.103	0.24
Chicken anemia virus; Gyrovirus; Apoptosis	4	4.17	110	81.606	0.43
HIV-1; Nef Gene Products, Human Immunodeficiency Virus; Infected cells	4	2.76	92	85.191	2.70
Swine; Picornaviridae; Vesicular disease	4	2.44	73	85.944	1.62
Influenza A Virus, H3N8 Subtype; Influenza, Human; H3N2 canine	4	2.14	69	84.540	0.75
Novirhabdovirus; Viral hemorrhagic septicemia virus; Infectious hematopoietic necrosis virus	4	1.24	84	87.752	0.88
Influenza A virus; Orthomyxoviridae; Viral polymerase	4	0.82	129	95.278	2.13
Influenza in birds; Influenza A virus; Poultry markets	4	0.72	166	97.670	0.64

续表

主题	发文量	发文占主题同期论文比(%)	引文量	主题显示度	FWCI 值
Toxoplasma; Toxoplasmosis; Gondii RH	4	0.52	73	96.663	1.12
Swine; HLA Antigens; Swine leukocyte	3	7.50	76	54.181	0.47
Haemophilus parasuis; Swine; Glässer's disease	3	2.70	74	74.027	0.51
Actinobacillus pleuropneumoniae; Pleuropneumonia; Porcine pleuropneumonia	3	2.24	62	83.181	0.82

3. 需求期刊及保障情况

经引文分析得知哈尔滨兽医研究所发文引用了 1 636 种外文期刊,与国家农业图书馆已订阅外文电子期刊品种进行比对,测算出其外文电子期刊全文保障率达到 86.07%,引文量前 40 的期刊见表 49。

表 49 哈尔滨兽医研究所引文量前 40 期刊

编号	期刊名称	引用数量	是否保障
1	Journal of Virology	1 799	是
2	Veterinary Microbiology	567	是
3	Journal of General Virology	483	是
4	Proceedings of the National Academy of Sciences of the United States of America	478	是
5	Virology	476	是
6	PLoS ONE	422	是
7	Virus Research	390	是
8	Journal of Biological Chemistry	361	是
9	Archives of Virology	361	是
10	Nature	336	是
11	Vaccine	299	是
12	PLoS Pathogens	280	是
13	Science	264	是
14	Avian Diseases	227	是

续表

编号	期刊名称	引用数量	是否保障
15	Avian Pathology	223	是
16	Emerging Infectious Diseases	209	是
17	Journal of Immunology	182	是
18	Cell	174	是
19	Journal of Virological Methods	168	是
20	Infection and Immunity	163	是
21	Infection, Genetics and Evolution	156	是
22	Virology Journal	153	是
23	Virus Genes	149	是
24	Scientific Reports	140	是
25	Viruses	139	是
26	Journal of Clinical Microbiology	136	是
27	Nucleic Acids Research	125	是
28	Transboundary and Emerging Diseases	113	是
29	Veterinary Immunology and Immunopathology	107	是
30	Antimicrobial Agents and Chemotherapy	105	是
31	Veterinary Research	105	是
32	Cell Host and Microbe	101	是
33	EMBO Journal	91	是
34	Immunity	87	是
35	Frontiers in Microbiology	87	是
36	Journal of Bacteriology	85	是
37	Antiviral Research	81	是
38	Veterinary Record	79	是
39	Research in Veterinary Science	78	是
40	Nature Immunology	74	是

4. 需求数据库分析

分析各直属研究所引用外文文献的来源数据库，从数据库层面把握各直属

研究所需求，是外文全文数据库建设的重要依据，同时也为各直属研究所参与电子资源共建选择数据库提供参考。根据各直属研究所需求期刊分析结果，将其与国家农业图书馆订阅的 27 种外文全文数据库期刊目录进行比对，发现 2017—2019 年哈尔滨兽医研究所引文主要来源数据库如图 53 所示，其中来源于 ScienceDirect（40.06%）、ASM（14.95%）、Springer（7.62%）、Nature（7.45%）和 Wiley（7.31%）的引用最多。

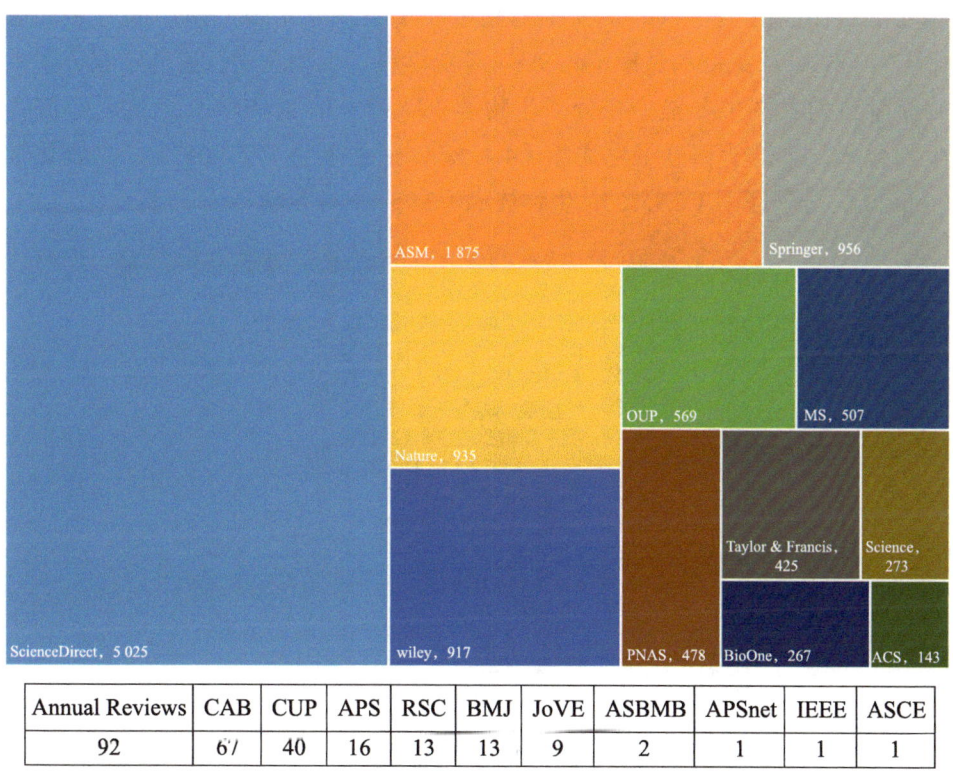

图 53 哈尔滨兽医研究所引文来源数据库分布

（二十三）兰州兽医研究所

1. 需求学科分析

采集兰州兽医研究所 2017—2019 年发表的外文期刊论文共计 526 篇，对其进行学科分析，可以看出该所发文主要集中在免疫与微生物学（67.77%），医学（53.41%），生物化学、遗传学和分子生物学（27.26%）这三大学科（图

54）。除此之外，在农业和生物科学，兽医学，化学，药理学、毒理学和药剂学等也有一定数量的发文，说明兰州兽医研究所的研究在这些领域也有涉足。

对免疫与微生物学，医学，生物化学、遗传学和分子生物学这三大学科的亚学科进行分析，结果如图54所示，在免疫与微生物学中，发文主要集中在寄生生物学（25.78%），微生物学（20.99%），病毒学（13.26%），免疫学（13.26%），综合免疫和微生物学（5.52%），应用微生物学和生物技术（3.13%）等亚学科中。医学学科的发文主要集中在传染病学（39.23%），微生物（医学）（12.89%），免疫和过敏（4.79%）等亚学科。生物化学、遗传学和分子生物学学科的发文主要集中在分子生物学（11.97%），遗传学（11.23%），综合生物化学、遗传学和分子生物学（4.42%），细胞生物学（4.05%），生物化学（3.68%），分子医学（2.95%），生物技术（2.95%）等亚学科。

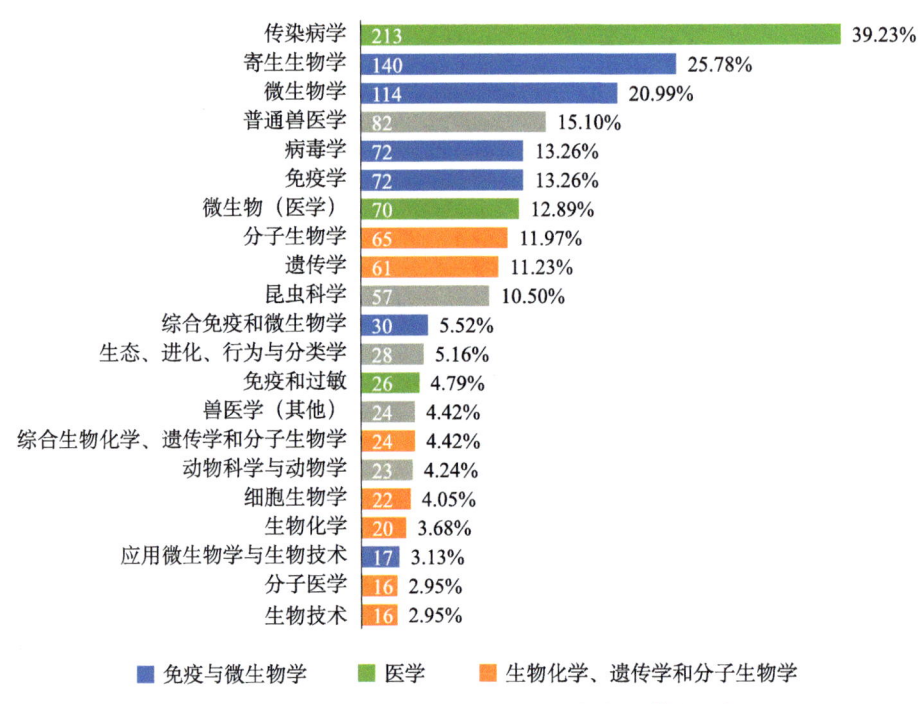

图54　兰州兽医研究所2017—2019年发文学科分布

2. 发文和引文主题分析

将文献按照主题组织，进行更细粒度的需求分析，是为了解决单纯按照学科为单元进行分析，针对性不强，导致资源建设成本高、利用不充分的问题。2017—2019年兰州兽医研究所发文共计涉及208个主题，通过相应的遴选指标，遴选出发文、引文涉及的主要主题（表50）。可以看出兰州兽医研究所在"Foot-and-Mouth Disease Virus; Foot-and-Mouth Disease; Cloven-hoofed animals"这个主题的发文和引文最多，由此判断该研究所较为侧重这一领域的研究，在该领域文献的需求强度也最高，同时这个主题的发文占该主题全球同期论文的7.67%，说明其在全球范围内对该领域的研究有较为突出的贡献；该所参与的最受关注、发展势头最好的主题为"Antiviral Agents; Interferons; Acid-inducible gene"，主题显示度值为99.756；而该所发文具有较高引文影响力的主题为"Polysaccharides; Antioxidants; Polysaccharide fractions"，发文FWCI值是同类论文的4.94倍。综上，通过主题分析的结果不仅从各个角度反映出兰州兽医研究所学科文献资源的精细化需求，同时也体现了研究所研究领域的分布态势，能够为其学科规划和发展提供参考。

表 50 兰州兽医研究所发文引文主要主题

主题	发文量	发文占主题同期论文比 (%)	引文量	主题显示度	FWCI 值
Foot-and-Mouth Disease Virus; Foot-and-Mouth Disease; Cloven-hoofed Animals	54	7.67	1 138	94.562	0.62
Toxoplasma; Toxoplasmosis; Gondii RH	31	4.05	824	96.663	1.18
Toxoplasma; Toxoplasmosis; Gondii Isolates	23	2.76	640	95.328	1.00
Theileria; Theileriasis; Tropical theileriosis	15	4.62	265	86.636	1.19
Antiviral Agents; Interferons; Acid-inducible gene	15	0.90	507	99.756	1.10
Fasciola hepatica; Fasciola; Gigantica infection	13	6.44	255	86.764	0.83
Schistosoma mansoni; *Schistosoma japonicum*; Adult worms	11	4.12	146	87.502	0.34
Peste-des-petits-ruminants virus; Peste-des-Petits-Ruminants; Lineage IV	11	3.57	214	83.079	1.77
Echinococcosis; *Echinococcus granulosus*; *Echinococcus multilocularis*	10	1.36	286	95.981	0.87
Enterocytozoon; Microsporidia; Bieneusi genotypes	9	2.54	288	88.875	1.47
Porcine epidemic diarrhea virus; Swine; Deltacoronavirus PDCoV	9	1.41	243	94.518	2.26
Swine; Picornaviridae; Vesicular disease	8	4.88	134	85.944	2.49

续表

主题	发文量	发文占主题同期论文比(%)	引文量	主题显示度	FWCI值
Hepatitis E virus; Hepatitis E; Wild boar	7	0.48	249	98.766	1.20
Anaplasma phagocytophilum; Ticks; Granulocytic anaplasmosis	7	1.43	153	94.052	2.47
Neospora; Cattle; Caninum antibodies	7	1.84	130	87.373	0.34
Echinococcosis; *Echinococcus granulosus*; Hepatic alveolar	7	1.77	120	89.138	0.60
Ticks; Theileria; *Theileria ovis*	7	4.55	180	80.969	0.47
Chlamydia; *Chlamydophila psittaci*; Psittaci infection	6	2.42	104	86.187	0.27
Cryptosporidium; Cryptosporidiosis; Nested PCR	5	0.58	194	97.727	0.85
Exosomes; Cells; Recipient cells	5	0.08	137	99.983	0.03
Hydrogen Sulfide; Cystathionine gamma-Lyase; Cystathionine γ-Lyase	5	0.24	146	99.740	1.71
MicroRNAs; Genes; Target prediction	5	0.31	117	99.336	1.43
Giardia lamblia; Giardia; Dehydrogenase Gdh	5	1.22	92	92.784	1.04
Anaplasma marginale; Anaplasmosis; Bovine anaplasmosis	5	2.98	118	78.706	0.50
Trichinella spiralis; Trichinellosis; Larval invasion	5	4.72	127	80.298	0.65
Orthomyxoviridae; Influenza in birds; Swine influenza	4	0.42	93	97.672	0.50
Bluetongue virus; Bluetongue; Epizootic hemorrhagic	4	1.06	93	88.304	0.36
Porcine respiratory and reproductive syndrome virus; Porcine reproductive and respiratory syndrome; Pathogenic porcine	4	0.50	84	96.354	0.51
Mycoplasma bovis; Mycoplasma; Contagious bovine	4	1.18	66	88.365	0.67
Codon; Genes; Mutation pressure	4	0.71	116	96.397	0.52
Babesia; Dogs; Canine babesiosis	4	1.66	129	85.322	0.81
Probes; Fluorescence; Biological thiols	4	0.38	138	99.531	2.84
Brucellosis; Brucella; Melitensis biovar	3	0.35	82	95.709	1.10
Polysaccharides; Antioxidants; Polysaccharide fractions	3	0.15	53	99.661	4.94
Enterovirus; Poliovirus; Replication organelles	3	1.61	66	88.786	1.22

续表

主题	发文量	发文占主题同期论文比(%)	引文量	主题显示度	FWCI值
Toxoplasmosis; Toxoplasma; Cerebral toxoplasmosis	3	1.54	106	78.519	3.65
Babesia; Babesia bovis; Bovine babesiosis	3	2.34	68	74.793	0.20
T-Lymphocytes; Cells; Molecule MR1	3	0.87	136	97.024	0.96

3. 需求期刊及保障情况

经引文分析得知兰州兽医研究所发文引用了 2 028 种外文期刊，与国家农业图书馆已订阅外文电子期刊品种进行比对，测算出其外文电子期刊全文保障率达到 84.41%，引文量前 40 的期刊见表 51。

表 51 兰州兽医研究所引文量前 40 期刊

编号	期刊名称	引用数量	是否保障
1	Journal of Virology	779	是
2	Veterinary Parasitology	625	是
3	PLoS ONE	548	是
4	Parasites and Vectors	461	是
5	Proceedings of the National Academy of Sciences of the United States of America	365	是
6	Zeitschrift für Parasitenkunde	336	是
7	Vaccine	317	是
8	Journal of Immunology	298	是
9	Nucleic Acids Research	291	是
10	Nature	279	是
11	International Journal for Parasitology	276	是
12	Veterinary Microbiology	258	是
13	Virology	257	是
14	Infection, Genetics and Evolution	250	是
15	Virus Research	233	是

续表

编号	期刊名称	引用数量	是否保障
16	Infection and Immunity	233	是
17	Journal of Biological Chemistry	223	是
18	Parasitology	215	是
19	PLoS Pathogens	199	是
20	Journal of General Virology	194	是
21	Science	187	是
22	Scientific Reports	170	是
23	PLoS Neglected Tropical Diseases	164	是
24	Emerging Infectious Diseases	154	是
25	Journal of Parasitology	153	是
26	Journal of Clinical Microbiology	152	是
27	Cell	146	是
28	Archives of Virology	140	是
29	Acta Tropica	139	是
30	Experimental Parasitology	138	是
31	Transboundary and Emerging Diseases	135	是
32	Journal of Virological Methods	129	是
33	Nature Immunology	125	是
34	Immunity	118	是
35	Frontiers in Microbiology	117	是
36	Bioinformatics	116	是
37	Trends in Parasitology	113	是
38	Clinical Microbiology Reviews	110	是
39	Journal of Experimental Medicine	109	是
40	Tropical Animal Health and Production	105	是

4. 需求数据库分析

分析各直属研究所引用外文文献的来源数据库，从数据库层面把握各直属研究所需求，是外文全文数据库建设的重要依据，同时也为各直属研究所参与电子资源共建选择数据库提供参考。根据各直属研究所需求期刊分析结果，将其与国家农业图书馆订阅的 27 种外文全文数据库期刊目录进行比对，发现 2017—2019 年兰州兽医研究所引文主要来源数据库如图 55 所示，其中来源于 ScienceDirect（46.40%）、Wiley（9.51%）、Nature（6.92%）、OUP（6.77%）和 ASM（6.23%）的引用最多。

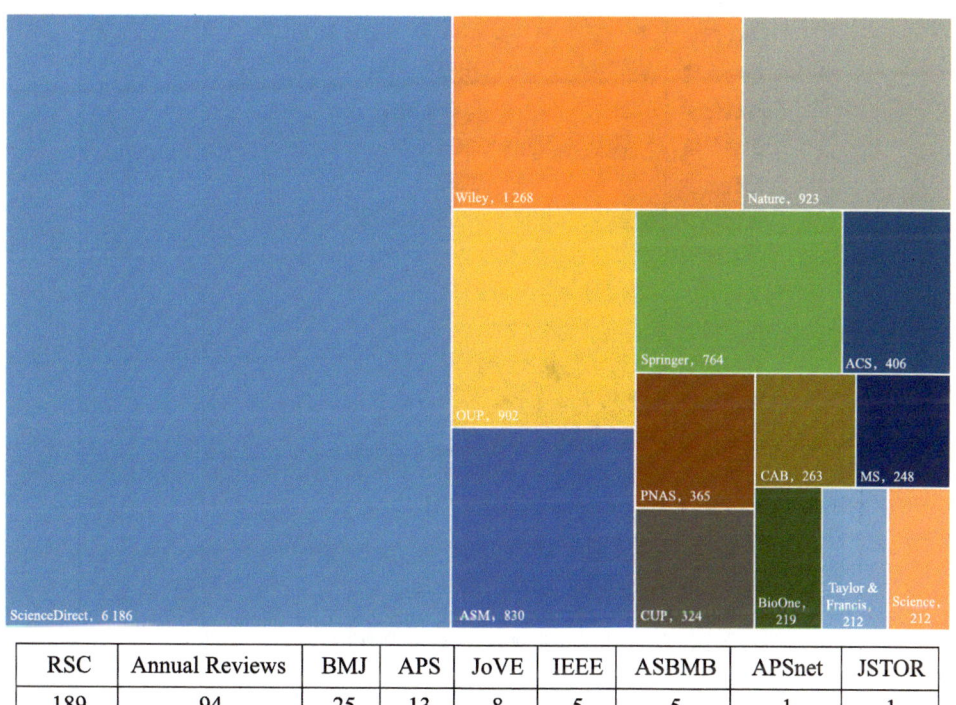

RSC	Annual Reviews	BMJ	APS	JoVE	IEEE	ASBMB	APSnet	JSTOR
189	94	25	13	8	5	5	1	1

图 55　兰州兽医研究所引文来源数据库分布

（二十四）兰州畜牧与兽药研究所

1. 需求学科分析

采集兰州畜牧与兽药研究所 2017—2019 年发表的外文期刊论文共计 160 篇，

对其进行学科分析，可以看出该所发文主要集中在生物化学、遗传学和分子生物学（44.19%），农业和生物科学（33.14%）这两大学科（图56）。除此之外，主要发文学科集中在化学，药理学、毒理学和药剂学，而医学、兽医学、环境科学等也有一定数量的发文，说明兰州畜牧与兽药研究所的研究在这些领域也有涉足。

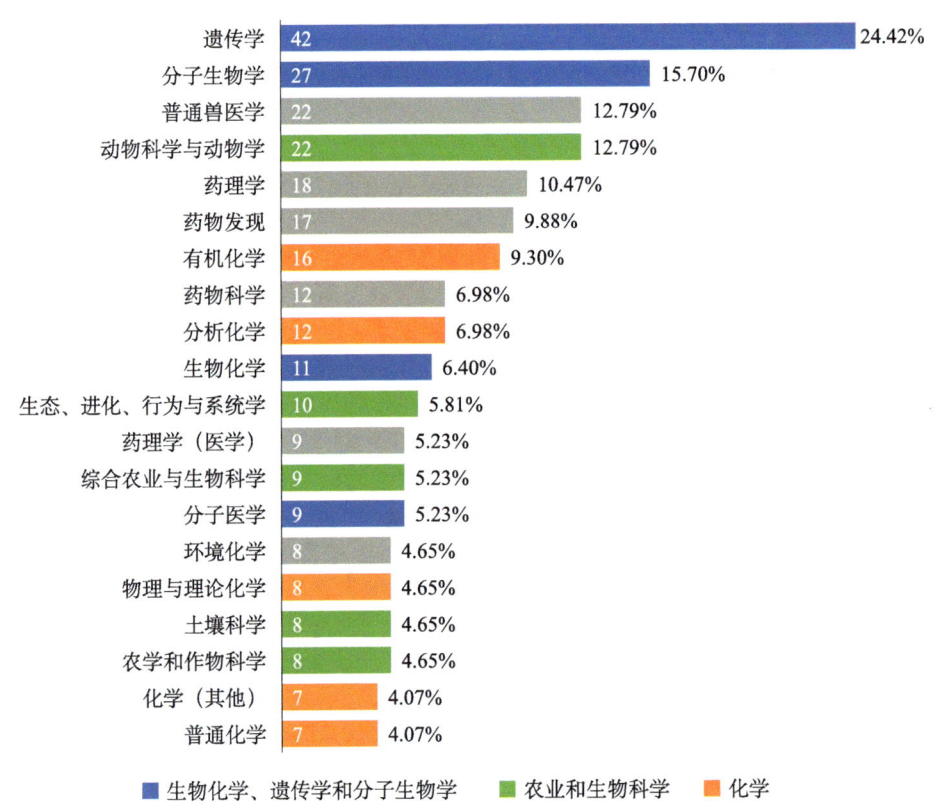

图56　兰州畜牧与兽药研究所2017—2019年发文学科分布

对生物化学、遗传学和分子生物学，农业和生物科学这两大学科的亚学科进行分析，结果如图56所示，在生物化学、遗传学和分子生物学中，发文主要集中在遗传学（24.42%），分子生物学（15.70%），生物化学（6.40%），分子医学（5.23%）等亚学科中。农业和生物科学学科的发文主要集中在动物科学与动物学（12.79%），生态、进化、行为与系统学（5.81%），综合农业和生物科学（5.23%），土壤科学（4.65%），农学和作物科学（4.65%）等亚学科。

2. 发文和引文主题分析

将文献按照主题组织，进行更细粒度的需求分析，是为了解决单纯按照学科为单元进行分析，针对性不强，导致资源建设成本高、利用不充分的问题。2017—2019年兰州畜牧与兽药研究所发文共计涉及115个主题，通过相应的遴选指标，遴选出发文、引文涉及的主要主题（表52）。可以看出兰州畜牧与兽药研究所在"Genome, Chloroplast; Genome, Mitochondrial; Copy SSC"这个主题的发文最多，由此判断该研究所较为侧重这一领域的研究，在"Genome; Polymorphism, Single Nucleotide; CNV regions"主题的引文最多，表明在该领域文献的需求强度最高；该所在"Placenta, Retained; Pacific Islands; Retained placenta"这个主题的发文占该主题全球同期论文的25.00%，说明其在全球范围内对该领域的研究有较为突出的贡献；该所参与的最受关注、发展势头最好的主题分别为"Polysaccharides; Antioxidants; Polysaccharide fractions"和"Polymers; Phase separation; Polymers MIPs"，主题显示度值分别为99.661和99.843；而该所发文具有较高引文影响力的主题为"Polysaccharides; Antioxidants; Polysaccharide fractions"，发文FWCI值是同类论文的4.94倍。综上，通过主题分析的结果不仅从各个角度反映出兰州畜牧与兽药研究所学科文献资源的精细化需求，同时也体现了研究所研究领域的分布态势，能够为其学科规划和发展提供参考。

表52 兰州畜牧与兽药研究所发文引文主要主题

主题	发文量	发文占主题同期论文比(%)	引文量	主题显示度	FWCI值
Genome, Chloroplast; Genome, Mitochondrial; Copy SSC	15	1.02	55	81.962	0.41
Diterpenes; Methicillin-Resistant Staphylococcus Aureus; Pleuromutilin derivatives	8	9.20	90	79.258	0.45
Eugenol; Eugenia; Clove oil	8	3.83	99	84.256	1.13
Genome; Polymorphism, Single Nucleotide; CNV regions	5	1.14	202	91.704	1.23
Horses; Genetic variation; Horse breeds	4	2.26	19	81.387	0.07
Albendazole; Anthelmintics; Albendazole ABZ	4	1.80	27	86.192	0.93
Cattle; Cattle breeds; Cattle populations	4	1.24	35	86.404	0.13
Soil moisture; Loess; Deep soil	4	0.77	54	93.964	0.21

续表

主题	发文量	发文占主题同期论文比(%)	引文量	主题显示度	FWCI值
Endometritis; Postpartum Period; Clinical endometritis	4	0.74	94	92.297	0.94
Psoroptidae; Mite infestations; Psoroptic mange	3	4.92	27	59.414	2.74
Shigella; Dysentery, Bacillary; Sonnei isolates	3	0.84	48	89.375	0.29
Polysaccharides; Antioxidants; Polysaccharide fractions	3	0.15	62	99.661	4.94
Polymers; Phase separation; Polymers MIPs	3	0.12	49	99.843	0.96
Manganese; Welding; Manganese levels	2	0.36	35	96.638	0.77
MicroRNAs; Adipocytes; Adipocyte differentiation	2	0.24	27	98.674	1.46
Biofilms; *Staphylococcus aureus*; Epidermidis biofilm	2	0.23	18	97.216	0.10
Genes; Gene expression; Stable genes	2	0.19	58	96.751	3.77
Placenta, Retained; Pacific Islands; Retained placenta	1	25.00	7	21.035	0.69
Arabinose; Vitex; Diabetic rats	1	12.50	0	22.253	1.31
Fungi; Porifera; Marine sponge	1	12.50	3	29.610	0.20
Glycoconjugates; Carbohydrates; Partner organisations	1	8.33	12	56.663	0.15
Zinc compounds; Transition metal compounds; Coordination polymers	1	6.25	3	5.102	0
Cell Membrane; Larva; Thiophenes	1	5.26	9	52.407	1.75
Soil prganic carbon; Organic carbon; Carbon	1	5.26	0	30.056	0.79
Niclosamide; Snails; Sea lamprey	1	4.55	3	56.816	3.37
Acids; Biological Agents; Total synthesis	1	3.03	2	66.685	0
Horns; Cattle; Polled animals	1	3.03	24	60.366	0.97
Alkaloids; Biological Agents; Natural products	1	2.63	1	72.482	3.77
Infiltration; Soil moisture; Soil infiltration	1	2.50	25	61.997	3.12
Metabolomics; Medicine, Chinese traditional; Differentially expressed	1	2.50	7	39.368	0.32
Spermatozoa; Fertilization; Sperm-egg fusion	1	2.08	14	42.740	2.02
Chromosomes; Buffaloes; River buffalo	1	1.96	4	60.522	0

续表

主题	发文量	发文占主题同期论文比(%)	引文量	主题显示度	FWCI值
Salt stress; Salt tolerance; NaCl stress	1	1.64	0	50.879	0.18
Swainsonine; Ipomoea; Indolizidine alkaloid	1	1.47	0	57.626	0
Follicular Fluid; Granulosa Cells; Cytokines	1	1.32	13	69.973	0.74
Elymus; Poaceae; Genetic diversity	1	1.15	0	64.655	0.11
Leukemia Inhibitory Factor; Receptors, OSM-LIF; Endometrium	1	1.14	0	69.284	0.86
Mastitis; Buffaloes; Sub-clinical mastitis	1	1.11	14	73.319	0
Ranunculaceae; Clematis; Chloroplast genome	1	1.10	2	61.027	2.06

3. 需求期刊及保障情况

经引文分析得知兰州畜牧与兽药研究所发文引用了1 537种外文期刊，与国家农业图书馆已订阅外文电子期刊品种进行比对，测算出其外文电子期刊全文保障率达到84.48%，引文量前40的期刊见表53。

表53 兰州畜牧与兽药研究所引文量前40期刊

编号	期刊名称	引用数量	是否保障
1	PLoS ONE	129	是
2	Journal of Dairy Science	86	是
3	BMC Genomics	81	是
4	Nature	77	是
5	Proceedings of the National Academy of Sciences of the United States of America	76	是
6	Veterinary Parasitology	65	是
7	Nucleic Acids Research	61	是
8	Journal of Ethnopharmacology	58	是
9	Scientific Reports	57	是
10	Journal of Animal Science	54	是

续表

编号	期刊名称	引用数量	是否保障
11	Journal of Natural Products	50	是
12	Nature Genetics	49	是
13	Land Degradation and Development	48	是
14	Carbohydrate Polymers	48	是
15	Science	47	是
16	Journal of Agricultural and Food Chemistry	44	是
17	Antimicrobial Agents and Chemotherapy	42	是
18	Journal of Antibiotics	42	是
19	Molecular Biology and Evolution	40	是
20	Theriogenology	39	是
21	Journal of Hydrology	38	是
22	Planta Medica	36	否
23	Journal of Biological Chemistry	35	是
24	Journal of Medicinal Chemistry	31	是
25	Gene	30	是
26	Natural Product Reports	30	是
27	Animal Genetics	29	是
28	Geoderma	28	是
29	International Journal of Biological Macromolecules	28	是
30	Bioinformatics	28	是
31	European Journal of Medicinal Chemistry	27	是
32	Journal of the American Chemical Society	26	是
33	Phytochemistry	26	是
34	Molecular Ecology	25	是
35	Food Chemistry	25	是
36	Livestock Science	24	是
37	PCR Methods and Applications	24	是
38	Veterinary Record	23	是

续表

编号	期刊名称	引用数量	是否保障
39	Journal of Chromatography A	23	是
40	Catena	23	是

4. 需求数据库分析

分析各直属研究所引用外文文献的来源数据库，从数据库层面把握各直属研究所需求，是外文全文数据库建设的重要依据，同时也为各直属研究所参与电子资源共建选择数据库提供参考。根据各直属研究所需求期刊分析结果，将其与国家农业图书馆订阅的 27 种外文全文数据库期刊目录进行比对，发现 2017—2019 年兰州畜牧与兽药研究所引文主要来源数据库如图 57 所示，其中来源于 ScienceDirect（46.70%）、Wiley（13.86%）、OUP（8.19%）、Nature（7.40%）和 Springer（7.20%）的引用最多。

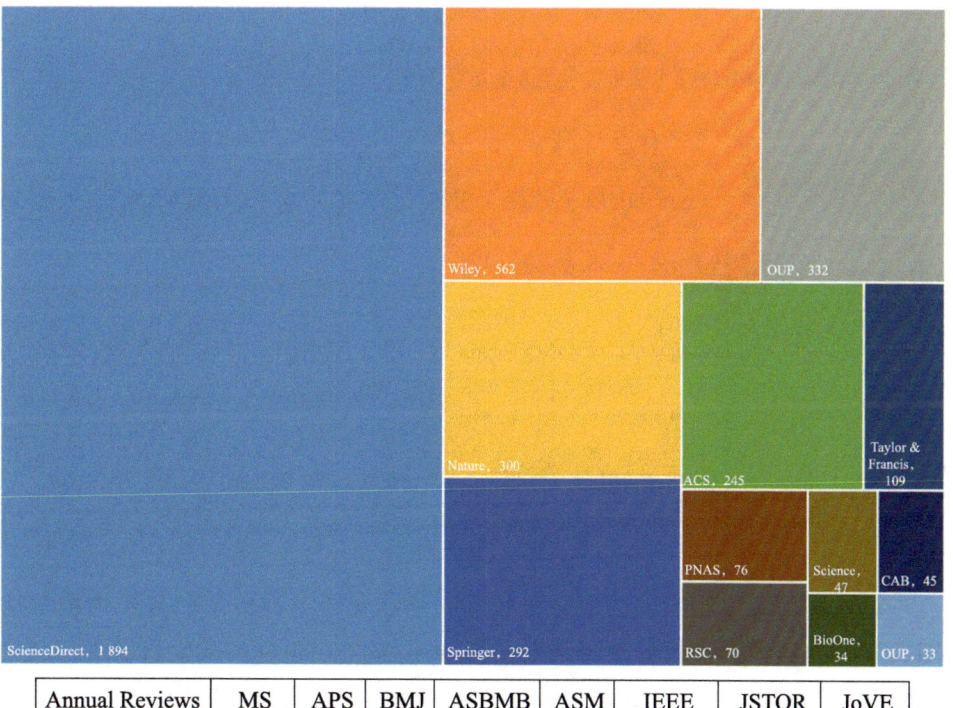

图 57　兰州畜牧与兽药研究所引文来源数据库分布

（二十五）上海兽医研究所

1. 需求学科分析

采集上海兽医研究所2017—2019年发表的外文期刊论文共计299篇，对其进行学科分析，可以看出该所发文主要集中在免疫与微生物学（62.62%），医学（36.10%），兽医学（26.20%），生物化学、遗传学和分子生物学（25.56%）这四大学科（图58）。除此之外，在农业和生物科学，药理学、毒理学和药剂学等也有一定数量的发文，说明上海兽医研究所的研究在这些领域也有涉足。

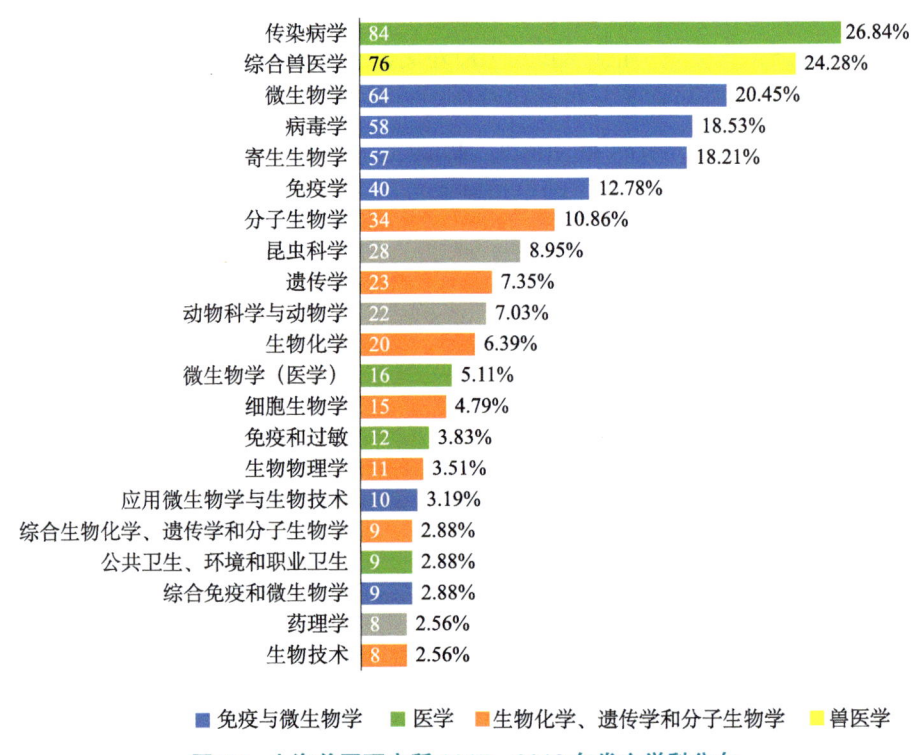

图58　上海兽医研究所2017—2019年发文学科分布

对免疫与微生物学，医学，兽医学，生物化学、遗传学和分子生物学这四大学科的亚学科进行分析，结果如图58所示，在免疫与微生物学中，发文主要集中在微生物学（20.45%），病毒学（18.53%），寄生生物学（18.21%），免疫学（12.78%），应用微生物学与生物技术（3.19%），综合免疫和微生物学（2.88%）等亚学科中。医学学科的发文主要集中在传染病学（26.84%），微生物（医学）（5.11%）、免疫和过敏（3.83%）、公共卫生、环境和职业卫生（2.88%）等亚学科。兽医学学科的发文主要集中在综合兽医学（24.28%）等亚学科。生物化学、遗传学和分子生物学学科的发文主要集中在分子生物学（10.86%）、遗传学（7.35%）、生物化学（6.39%）、细胞生物学（4.79%）、生物物理学（3.51%）、综合生物化学、遗传学和分子生物学（2.88%）、生物技术（2.56%）等亚学科。

2. 发文和引文主题分析

将文献按照主题组织，进行更细粒度的需求分析，是为了解决单纯按照学科为单元进行分析，针对性不强，导致资源建设成本高、利用不充分的问题。2017—2019年上海兽医研究所发文共计涉及153个主题，通过相应的遴选指标，遴选出发文、引文涉及的主要主题（表54）。可以看出上海兽医研究所在"Porcine respiratory and reproductive syndrome virus; Porcine Reproductive and Respiratory Syndrome; Pathogenic porcine"这个主题的发文和引文最多，由此判断该研究所较为侧重这一领域的研究，在该领域文献的需求强度也最高；该所在"Riemerella; Ducks; Anatipestifer isolates"这个主题的发文占该主题全球同期论文的8.62%，说明其在全球范围内对该领域的研究有较为突出的贡献；该所参与的最受关注、发展势头最好的主题为"Antiviral Agents; Interferons; Acid-inducible gene"，主题显示度值为99.756；而该所发文具有较高引文影响力的主题为"Porcine epidemic diarrhea virus; Swine; Deltacoronavirus PDCoV"，发文FWCI值是同类论文的3.65倍。综上，通过主题分析的结果不仅从各个角度反映出上海兽医研究所学科文献资源的精细化需求，同时也体现了研究所研究领域的分布态势，能够为其学科规划和发展提供参考。

表54　上海兽医研究所发文引文主要主题

主题	发文量	发文占主题同期论文比(%)	引文量	主题显示度	FWCI值
Porcine respiratory and reproductive syndrome virus; Porcine Reproductive and Respiratory Syndrome; Pathogenic porcine	20	2.48	467	96.354	1.42
Schistosoma mansoni; *Schistosoma japonicum*; Adult worms	16	5.99	241	87.502	0.52

续表

主题	发文量	发文占主题同期论文比(%)	引文量	主题显示度	FWCI值
Newcastle disease virus; Newcastle Disease; Avian paramyxovirus	15	2.75	391	93.141	0.81
Eimeria; Coccidiosis; Avian coccidiosis	13	3.39	171	89.059	1.36
Orthomyxoviridae; Influenza in birds; Swine influenza	8	0.83	177	97.672	0.66
Ticks; Rhipicephalus; Tick saliva	8	2.16	185	93.726	1.11
Influenza A virus; Orthomyxoviridae; IAV Infection	7	1.23	152	97.178	0.63
Brucella; *Brucella abortus*; Abortus infection	7	1.36	168	91.791	1.42
Herpesvirus 1, Suid; Pseudorabies; Pseudorabies virus	7	3.41	109	84.856	0.68
Antiviral Agents; Interferons; Acid-inducible gene	6	0.36	172	99.756	1.09
Encephalitis Viruses, Japanese; Encephalitis, Japanese; Japanese Encephalitis Vaccines	6	1.53	155	90.789	1.20
Autophagy; Infection; Antigen presentation	5	0.65	117	98.462	1.66
Riemerella; Ducks; Anatipestifer isolates	5	8.62	87	58.933	0.77
Quorum Sensing; Biofilms; Homoserine lactones	4	0.25	69	99.337	0.38
Anthelmintics; Haemonchus; Benzimidazole resistance	4	0.81	60	93.638	0.87
Babesiosis; Babesia; Human babesiosis	4	1.23	67	88.120	0.28
Hemorrhagic disease virus, Rabbit; Rabbits; Rabbit haemorrhagic	4	2.13	58	88.073	0.59
Schistosomiasis; Snails; Hupensis snail	4	1.13	82	67.759	0.68
Endoplasmic Reticulum Stress; Unfolded Protein Response; Homologous protein	3	0.12	116	99.742	2.16
Schistosomiasis; Helminths; Preventive chemotherapy	3	0.24	130	98.522	0.18
Ducks; Viruses; DTMUV Infection	3	3.23	49	73.343	2.55
Schistosomiasis; *Schistosoma mansoni*; Worm burden	3	3.00	53	72.672	0.55

续表

主题	发文量	发文占主题同期论文比(%)	引文量	主题显示度	FWCI值
Malaria; Antimalarials; Reactive oxygen	3	4.76	45	72.642	0.31
Newcastle disease virus; Neoplasms; Virus NDV	3	2.94	66	72.236	0.95
Exosomes; Cells; Recipient cells	2	0.03	86	99.983	0.26
Graphite; Graphene; Mesenchymal stem	2	0.09	8	99.930	0
Colistin; *Escherichia coli*; Gene *Mcr-1*	2	0.20	46	99.515	1.48
Influenza Vaccines; Influenza, Human; Universal influenza	2	0.21	49	99.237	1.85
Oncolytic Viruses; Neoplasms; Oncolytic herpes	2	0.25	37	98.712	0.56
Influenza in birds; Influenza A virus; Poultry markets	2	0.36	52	97.670	0.72
RNA, Messenger; RNA Stability; SG assembly	2	0.53	44	97.225	0.51
MicroRNAs; Herpesvirus 4, Human; Virus EBV	2	0.46	24	95.839	1.29
Viruses; Metagenomics; Viral genomes	2	0.45	43	95.398	1.78
Porcine epidemic diarrhea virus; Swine; Deltacoronavirus PDCoV	2	0.31	82	94.518	3.65
Porphyromonas gingivalis; Periodontitis; Periodontal pathogen	2	0.48	42	93.655	0
Electrophoresis, Capillary; Capillaries; Capillary isoelectric	2	1.10	6	90.024	0.31
Biomphalaria; Snails; *Biomphalaria glabrata*	2	1.23	46	84.514	0.83
Escherichia coli; Vaccines; Cell envelopes	2	3.17	21	76.876	0.89

3. 需求期刊及保障情况

经引文分析得知上海兽医研究所发文引用了1 481种外文期刊,与国家农业图书馆已订阅外文电子期刊品种进行比对,测算出其外文电子期刊全文保障率达到85.59%,引文量前40的期刊见表55。

表 55 上海兽医研究所引文量前 40 期刊

编号	期刊名称	引用数量	是否保障
1	Journal of Virology	703	是
2	PLoS ONE	315	是
3	Veterinary Microbiology	271	是
4	Proceedings of the National Academy of Sciences of the United States of America	257	是
5	Journal of General Virology	205	是
6	Journal of Biological Chemistry	197	是
7	Nature	188	是
8	Virology	167	是
9	Poultry Science	165	是
10	PLoS Pathogens	165	是
11	Vaccine	154	是
12	Archives of Virology	152	是
13	Infection and Immunity	146	是
14	Virus Research	144	是
15	Veterinary Parasitology	142	是
16	Science	138	是
17	Zeitschrift für Parasitenkunde	125	是
18	Cell	122	是
19	International Journal for Parasitology	118	是
20	Journal of Bacteriology	117	是
21	Scientific Reports	112	是
22	Parasites and Vectors	109	是
23	Emerging Infectious Diseases	100	是
24	Avian Pathology	98	是

续表

编号	期刊名称	引用数量	是否保障
25	PLoS Neglected Tropical Diseases	97	是
26	Journal of Immunology	92	是
27	Nucleic Acids Research	90	是
28	Virology Journal	84	是
29	Journal of Parasitology	76	是
30	Molecular Microbiology	71	是
31	Parasitology	68	是
32	Experimental Parasitology	67	是
33	Veterinary Research	66	是
34	Avian Diseases	64	是
35	Cell Host and Microbe	61	是
36	Infection, Genetics and Evolution	60	是
37	Frontiers in Microbiology	59	是
38	Journal of Clinical Microbiology	59	是
39	Molecular and Biochemical Parasitology	58	是
40	Journal of Experimental Medicine	53	是

4. 需求数据库分析

分析各直属研究所引用外文文献的来源数据库，从数据库层面把握各直属研究所需求，是外文全文数据库建设的重要依据，同时也为各直属研究所参与电子资源共建选择数据库提供参考。根据各直属研究所需求期刊分析结果，将其与国家农业图书馆订阅的27种外文全文数据库期刊目录进行比对，发现2017—2019年上海兽医研究所引文主要来源数据库如图59所示，其中来源于ScienceDirect（43.80%）、ASM（9.51%）、Wiley（8.71%）和Nature（7.84%）的引用最多。

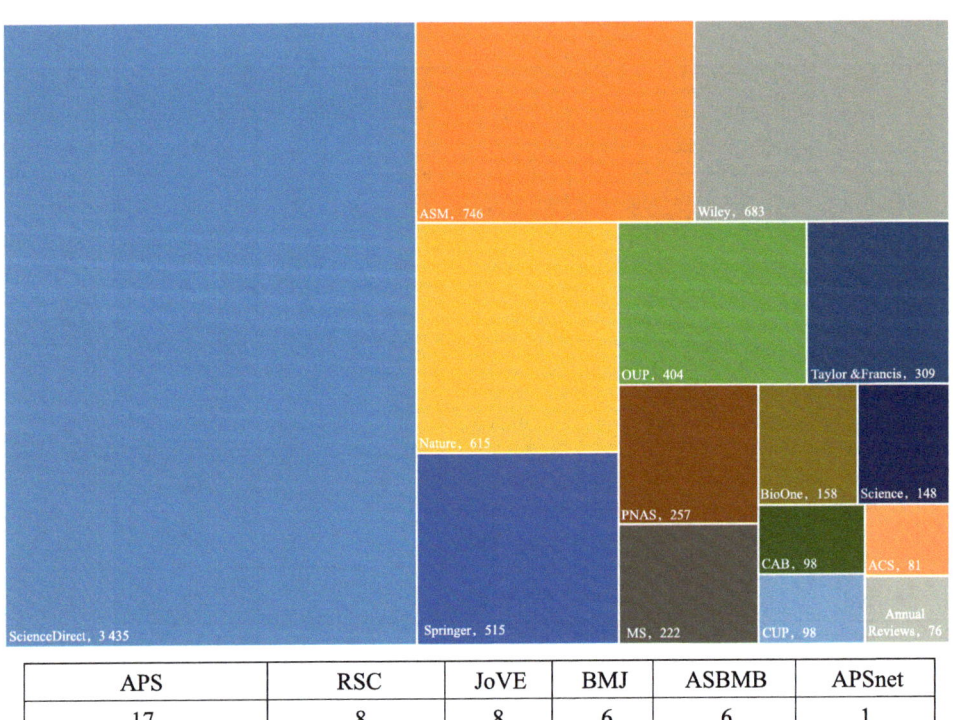

APS	RSC	JoVE	BMJ	ASBMB	APSnet
17	8	8	6	6	1

图 59　上海兽医研究所引文来源数据库分布

（二十六）草原研究所

1. 需求学科分析

采集草原研究所 2017—2019 年发表的外文期刊论文共计 163 篇，对其进行学科分析，可以看出该所发文主要集中在农业和生物科学（65.28%），环境科学（41.67%）这两大学科（图 60）。除此之外，在生物化学、遗传学和分子生物学，地球与行星科学，社会科学等也有一定数量的发文，说明草原研究所的研究在这些领域也有涉足。

对农业和生物科学、环境科学这两大学科的亚学科进行分析，结果如图 60 所示，在农业和生物科学中，发文主要集中在植物科学（29.17%），农学和作物科学（22.69%），土壤科学（19.91%），生态、进化、行为与系统学（17.13%），综合农业和生物科学（10.19%），动物科学与动物学（4.63%），环境工程学（3.70%）等亚学科中。环境科学学科的发文主要集中在自然和景观保护（18.06%）、生态学（12.50%）、管理监测与政策法规学（6.48%）、环境化学（5.56%）、综合环境科学（4.17%）、污染学（3.70%）等亚学科。

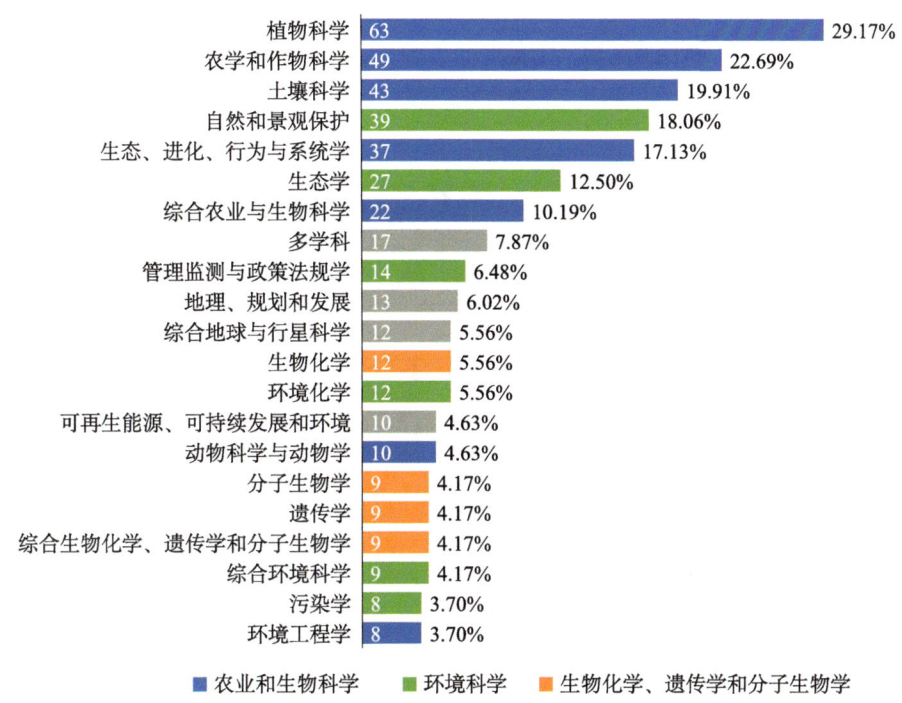

图 60　草原研究所 2017—2019 年发文学科分布

2. 发文和引文主题分析

将文献按照主题组织，进行更细粒度的需求分析，是为了解决单纯按照学科为单元进行分析，针对性不强，导致资源建设成本高、利用不充分的问题。2017—2019 年草原研究所发文共计涉及 124 个主题，通过相应的遴选指标，遴选出发文、引文涉及的主要主题（表 56）。可以看出草原研究所在"Grazing; Grasslands; Grazing exclusion"这个主题的发文最多，由此判断该研究所较为侧重这一领域的研究，在"Functional diversity; Traits; Trait values"主题的引文最多，表明在该领域文献的需求强度最高；该所在"Alfalfa; China; Han dynasty"这个主题的发文占该主题全球同期论文的 42.86%，说明其在全球范围内对该领域的研究有较为突出的贡献；该所参与的最受关注、发展势头最好的主题为"Functional diversity; Traits; Trait values"，主题显示度值为 99.872；而该所发文具有较高引文影响力的主题分别为"Evapotranspiration; Energy balance; Evaporative fraction"和"Polysaccharides; Antioxidants; Polysaccharide fractions",发文FWCI值分别是同类论文的5.89倍和4.35倍。综上,通过主题分析的结果不仅从各个角度反映出草原研究所学科文献资源的精细化需求,同时也体现了研究所研究领域的分布态势,能够为其学科规划和发展提供参考。

表56 草原研究所发文引文主要主题

主题	发文量	发文占主题同期论文比(%)	引文量	主题显示度	FWCI值
Grazing; Grasslands; Grazing exclusion	20	4.03	267	96.414	0.72
Alfalfa; China; Han dynasty	12	42.86	0	36.946	0.30
Functional diversity; Traits; Trait values	8	0.29	277	99.872	2.59
Polysaccharides; Antioxidants; Polysaccharide fractions	6	0.30	167	99.661	4.35
Stoichiometry; Phosphorus; Stoichiometric ratios	6	0.72	149	96.249	2.51
Mongolia; Rangeland; Natural resources	6	1.64	69	89.924	1.03
Salinity; Salt tolerance; Salt tolerant	5	0.28	60	98.949	0.25
Soil; Microbial community; Soil fungal	5	0.36	74	99.229	1.99
Silage; Corn silage; Silage fermentation	4	0.55	38	94.538	0
Saccharopolyspora; Macrolides; Spinosad production	4	6.56	29	69.564	0.32
Drought; Stream flow; Evapotranspiration index	3	0.15	68	99.361	2.71
Land surface; Surface measurement; Emissivity separation	3	0.35	63	95.902	1.01
Soil quality; Soil; Soil biological	2	0.18	22	98.369	0
Optical radar; Cirrus; Ice cloud	2	0.34	16	94.007	1.58
Wildfire; Fire; Water repellent	2	0.26	55	97.790	0.69
Ecosystem service; Ecosystem services; Multiple ecosystem	2	0.06	28	99.932	1.11
Soil moisture; Radiometers; Moisture retrievals	2	0.16	26	99.316	1.93
Eddy covariance; Net ecosystem exchange; Carbon flux	2	0.22	76	98.486	0.42

续表

主题	发文量	发文占主题同期论文比(%)	引文量	主题显示度	FWCI值
Input-output analysis; Carbon emission; Multi-regional input-output	2	0.09	35	99.895	0.51
Evapotranspiration; Energy balance; Evaporative fraction	2	0.22	86	98.195	5.89
Droughts; Transcription factors; Freezing tolerance	2	0.17	36	98.632	0.18
Temperature; Extreme event; Precipitation indices	2	0.12	53	99.401	1.37
Genes; Gene expression; Stable genes	2	0.19	33	96.751	0.38
Phosphorus; Phosphates; Phosphate starvation	2	0.25	43	97.851	1.31
Genome, Mitochondrial; RNA, Transfer; T-rich region	2	0.13	34	93.662	1.22
Copper; Water Pollutants, Chemical; Ligand model	2	0.52	37	93.980	0.77
Calves; Dairies; Starter intake	2	0.46	33	90.803	2.59
Grassland; Precipitation; Annual precipitation	2	0.43	167	96.137	1.24
Elymus; Poaceae; Genetic diversity	2	2.30	14	64.655	0.29
Methane; Soil emission; Soil CH	2	1.06	39	89.076	0.72
Empididae; Diptera; Dance flies	2	2.30	19	53.403	0.11
Rangeland; Grazing; Continuous grazing	2	1.85	11	78.471	0.51
Grassland; Vegetation; Remote sensing	2	4.00	24	63.007	0.69
Alkalis; Seedlings; Alkaline stress	2	1.94	31	78.576	0.34
Vicia sativa subsp. *Sativa*; *Elymus sibiricus*; Gray mold	2	16.67	2	49.175	0.30
Oats; Forage; Fall-grown oat	2	9.52	4	25.881	0.40

3. 需求期刊及保障情况

经引文分析得知草原研究所发文引用了1 136种外文期刊，与国家农业图书馆已订阅外文电子期刊品种进行比对，测算出其外文电子期刊全文保障率达到91.21%，引文量前40的期刊见表57。

表 57 草原研究所引文量前 40 期刊

编号	期刊名称	引用数量	是否保障
1	Remote Sensing of Environment	170	是
2	PLoS ONE	147	是
3	Global Change Biology	138	是
4	Ecology	135	是
5	Plant and Soil	133	是
6	Proceedings of the National Academy of Sciences of the United States of America	120	是
7	Soil Biology and Biochemistry	114	是
8	Nature	107	是
9	Journal of Physiology	102	是
10	Science	100	是
11	Plant Physiology	90	是
12	Journal of Geophysical Research	87	是
13	Oecologia	83	是
14	Journal of Ecology	77	是
15	Ecology Letters	75	是
16	Carbohydrate Polymers	73	是
17	Scientific Reports	69	是
18	International Journal of Biological Macromolecules	67	是
19	International Journal of Remote Sensing	66	是
20	Agriculture, Ecosystems and Environment	66	是
21	Journal of Experimental Botany	65	是
22	Agricultural and Forest Meteorology	64	是
23	Journal of Hydrology	62	是
24	IEEE Transactions on Geoscience and Remote Sensing	61	是

续表

编号	期刊名称	引用数量	是否保障
25	Journal of Arid Environments	60	是
26	Remote Sensing	55	是
27	Science of the Total Environment	51	是
28	Food Chemistry	49	是
29	Functional Ecology	47	是
30	Geoderma	47	是
31	Rangeland Journal	45	是
32	Plant Cell	42	是
33	Journal of Dairy Science	41	是
34	Frontiers in Plant Science	39	是
35	Plant Journal	38	是
36	Journal of Vegetation Science	37	是
37	Journal of Applied Ecology	37	是
38	Soil Science Society of America Journal	36	是
39	Catena	35	是
40	Crop Science	34	是

4. 需求数据库分析

分析各直属研究所引用外文文献的来源数据库，从数据库层面把握各直属研究所需求，是外文全文数据库建设的重要依据，同时也为各直属研究所参与电子资源共建选择数据库提供参考。根据各直属研究所需求期刊分析结果，将其与国家农业图书馆订阅的 27 种外文全文数据库期刊目录进行比对，发现 2017—2019 年草原研究所引文主要来源数据库如图 61 所示，其中来源于 ScienceDirect（39.44%）、Wiley（25.18%）和 Springer（14.53%）的引用最多。

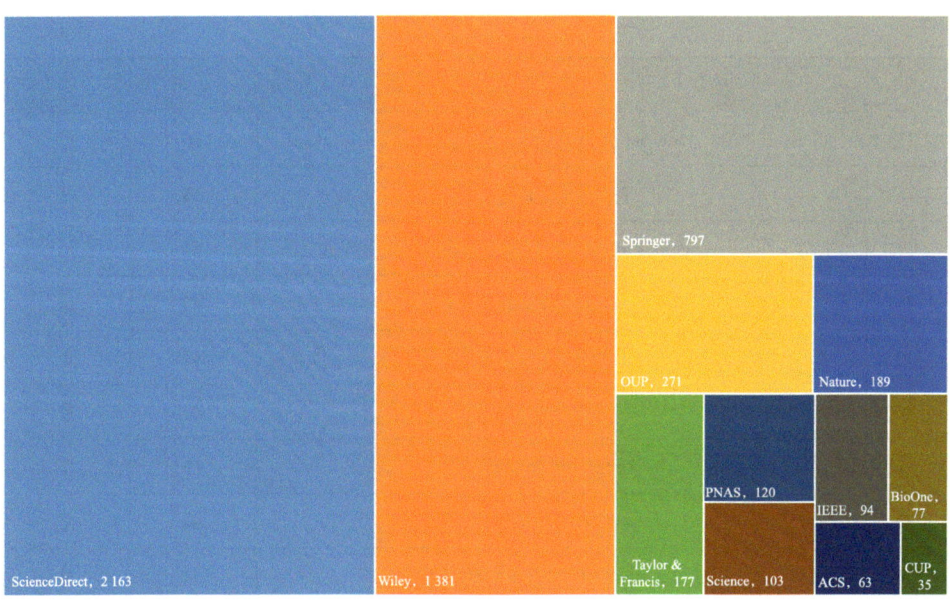

图 61　草原研究所引文来源数据库分布

（二十七）特产研究所

1. 需求学科分析

采集特产研究所 2017—2019 年发表的外文期刊论文共计 213 篇，对其进行学科分析，可以看出该所发文主要集中在生物化学、遗传学和分子生物学（43.20%），农业和生物科学（27.60%），化学（25.60%）这三大学科（图 62）。除此之外，在免疫与微生物学，药理学、毒理学和药剂学，兽医学，化学工程等也有一定数量的发文，说明特产研究所的研究在这些领域也有涉足。

对生物化学、遗传学和分子生物学，农业和生物科学，化学这三大学科的亚学科进行分析，结果如图 62 所示，在生物化学、遗传学和分子生物学中，发文主要集中在分子生物学（12.00%），遗传学（11.20%），生物化学（9.20%），生物技术（6.80%），分子医学（5.60%），细胞生物学（5.20%）等亚学科中。农业和生物科学学科的发文主要集中在动物科学与动物学（11.20%），食品科学（4.80%）等亚学科。化学学科的发文主要集中在分析化学（7.60%），有机化学

（6.80%），普通化学（5.60%），物理与理论化学（5.20%），无机化学（4.80%）等亚学科。

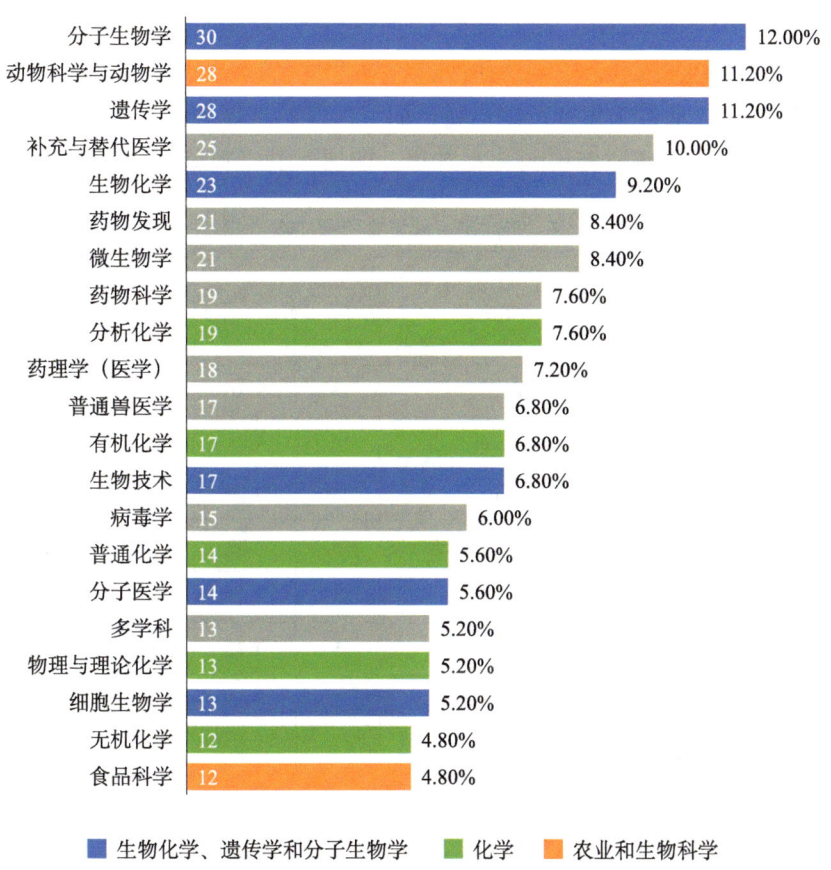

图62　特产研究所2017—2019年发文学科分布

2. 发文和引文主题分析

将文献按照主题组织，进行更细粒度的需求分析，是为了解决单纯按照学科为单元进行分析，针对性不强，导致资源建设成本高、利用不充分的问题。2017—2019年特产研究所发文共计涉及149个主题，通过相应的遴选指标，遴选出发文、引文涉及的主要主题（表58）。可以看出特产研究所在"Antlers; Deer; Antler growth"这个主题的发文最多，由此判断该研究所较为侧重这一领域的研究，并且该所在这个主题的发文占该主题全球同期论文的15.03%，说明其在全球范围内对该领域的研究有较为突出的贡献；在"Ginsenosides; Panax;

Ginseng extract"主题的引文最多,表明在该领域文献的需求强度最高;该所参与的最受关注、发展势头最好的主题为"RNA, Long Untranslated; Neoplasms; Proliferation migration"和"Ginsenosides; Panax; Ginseng extract",主题显示度值分别为99.984和98.544;而该所发文具有较高引文影响力的主题为"Miocene; Fossil; Northern Pakistan",发文 FWCI 值是同类论文的 7.13 倍。综上,通过主题分析的结果不仅从各个角度反映出特产研究所学科文献资源的精细化需求,同时也体现了研究所研究领域的分布态势,能够为其学科规划和发展提供参考。

表 58　特产研究所发文引文主要主题

主题	发文量	发文占主题同期论文比 (%)	引文量	主题显示度	FWCI 值
Antlers; Deer; Antler growth	23	15.03	244	67.225	0.40
Ginsenosides; Panax; Ginseng extract	16	1.00	376	98.544	1.00
Mink; Neovison vison; Female mink	6	7.79	31	57.676	0.27
Aluminum; Aluminum Compounds; Aluminium Chloride	6	1.32	86	92.260	0.95
Rumen; Metagenome; Rumen bacterial	6	1.08	139	97.609	1.08
Parvovirus, Canine; Dogs; CPV infection	5	1.72	95	86.539	1.66
Distemper Virus, Canine; Distemper; CDV infection	5	1.63	64	87.146	0.62
Zinc; Copper; Mg Zn/Kg	4	1.07	67	89.157	0.09
Hair Follicle; Hair; DP cells	4	0.83	75	93.756	1.72
Polymorphism, Single Nucleotide; Single nucleotide polymorphism; Site-associated DNA	4	0.71	48	97.644	0.61
Acetaminophen; Liver; APAP-induced hepatotoxicity	4	0.63	67	96.336	5.53
Porcine respiratory and reproductive syndrome virus; Porcine Reproductive and Respiratory Syndrome; Pathogenic porcine	4	0.50	93	96.354	0.26
RNA, Long Untranslated; Neoplasms; Proliferation migration	4	0.03	80	99.984	1.33
Parvovirus; Aleutian mink Disease virus; Mink	3	2.88	34	74.574	0
Odor compounds; Carrier proteins; Chemosensory proteins	3	0.73	85	93.839	0.52

续表

主题	发文量	发文占主题同期论文比(%)	引文量	主题显示度	FWCI值
Metagenome; Obesity; Microbial composition	3	0.04	63	99.985	2.36
Blastocyst; Mink; Embryonic diapause	2	6.67	10	54.516	0.58
Fever; Herpesviridae; Catarrhal fever	2	3.03	27	53.745	1.05
Thogotovirus; Influenzavirus C; Respiratory disease	2	2.41	6	74.442	1.14
Cutis laxa; Syndrome; Recessive cutis	2	1.94	16	72.812	1.76
Miocene; Fossil; Northern Pakistan	2	1.72	21	60.375	7.13
Color; Receptor, Melanocortin, Type 1; Coat colour	2	0.66	21	81.929	0.33
S100 Proteins; Proteins; Calcium-binding protein	2	0.58	44	89.154	0.85
Enterocytozoon; Microsporidia; Bieneusi genotypes	2	0.56	57	88.875	1.78
Brucella; *Brucella abortus*; Abortus infection	2	0.39	31	91.791	0.30
Colletotrichum; Anthracnose; Anthracnose symptoms	2	0.34	9	91.034	0.20
Porcine epidemic diarrhea virus; Swine; Deltacoronavirus PDCoV	2	0.31	33	94.518	0.99
Silage; Corn silage; Silage fermentation	2	0.27	17	94.538	0
Fatty acid composition; Lambs; Lamb meat	2	0.22	22	95.875	1.18
DNA methylation; Epigenetics; Methylation RdDM	2	0.20	29	99.098	0.18
Glycosylation End Products, Advanced; Skin; SRAGE levels	2	0.15	36	98.576	0.12
Ebolavirus; Hemorrhagic Fever, Ebola; Ebola virus	2	0.07	46	99.792	0.80
Reactive Oxygen Species; Antioxidants; Oxidative stress	1	8.33	2	43.933	2.70
Beta-Glucosidase; Glucosylceramides; Spastic paraplegia	1	4.76	5	52.499	2.51
South Korea; Formicidae; Ant	1	4.35	7	31.620	2.83

3. 需求期刊及保障情况

经引文分析得知特产研究所发文引用了1 770种外文期刊，与国家农业图书馆已订阅外文电子期刊品种进行比对，测算出其外文电子期刊全文保障率达到 84.27%，引文量前 40 的期刊见表 59。

表 59 特产研究所引文量前 40 期刊

编号	期刊名称	引用数量	是否保障
1	PLoS ONE	230	是
2	Journal of Virology	109	是
3	Science	105	是
4	Proceedings of the National Academy of Sciences of the United States of America	100	是
5	Journal of Biological Chemistry	85	是
6	Nature	84	是
7	Journal of Animal Science	81	是
8	Journal of Agricultural and Food Chemistry	78	是
9	Journal of Ginseng Research	77	是
10	Nucleic Acids Research	75	是
11	Scientific Reports	70	是
12	Biology of Reproduction	68	是
13	Bioinformatics	67	是
14	Journal of Dairy Science	67	是
15	Veterinary Microbiology	64	是
16	Applied and Environmental Microbiology	64	是
17	Cell	63	是
18	Soil Biology and Biochemistry	58	是
19	Journal of Ethnopharmacology	52	是
20	Biological Trace Element Research	51	是
21	Food Chemistry	50	是
22	Journal of General Virology	49	是

续表

编号	期刊名称	引用数量	是否保障
23	Journal of Nutrition	49	是
24	Journal of Pharmaceutical and Biomedical Analysis	45	是
25	Virology	45	是
26	Archives of Virology	44	是
27	Food and Chemical Toxicology	42	是
28	Frontiers in Microbiology	36	是
29	PCR Methods and Applications	35	是
30	Virus Research	35	是
31	Vaccine	35	是
32	Poultry Science	33	是
33	Theriogenology	32	是
34	Nature Methods	32	是
35	Journal of Virological Methods	32	是
36	Biochemical and Biophysical Research Communications	30	是
37	International Journal of Molecular Sciences	28	是
38	Animal Feed Science and Technology	28	是
39	Journal of Investigative Dermatology	28	是
40	Nature Genetics	26	是

4. 需求数据库分析

分析各直属研究所引用外文文献的来源数据库，从数据库层面把握各直属研究所需求，是外文全文数据库建设的重要依据，同时也为各直属研究所参与电子资源共建选择数据库提供参考。根据各直属研究所需求期刊分析结果，将其与国家农业图书馆订阅的27种外文全文数据库期刊目录进行比对，发现2017—2019年特产研究所引文主要来源数据库如图63所示，其中来源于ScienceDirect（42.90%）、Wiley（13.74%）和OUP（10.87%）的引用最多。

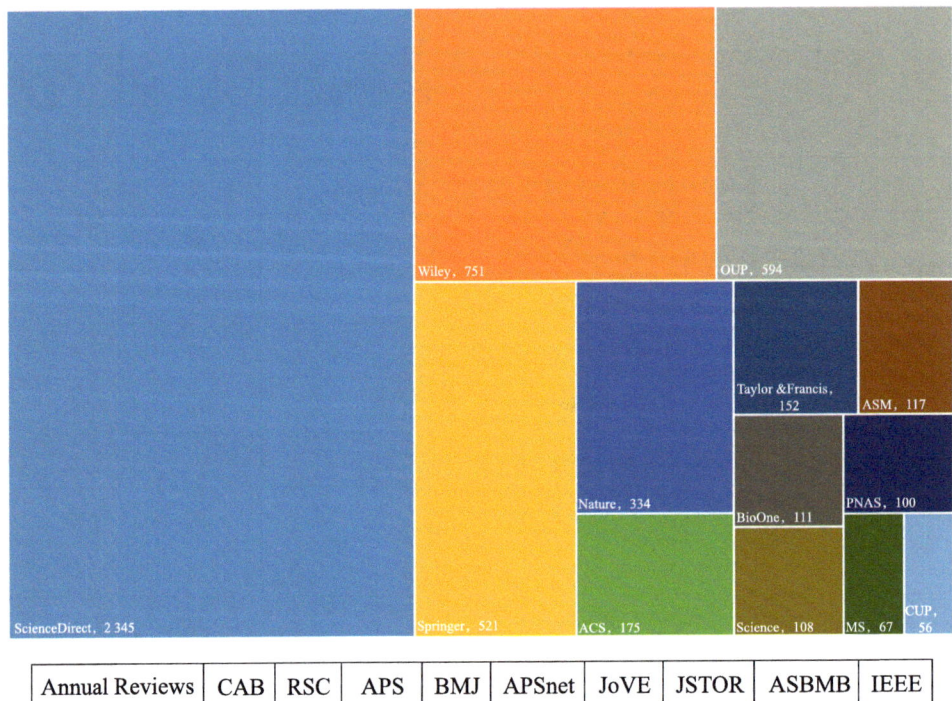

图63　特产研究所引文来源数据库分布

（二十八）环境保护科研监测所

1. 需求学科分析

采集环境保护科研检测所（简称环保所）2017—2019年发表的外文期刊论文共计283篇，对其进行学科分析，可以看出该所发文主要集中在环境科学（72.81%）、农业和生物科学（38.25%）、化学（17.51%）这三大学科（图64）。除此之外，在化学工程，工程学，药理学、毒理学和药剂学，医学，材料科学等也有一定数量的发文，说明环保所的研究在这些领域也有涉足。

对环境科学、农业和生物科学、化学这三大学科的亚学科进行分析，结果如图64所示，在环境科学中，发文主要集中在环境化学（36.18%），污染学（26.96%），生态学（23.50%），健康、毒理学和突变（19.82%），环境工程学（17.05%），管理监测与政策法规学（15.21%），自然和景观保护（14.06%），废物管理和处置（11.98%），综合环境科学（11.06%），水科学与技术（3.23%）等亚学科。农业和生物科学学科的发文主要集中在生态、进化、行为与系统学（23.27%），农学和作物科学（17.97%），土壤科学（17.74%），综合农业和生物科学（5.30%），植物科学（4.38%）等亚学科。化学学科的发文主要集中在普通化学（12.21%），分析化学（3.92%）等亚学科。

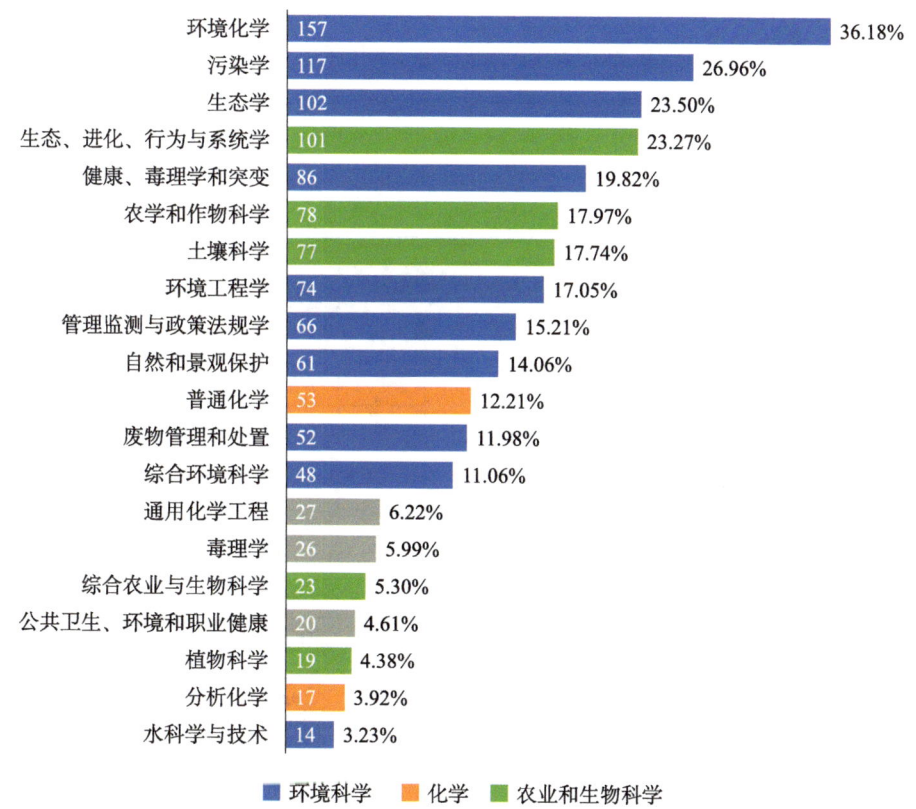

图 64　环境保护科研监测所 2017—2019 年发文学科分布

2. 发文和引文主题分析

将文献按照主题组织，进行更细粒度的需求分析，是为了解决单纯按照学科为单元进行分析，针对性不强，导致资源建设成本高、利用不充分的问题。2017—2019 年环境保护科研监测所发文共计涉及 186 个主题，通过相应的遴选指标，遴选出发文、引文涉及的主要主题（表 60）。可以看出环保所在 "Pyrolysis; Soil amendment; Biochar amendment" 这个主题的发文和引文最多，由此判断该研究所较为侧重这一领域的研究，在该领域文献的需求强度也最高；该所在"Cadmium; Sepiolite; Paddy soil"这个主题的发文占该主题全球同期论文的16.67%，说明其在全球范围内对该领域的研究有较为突出的贡献；该所参与的最受关注、发展势头最好的主题为"Pyrolysis; Soil amendment; Biochar amendment"和"Microbial fuel cells; Fuel cell; Cells MFCs"，主题显示度值分别为99.968和99.971；而该所发文具有较高引文影响力的主题为"Cellulose; Hydrolysis; Hydrolytic hydrogenation"，发文FWCI值是同类论文的3.47倍。综上，通过主题分析的结果不仅从各个角度反映出环保所学科文献资源的精细化需求，同时也体现了研究所研究领域的分布态势，能够为其学科规划和发展提供参考。

表60 环境保护科研监测所发文引文主要主题

主题	发文量	发文占主题同期论文比(%)	引文量	主题显示度	FWCI值
Pyrolysis; Soil amendment; Biochar amendment	26	0.47	501	99.968	1.84
Cadmium; Heavy metal; Hazard quotient	19	1.54	244	98.800	1.03
Arsenic; *Oryza sativa*; Arsenic accumulation	12	1.09	317	99.216	1.72
Heavy metal; Heavy metals; Urban soils	12	0.65	135	99.544	1.44
Microbial fuel cells; Fuel cell; Cells MFCs	12	0.27	373	99.971	1.48
Cadmium; Sepiolite; Paddy soil	9	16.67	74	72.355	2.06
Phytoremediation; Cadmium; Pot experiment	8	0.65	166	98.956	1.17
Graphite; Graphene; Mesenchymal stem	8	0.35	165	99.930	1.53
Arsenic; Pollution control; Arsenic adsorption	7	0.47	187	99.494	1.64
Antibiotic resistance; Drug resistance, Microbial; Antibiotic-resistant bacteria	7	0.33	156	99.881	1.02
Soil organic carbon; Organic carbon; Soil aggregation	7	0.29	90	99.574	1.10
Furfural; Catalysts; Furfural yield	7	0.22	262	99.958	1.77
Anaerobic digestion; Biogas; Methane yields	7	0.19	83	99.935	0.46
Selenium; Selenites; Inorganic selenium	6	0.64	130	98.321	1.44
Pesticides; Pesticide Residues; Quick easy	6	0.44	96	99.141	0.62
Nanoparticles; Plants; Seedling growth	6	0.36	124	99.695	1.56

续表

主题	发文量	发文占主题同期论文比(%)	引文量	主题显示度	FWCI值
Antibiotics; Oxytetracycline; Veterinary antibiotics	6	0.27	187	99.816	1.26
Ferrihydrite; Adsorption; Ionic strength	5	1.61	110	94.152	1.22
Colloid; Colloids; Colloid transport	5	1.24	127	94.383	1.49
Cellulose; Hydrolysis; Hydrolytic hydrogenation	5	1.06	102	97.858	3.47
Net primary production; Productivity; Annual NPP	5	0.75	4	96.869	0
Methylmercury; Mercury (element); Mercury methylation	5	0.54	5	98.811	0.22
Capacitance; Carbonization; Aqueous electrolyte	5	0.12	139	99.972	1.78
Nonpoint source pollution; Watersheds; Source NPS	4	2.02	5	75.925	0.10
Drought; Disaster; Drought disaster	4	2.02	0	66.907	0
Volatilization; Urea; Urease inhibitors	4	1.19	17	92.679	0.39
Litter; Decomposition; Root decomposition	4	0.46	112	97.944	0.45
Nitrous oxide; Soil emission; Oxide emissions	4	0.28	82	99.321	1.76
Composting; Compost; Thermophilic phase	4	0.27	96	99.479	0.48
Mercury (element); Methylmercury; MeHg concentrations	3	2.31	7	84.556	0
Electrochemical sensors; Phenols; Oxidation peak	3	1.06	47	96.993	2.06
Atrazine; Herbicides; Atrazine degradation	3	1.06	40	95.215	1.53
Phthalate; Ester; Phthalate DMP	3	0.58	50	96.331	1.04
Phosphorus; Soil; Dissolved reactive	3	0.48	30	94.649	0.17
EDTA; Phytoremediation; Soil washing	3	0.47	94	97.083	0.42
Phosphate; Phosphates; Phosphate concentration	3	0.27	57	98.991	1.35
Halogenated Diphenyl Ethers; Flame Retardants; Halogenated flame	3	0.17	70	99.675	0.62
Degradation; Radical; Activated persulfate	3	0.12	46	99.942	1.92
Silver; Nanoparticles; CuO NPs	3	0.08	221	99.946	1.40

3. 需求期刊及保障情况

经引文分析得知环境保护科研监测所发文引用了 1 362 种外文期刊，与国家农业图书馆已订阅外文电子期刊品种进行比对，测算出其外文电子期刊全文保障率达到 93.50%，引文量前 40 的期刊见表 61。

表 61 环境保护科研监测所引文量前 40 期刊

编号	期刊名称	引用数量	是否保障
1	Environmental Science and Technology	839	是
2	Chemosphere	428	是
3	Bioresource Technology	378	是
4	Journal of Hazardous Materials	370	是
5	Science of the Total Environment	361	是
6	Environmental Pollution	336	是
7	Chemical Engineering Journal	260	是
8	Water Research	246	是
9	Environmental Science and Pollution Research	185	是
10	Soil Biology and Biochemistry	178	是
11	Plant and Soil	167	是
12	Ecotoxicology and Environmental Safety	162	是
13	Geoderma	130	是
14	Nature	105	是
15	Carbon	105	是
16	Journal of Agricultural and Food Chemistry	104	是
17	Journal of Environmental Management	103	是
18	Proceedings of the National Academy of Sciences of the United States of America	94	是
19	Journal of Colloid and Interface Science	92	是
20	RSC Advances	92	是
21	Science	90	是

续表

编号	期刊名称	引用数量	是否保障
22	Green Chemistry	87	是
23	Journal of Physiology	80	是
24	Applied Catalysis B: Environmental	79	是
25	Journal of Environmental Sciences	77	是
26	Agriculture, Ecosystems and Environment	75	是
27	Scientific Reports	75	是
28	Analytical Chemistry	71	是
29	Applied and Environmental Microbiology	67	是
30	Environment International	67	是
31	Ecological Engineering	64	是
32	ACS Applied Materials and Interfaces	64	是
33	Biosensors and Bioelectronics	64	是
34	Journal of Environmental Quality	63	是
35	PLoS ONE	62	是
36	ACS Nano	61	是
37	Field Crops Research	61	是
38	Environmental and Experimental Botany	59	是
39	Journal of Chromatography A	59	是
40	Geochimica et Cosmochimica Acta	58	是

4. 需求数据库分析

分析各直属研究所引用外文文献的来源数据库，从数据库层面把握各直属研究所需求，是外文全文数据库建设的重要依据，同时也为各直属研究所参与电子资源共建选择数据库提供参考。根据各直属研究所需求期刊分析结果，将其与国家农业图书馆订阅的27种外文全文数据库期刊目录进行比对，发现2017—2019年环境保护科研监测所引文主要来源数据库如图65所示，其中来源于ScienceDirect（54.41%）、ACS（13.48%）和Springer（10.98%）的引用最多。

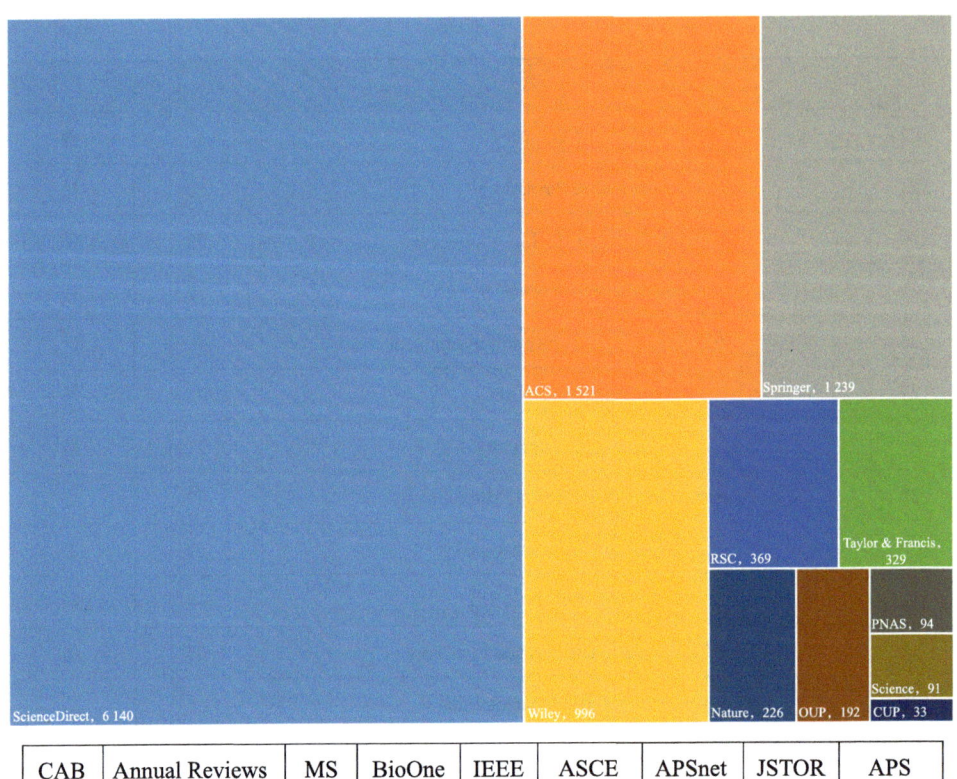

图 65　环境保护科研监测所引文来源数据库分布

（二十九）沼气科学研究所

1. 需求学科分析

采集沼气科学研究所（简称沼气所）2017—2019年发表的外文期刊论文共计157篇，对其进行学科分析，可以看出该所发文主要集中在环境科学（51.67%），化学工程（36.67%），能源（30.00%），生物化学、遗传学和分子生物学（25.56%）这四大学科（图66）。除此之外，在免疫与微生物学，农业和生物科学，化学，工程学等也有一定数量的发文，说明沼气所的研究在这些领域也有涉足。

对环境科学，化学工程，能源，生物化学、遗传学和分子生物学这四大学科的亚学科进行分析，结果如图66所示，在环境科学中，发文主要集中在废物管理和处置（23.89%），环境工程学（20.56%），环境化学（15.00%），污染学（13.89%），管理监测与政策法规学（7.78%）等亚学科。化学工程学科的发文主要集中在生物工程（20.56%），综合化学工程（13.33%）等亚学科。能源学科的发文主要集中在可再生能源、可持续发展与环境（24.44%），能源工程和电力技术（7.78%），燃料工艺（6.11%），通用能源（5.00%）等亚学科。生物化学、遗传学和分子生物学学科的发文主要集中在生物技术（13.89%），分子生物学（7.22%），生物化学（6.67%）等亚学科。

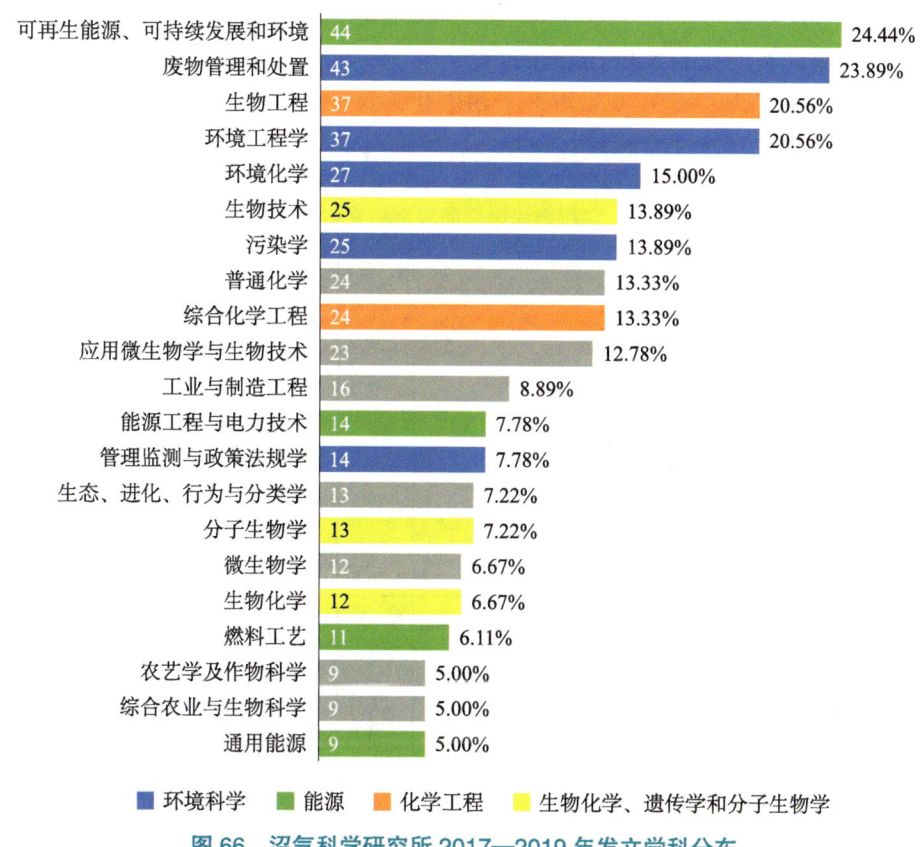

图 66　沼气科学研究所 2017—2019 年发文学科分布

2. 发文和引文主题分析

将文献按照主题组织，进行更细粒度的需求分析，是为了解决单纯按照学科为单元进行分析，针对性不强，导致资源建设成本高、利用不充分的问题。2017—2019 年沼气科学研究所发文共计涉及 91 个主题，通过相应的遴选指标，遴选出发文、引文涉及的主要主题（表 62）。可以看出沼气所在

"Anaerobic digestion; Biogas; Methane yields"这个主题的发文和引文最多,由此判断该研究所较为侧重这一领域的研究,在该领域文献的需求强度也最高;该所在"Boiling; Drought; Plant lectins"这个主题的发文占该主题全球同期论文的25.00%,说明其在全球范围内对该领域的研究有较为突出的贡献;该所参与的最受关注、发展势头最好的主题为"Degradation; Radical; Activated persulfate"和"Anaerobic digestion; Biogas; Methane yields",主题显示度值为99.942和99.935;而该所发文具有较高引文影响力的主题为"Degradation; Radical; Activated persulfate"和"Pyrolysis; Soil amendment; Biochar amendment",发文FWCI值是同类论文的6.39倍和3.37倍。综上,通过主题分析的结果不仅从各个角度反映出沼气所学科文献资源的精细化需求,同时也体现了研究所研究领域的分布态势,能够为其学科规划和发展提供参考。

表62 沼气科学研究所发文引文主要主题

主题	发文量	发文占主题同期论文比(%)	引文量	主题显示度	FWCI值
Anaerobic digestion; Biogas; Methane yields	24	0.66	472	99.935	0.77
Degradation; Radical; Activated persulfate	8	0.31	304	99.942	6.39
Enzymatic hydrolysis; Saccharification; Pretreatment conditions	6	0.17	130	99.919	0.95
Xylose; Fermentation; Xylose fermentation	5	0.65	125	98.423	0.58
Vitamin K 2; Bacterial Typing Techniques; Designated strain	5	0.21	84	99.020	0.33
Pyrolysis; Soil amendment; Biochar amendment	5	0.09	143	99.968	3.37
Zymomonas mobilis; Ethanol production; Glucose-fructose oxidoreductase	4	4.60	131	78.410	1.25
Dissolved organic matter; Biogeochemistry; Humic-like components	4	0.28	76	99.062	0.80
Algae; Microalga; Microalgae biomass	4	0.20	69	99.868	0.49
Iron; Dechlorination; Nanoscale aero-valent	4	0.19	120	99.800	1.62
Petroleum; Oil and gas fields; Anaerobic degradation	3	0.78	96	95.654	0.79
Anaerobic digestion; Methanogenesis; Direct interspecies	3	0.68	88	98.273	1.15
Biogas; Anaerobic digestion; Biogas digesters	3	0.66	46	93.075	0.37

续表

主题	发文量	发文占主题同期论文比 (%)	引文量	主题显示度	FWCI 值
Lactic acid; Fermentation; L-lactic acid	3	0.62	61	95.719	0.96
Municipal solid waste; Solid wastes; MSW generation	3	0.56	39	93.514	1.02
Phosphorus; Phosphates; Phosphate starvation	3	0.38	41	97.851	0.62
Butenes; Clostridium; Acetobutylicum ATCC	3	0.32	72	99.205	1.27
Adsorption; Ionic Strength; pH ionic	3	0.30	52	99.631	5.15
Nitrogen Removal; Wastewater treatment; Anaerobic ammonia	3	0.22	76	99.569	0.67
Biogas; Manures; Biogas alurry	2	6.67	8	63.082	0.64
Anaerobic digestion; Sludge; Digested sludge	2	1.13	46	87.883	0.15
Enzymatic hydrolysis; Saccharification; Fermentation SSF	2	0.64	27	96.141	0.62
Nanofiltration; Nanofiltration membranes; NF Membrane	2	0.59	12	95.382	1.28
Walls (structural partitions); Thermal insulation; Optimum insulation	2	0.34	25	95.272	1.86
Pervaporation; Membranes; Pervaporation dehydration	2	0.27	82	98.664	0.78
Ozonization; Ozone water treatment; Photocatalytic ozonation	2	0.26	80	98.527	0.14
Leachate; Landfill; Landfill leachates	2	0.20	27	98.232	0.21
Metabolic engineering; Yeast; Isobutanol production	2	0.18	94	99.613	0.23
Anaerobic digestion; Activated sludge; Sludge disintegration	2	0.16	68	99.475	1.32
Graphene; Adsorption; Adsorption kinetics	2	0.16	18	99.624	5.35
Behavior; Recycling; Green purchase	2	0.08	36	99.731	4.17
Boiling; Drought; Plant lectins	1	25.00	1	33.095	2.92
Liquefaction; Lignite; Red maple	1	5.56	0	69.054	0
Bioethanol; Biofuels; Bioethanol production	1	3.23	1	64.948	0.54
Biogas; Anaerobic digestion; Anaerobic fermentation	1	2.56	12	38.377	0

续表

主题	发文量	发文占主题同期论文比 (%)	引文量	主题显示度	FWCI 值
Sex attractants; Sex pheromones; Activating neuropeptide	1	1.19	31	68.181	1.93
Microbial consortia; Straw; Microbial consortium	1	1.19	21	76.793	1.06

3. 需求期刊及保障情况

经引文分析得知沼气科学研究所发文引用了 1 025 种外文期刊，与国家农业图书馆已订阅外文电子期刊品种进行比对，测算出其外文电子期刊全文保障率达到 91.89%，引文量前 40 的期刊见表63。

表63 沼气科学研究所引文量前 40 期刊

编号	期刊名称	引用数量	是否保障
1	Bioresource Technology	701	是
2	Chemical Engineering Journal	263	是
3	Water Research	226	是
4	Environmental Science and Technology	169	是
5	Journal of Hazardous Materials	164	是
6	International Journal of Systematic and Evolutionary Microbiology	159	是
7	Applied Microbiology and Biotechnology	122	是
8	Applied and Environmental Microbiology	112	是
9	Applied Catalysis B: Environmental	102	是
10	Renewable and Sustainable Energy Reviews	99	是
11	Waste Management	98	是
12	Chemosphere	93	是
13	Biotechnology for Biofuels	93	是
14	PLoS ONE	85	是
15	Applied Energy	65	是
16	Proceedings of the National Academy of Sciences of the United States of America	62	是

续表

编号	期刊名称	引用数量	是否保障
17	Science	60	是
18	Nature	58	是
19	Biomass and Bioenergy	58	是
20	Biotechnology and Bioengineering	56	是
21	Journal of Environmental Management	55	是
22	Science of the Total Environment	54	是
23	Journal of Cleaner Production	52	是
24	Journal of Bacteriology	46	是
25	Water Science and Technology	46	是
26	Journal of Membrane Science	42	是
27	International Journal of Hydrogen Energy	41	是
28	Energy and Buildings	39	是
29	Nucleic Acids Research	38	是
30	Process Biochemistry	38	是
31	Applied Biochemistry and Biotechnology	36	是
32	Biotechnology Advances	34	是
33	International Journal of Systematic Bacteriology	34	是
34	Scientific Reports	31	是
35	Journal of Biotechnology	31	是
36	Separation and Purification Technology	31	是
37	Renewable Energy	31	是
38	Organic Geochemistry	30	是
39	Plant Physiology	29	是
40	Journal of Bioscience and Bioengineering	29	是

4. 需求数据库分析

分析各直属研究所引用外文文献的来源数据库，从数据库层面把握各直属

研究所需求,是外文全文数据库建设的重要依据,同时也为各直属研究所参与电子资源共建选择数据库提供参考。根据各直属研究所需求期刊分析结果,将其与国家农业图书馆订阅的 27 种外文全文数据库期刊目录进行比对,发现 2017—2019 年沼气科学研究所引文主要来源数据库如图 67 所示,其中来源于 ScienceDirect(63.86%)和 Springer(9.33%)的引用最多。

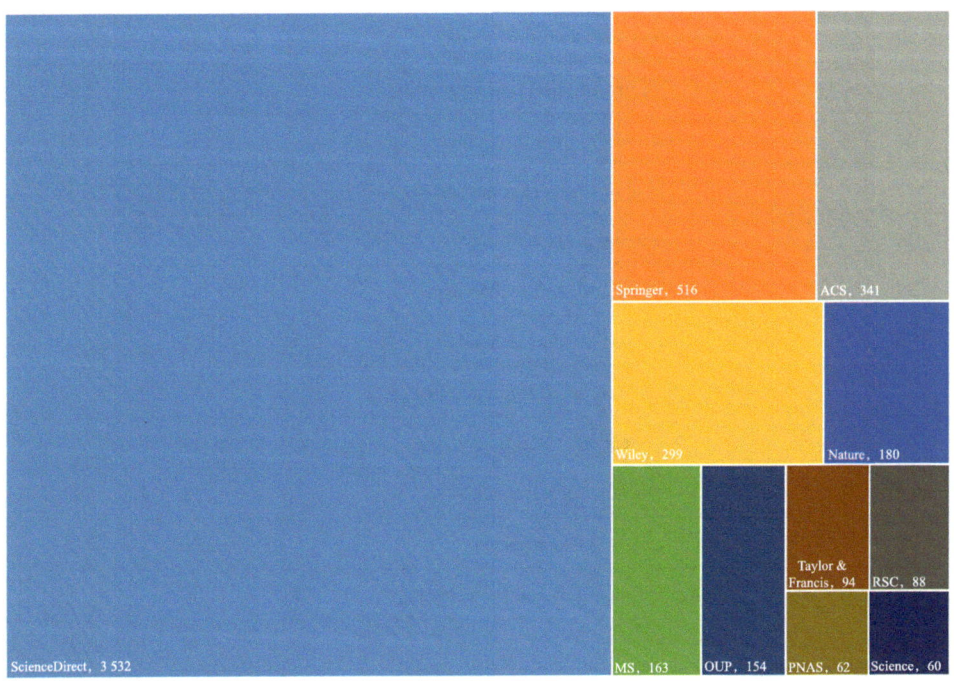

Annual Reviews	CUP	BMJ	ASCE	ASM	BioOne	ACM
23	11	11	7	6	5	3
IEEE	JSTOR	Emerald	APSnet	CAB		
2	2	2	1	1		

图 67 沼气科学研究所引文来源数据库分布

(三十)南京农业机械化研究所

1. 需求学科分析

采集南京农业机械化研究所 2017—2019 年发表的外文期刊论文共计 119 篇,对其进行学科分析,可以看出该所发文主要集中在工程学(80.10%)、农业和生物科学（70.87%）这两大学科（图68）。除此之外，在计算机科学、材料科学、能源等学科也有一定数量的发文，说明南京农业机械化研究所的研究在这些领域也有涉足。

对工程学，农业和生物科学这两大学科的亚学科进行分析，结果如图68所示，在工程学中，发文主要集中在机械工程学（59.22%），综合工程学（12.62%），工业和制造工程学（5.34%），材料力学（2.91%），电气与电子工程学（2.43%）等亚学科。农业和生物科学的发文主要集中在综合农业和生物科学（57.28%），农学和作物科学（8.25%），食品科学（5.83%），林业科学（4.85%），园艺学（4.37%）等亚学科。

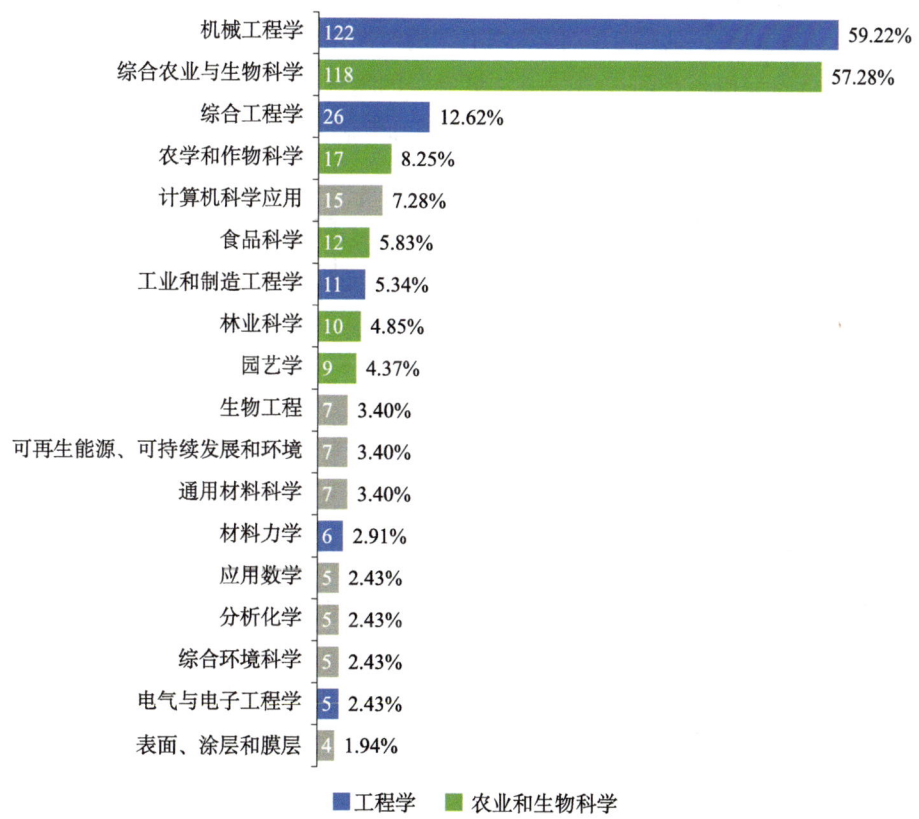

图 68　南京农业机械化研究所 2017—2019 年发文学科分布

2. 发文和引文主题分析

将文献按照主题组织，进行更细粒度的需求分析，是为了解决单纯按照学科为单元进行分析,针对性不强,导致资源建设成本高、利用不充分的问题。2017—2019年南京农业机械化研究所发文共计涉及80个主题,通过相应的遴选指标,遴选出发文、引文涉及的主要主题(表64)。可以看出南京农业机械化研究所在"Harvesters; Cutting; Cotton stalk"这个主题的发文最多,由此判断该研究所较为侧重这一领域的研究,在"Nozzles; Sprayers; Spray drift"主题的引文最多,表明在该领域文献的需求强度最高;该所在"Harvesters; Peanuts; Damage rate"这个主题的发文占该主题全球同期论文的13.85%,说明其在全球范围内对该领域的研究有较为突出的贡献;该所参与的最受关注、发展势头最好的主题为"Drying; Solar dryers; Drying models",主题显示度值为99.179;而该所发文具有较高引文影响力的主题为"Fruits; Harvesting; Fruit detection",发文FWCI值是同类论文的2.39倍。综上,通过主题分析的结果不仅从各个角度反映出南京农业机械化研究所学科文献资源的精细化需求,同时也体现了研究所研究领域的分布态势,能够为其学科规划和发展提供参考。

表64 南京农业机械化研究所发文引文主要主题

主题	发文量	发文占主题同期论文比(%)	引文量	主题显示度	FWCI值
Harvesters; Cutting; Cotton stalk	21	5.85	67	78.89	0.43
Harvesters; Peanuts; Damage rate	18	13.85	69	66.531	0.32
Nozzles; Sprayers; Spray drift	15	1.86	103	95.379	1.36
Agricultural machinery; Tillage; Rotary tillage	13	3.31	35	85.928	1.03
Fertilizers; Spreaders; Rate fertilization	8	5.59	90	77.776	1.12
Harvesters; Combine harvesters; Threshing cylinder	8	2.34	42	76.615	0.28
Modal analysis; Structural dynamics; Spray boom	7	11.86	51	63.084	1.29
Drying; Solar dryers; Drying models	6	0.31	32	99.179	0.48
Mulching; Plastic film; Residual plastic	5	0.83	9	94.587	1.45
Magnetorheological fluids; Brakes; CI Particles	5	0.71	50	96.263	0.21
Agricultural machinery; Transplanters; Pick-up Mechanism	4	1.59	33	80.183	0.15
Image analysis; Meats; Optimal wavelengths	4	0.24	39	99.123	0.19
Straw; Pelletizing; Moisture content	3	2.14	27	71.501	0.21

续表

主题	发文量	发文占主题同期论文比(%)	引文量	主题显示度	FWCI值
Physical properties; Water content; Width thickness	3	0.81	12	81.623	0
Input-output analysis; Carbon emission; Multi-regional input-output	3	0.14	42	99.895	0.94
Soil organic carbon; Organic carbon; Soil aggregation	3	0.12	1	99.574	0.78
Modal analysis; Vibration; Combine harvester	2	4.55	8	48.841	0.44
Drying; Moisture determination; Brown rice	2	4.00	2	28.533	0.25
Drops; Spraying; Electrostatic spraying	2	3.77	1	55.979	0.60
Cotton; Cotton fibers; Foreign fiber	2	1.24	6	67.482	0.08
Agricultural machinery; Motion planning; Harvesting	2	0.88	31	78.915	1.07
Vibration analysis; Cantilever beams; Rotating beam	2	0.58	6	85.589	0.80
Rice; *Oryza sativa*; Rice kernels	2	0.38	36	91.414	0.76
Meters (equipment); Sowing; Precision seeding	2	0.37	14	90.827	0
Wood products; Wood; Composites WPCs	2	0.29	34	95.831	1.44
Fruits; Harvesting; Fruit detection	2	0.22	24	96.026	2.39
Agriculture; Crops; Weed detection	2	0.17	35	97.580	0.95
Tribology; Wear of materials; Wear mechanisms	2	0.15	24	97.911	0
Vegetation; Chlorophyll; Hyperspectral reflectance	2	0.10	31	99.410	1.33
Pyrolysis; Biomass; Torrefaction temperature	2	0.07	33	99.853	1.34
Natural fibers; Composite materials; Natural fibres	2	0.04	30	99.813	0

3. 需求期刊及保障情况

经引文分析得知南京农业机械化研究所发文引用了643种外文期刊，与国家农业图书馆已订阅外文电子期刊品种进行比对，测算出其外文电子期刊全文保障率达到67.85%，引文量前40的期刊见表65。

表 65　南京农业机械化研究所引文量前 40 期刊

编号	期刊名称	引用数量	是否保障
1	Biosystems Engineering	105	是
2	Computers and Electronics in Agriculture	66	是
3	Journal of Food Engineering	54	是
4	Renewable and Sustainable Energy Reviews	49	是
5	Energy Policy	42	是
6	International Journal of Agricultural and Biological Engineering	41	是
7	Transactions - American Society of Agricultural Engineers: General Edition	35	是
8	Journal of Cleaner Production	33	是
9	Journal of Agricultural and Engineering Research	27	是
10	Energy	25	是
11	Environmental Science and Technology	22	是
12	Biomass and Bioenergy	21	是
13	Applied Energy	19	是
14	Transactions of the ASABE	18	是
15	Wear	17	是
16	Renewable Energy	17	是
17	Postharvest Biology and Technology	16	是
18	International Agricultural Engineering Journal	16	是
19	Bioresource Technology	16	是
20	Powder Technology	15	是
21	Soil and Tillage Research	13	是
22	Journal of Agricultural and Food Chemistry	13	是
23	Crop Protection	13	是
24	Applied Engineering in Agriculture	13	是

续表

编号	期刊名称	引用数量	是否保障
25	Field Crops Research	12	是
26	Precision Agriculture	12	是
27	Materials and Design	12	是
28	Food Chemistry	11	是
29	Smart Materials and Structures	11	否
30	Journal of Intelligent Material Systems and Structures	10	否
31	Composites Part B: Engineering	10	是
32	Carbohydrate Polymers	10	是
33	Journal of Applied Polymer Science	10	是
34	European Journal of Operational Research	9	是
35	Surface and Coatings Technology	9	是
36	Applied Soft Computing Journal	9	是
37	Atmospheric Environment	8	是
38	Electrochimica Acta	8	是
39	Industrial Crops and Products	8	是
40	Multibody System Dynamics	7	是

4. 需求数据库分析

分析各直属研究所引用外文文献的来源数据库，从数据库层面把握各直属研究所需求，是外文全文数据库建设的重要依据，同时也为各直属研究所参与电子资源共建选择数据库提供参考。根据各直属研究所需求期刊分析结果，将其与国家农业图书馆订阅的27种外文全文数据库期刊目录进行比对，发现2017—2019年南京农业机械化研究所引文主要来源数据库如图69所示，其中来源于ScienceDirect（70.63%）和Springer（9.17%）的引用最多。

ASME	Nature	RSC	JSTOR	Annual Reviews	BioOne	PNAS
12	7	6	5	4	2	1
Science	APSnet	CUP	ASCE	ACM		
1	1	1	1	1		

图 69　南京农业机械化研究所引文来源数据库分布

（三十一）烟草研究所

1. 需求学科分析

采集烟草研究所 2017—2019 年发表的外文期刊论文共计 265 篇，对其进行学科分析，可以看出该所发文主要集中在农业和生物科学（53.14%），生物化学、遗传学和分子生物学（33.96%），化学（22.01%）这三大学科（图 70）。除此之外，在环境科学，免疫与微生物学，医学，化学工程，药理学、毒理学和药剂学等也有一定数量的发文，说明烟草研究所的研究在这些领域也有涉足。

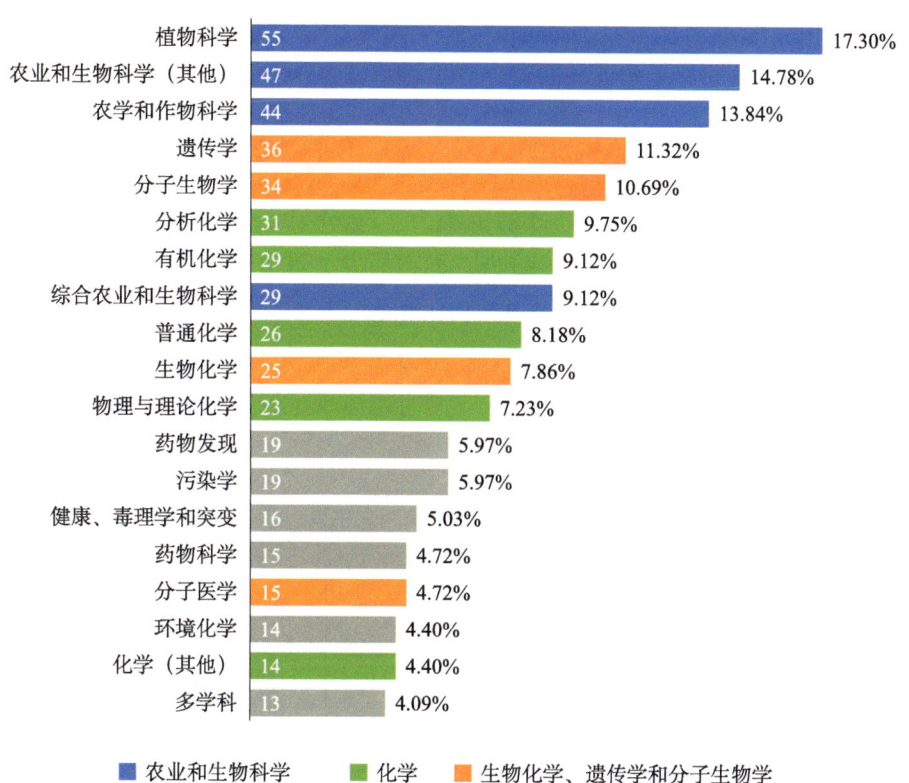

图 70 烟草研究所 2017—2019 年发文学科分布

对农业和生物科学，生物化学、遗传学和分子生物学，化学这三大学科的亚学科进行分析，结果如图 70 所示，在农业和生物科学中，发文主要集中在植物科学（17.30%），农业和生物科学（其他）（14.78%），农学和作物科学（13.84%），综合农业和生物科学（9.12%）等亚学科。生物化学、遗传学和分子生物学学科的发文主要集中在遗传学（11.32%），分子生物学（10.69%），生物化学（7.86%），分子医学（4.72%）等亚学科。化学学科的发文主要集中在分析化学（9.75%），有机化学（9.12%），普通化学（8.18%），物理与理论化学（7.23%），化学（其他）（4.40%）等亚学科。

2. 发文和引文主题分析

将文献按照主题组织，进行更细粒度的需求分析，是为了解决单纯按照学科为单元进行分析，针对性不强，导致资源建设成本高、利用不充分的问题。2017—2019 年烟草研究所发文共计涉及 203 个主题，通过相应的遴选指标，遴选出发文、引文涉及的主要主题（表 66）。可以看出烟草研究所在 "Senescence;

Transcription factors; Leaf senescence"这个主题的发文和引文最多,由此判断该研究所较为侧重这一领域的研究,在该领域文献的需求强度也最高;该所在"Wild rice; *Oryza sativa*; *Zizania palustris*"这个主题的发文占该主题全球同期论文的 13.33%,说明其在全球范围内对该领域的研究有较为突出的贡献;该所参与的最受关注、发展势头最好的主题为"Pyrolysis; Soil amendment; Biochar amendment",主题显示度值为 99.968;而该所发文具有较高引文影响力的主题为"Anthocyanins; Transcription factors; Anthocyanin biosynthetic",发文 FWCI 值是同类论文的 2.45 倍。综上,通过主题分析的结果不仅从各个角度反映出烟草研究所学科文献资源的精细化需求,同时也体现了研究所研究领域的分布态势,能够为其学科规划和发展提供参考。

表 66 烟草研究所发文引文主要主题

主题	发文量	发文占主题同期论文比(%)	引文量	主题显示度	FWCI 值
Senescence; Transcription factors; Leaf senescence	10	1.58	323	96.753	1.13
Pyrolysis; Soil amendment; Biochar amendment	8	0.15	191	99.968	1.24
Tobacco; *Nicotiana tabacum*; Tobacco cultivars	7	8.64	85	55.258	0.72
Tobacco; Flue-cured tobacco; Aroma components	6	5.08	4	49.705	0.17
Lignin; Cell walls; Lignin biosynthesis	5	0.58	169	98.238	0.98
Wild rice; *Oryza sativa*; *Zizania palustris*	4	13.33	58	61.442	2.27
Mucilages; Testa; Seed mucilage	4	6.90	55	74.838	0.97
Cell walls; Cell wall; Wall polysaccharides	4	1.11	114	96.429	0.91
Jasmonic acid; Oxylipins; Jasmonate signaling	4	0.60	103	98.285	0.65
Herbivores; Herbivory; Volatiles HIPVs	4	0.41	20	98.624	0.18
Eutectics; Solvents; Chloride ChCl	4	0.27	68	99.755	1.31
Anthocyanins; Transcription factors; Anthocyanin biosynthetic	4	0.26	114	98.997	2.45
Densovirus; Bombyx; Mori bidensovirus	3	4.35	61	57.574	0.09
Endoplasmic reticulum; Unfolded protein response; Endoplasmic reticulum stress	3	3.23	49	85.048	0.35

续表

主题	发文量	发文占主题同期论文比(%)	引文量	主题显示度	FWCI值
Intercropping; Rhizosphere; Continuous cropping	3	2.36	9	67.053	0.08
Fungi; Aspergillus; Electronic circular	3	1.36	20	89.762	0.54
Phosphates; Terpenes; Phosphate MEP	3	1.05	55	89.317	0.23
Photosynthesis; Photocurrents; Photocurrent generation	3	1.00	50	96.078	0.23
Enantiomers; Enantioselectivity; Chiral pesticides	3	0.97	39	93.364	1.39
Volatile organic compounds; Fungi; Mycelial growth	3	0.90	9	95.067	1.14
Disease resistance; Plant immunity; NLR proteins	3	0.50	72	97.722	0.65
Chitosan; Chitin; Weight chitosan	3	0.36	42	98.547	1.88
Eddy covariance; Net ecosystem exchange; Carbon flux	3	0.34	5	98.486	0.34
Water stress; Antioxidants; Glutathione reductase	3	0.32	71	95.554	1.07
Indoleacetic Acids; Auxins; Auxin efflux	3	0.31	105	98.907	0.57
Rice; *Oryza sativa*; Cultivated rice	3	0.24	33	98.470	0.53
Tobacco; Coenzymes; Tobacco waste	2	6.06	51	52.977	0.33
Sucrose; Isomerases; Sucrose isomerase	2	4.65	23	70.313	1.33
Babuvirus; Musa; Banana bunchy	2	3.08	15	65.627	0.55
Oxidation; Manganese oxide; Potassium permanganate	2	2.94	23	73.345	1.33
Endonucleases; Genome, Mitochondrial; Homing endonucleases	2	2.38	10	73.116	1.02
Miridae; Hemiptera; Tarnished plant	2	2.08	13	66.959	0.19
Polyketide synthases; Chalcone; Synthase CHS	2	1.98	33	77.636	0.90
Fungicides; Fungicides, Industrial; Maximum residue	2	1.59	9	85.336	0.58
Glucans; Ascomycota; Pullulan production	2	1.31	55	87.725	0.81
Alternative splicing; Arabidopsis; Intron retention	2	1.13	26	91.101	1.38
Droughts; Transcription factors; Freezing tolerance	2	0.17	131	98.632	1.64

3. 需求期刊及保障情况

经引文分析得知烟草研究所发文引用了 1 514 种外文期刊,与国家农业图书馆已订阅外文电子期刊品种进行比对,测算出其外文电子期刊全文保障率达到 92.98%,引文量前 40 的期刊见表 67。

表 67 烟草研究所引文量前 40 期刊

编号	期刊名称	引用数量	是否保障
1	Plant Physiology	427	是
2	Plant Cell	321	是
3	Plant Journal	263	是
4	Proceedings of the National Academy of Sciences of the United States of America	233	是
5	Journal of Agricultural and Food Chemistry	207	是
6	Journal of Experimental Botany	197	是
7	Food Chemistry	176	是
8	PLoS ONE	175	是
9	Frontiers in Plant Science	154	是
10	Science	149	是
11	Plant Molecular Biology	123	是
12	Chemosphere	121	是
13	Carbohydrate Polymers	109	是
14	Nucleic Acids Research	106	是
15	Nature	106	是
16	Plant and Cell Physiology	102	是
17	Trends in Plant Science	99	是
18	Planta	98	是
19	Journal of Physiology	91	是
20	Scientific Reports	87	是
21	Bioinformatics	84	是

续表

编号	期刊名称	引用数量	是否保障
22	Science of the Total Environment	79	是
23	Journal of Biological Chemistry	78	是
24	Bioresource Technology	77	是
25	Theoretical and Applied Genetics	74	是
26	Annual Review of Plant Biology	73	是
27	Current Opinion in Plant Biology	67	是
28	Environmental Science and Technology	67	是
29	Plant, Cell and Environment	67	是
30	Molecular Plant	66	是
31	Molecular Plant-Microbe Interactions	66	是
32	Applied and Environmental Microbiology	63	是
33	Molecules	62	是
34	BMC Plant Biology	61	是
35	Plant Disease	59	是
36	Soil Biology and Biochemistry	57	是
37	Nature Biotechnology	56	是
38	Plant Cell Reports	55	是
39	Journal of virology	55	是
40	Journal of Chromatography A	53	是

4. 需求数据库分析

分析各直属研究所引用外文文献的来源数据库，从数据库层面把握各直属研究所需求，是外文全文数据库建设的重要依据，同时也为各直属研究所参与电子资源共建选择数据库提供参考。根据各直属研究所需求期刊分析结果，将其与国家农业图书馆订阅的27种外文全文数据库期刊目录进行比对，发现2017—2019年烟草研究所引文主要来源数据库如图71所示，其中来源于ScienceDirect（37.62%）、Springer（15.66%）和Wiley（13.48%）的引用最多。

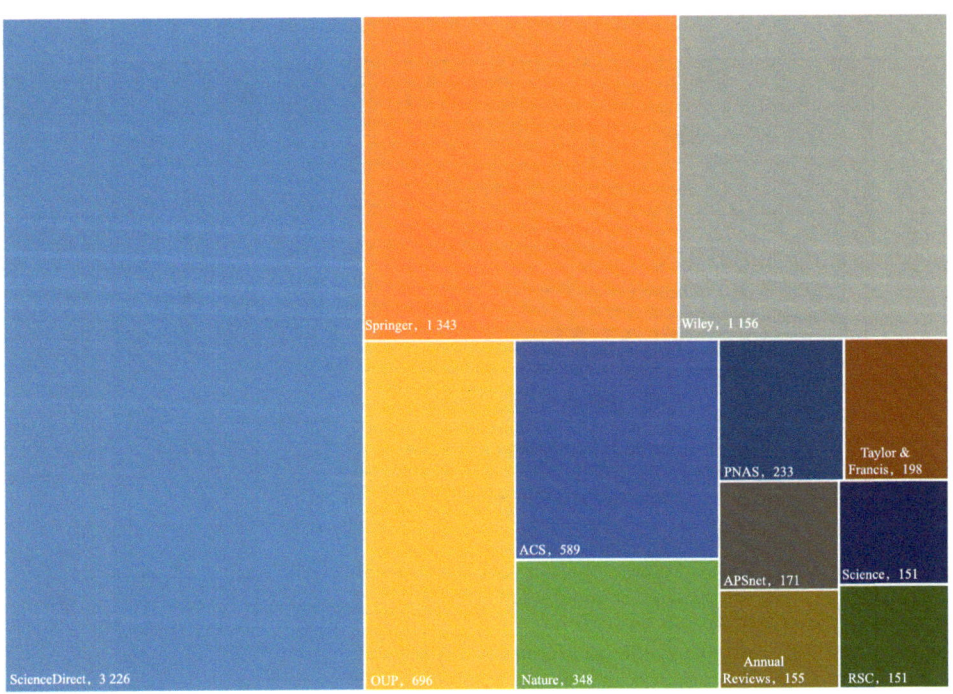

ASM	MS	CAB	BioOne	CUP	BMJ	APS	ASBMB	ASCE	JoVE
59	53	41	36	34	6	6	2	1	1

图 71 烟草研究所引文来源数据库分布

（三十二）深圳农业基因组研究所

1. 需求学科分析

采集深圳农业基因组研究所（简称基因组所）2017—2019 年发表的外文期刊论文共计 173 篇，对其进行学科分析，可以看出该所发文主要集中在生物化学、遗传学和分子生物学（66.49%），农业和生物科学（45.41%）这两大学科（图 72）。除此之外，在化学、免疫与微生物学、化学工程等也有一定数量的发文，说明基因组所的研究在这些领域也有涉足。

对生物化学、遗传学和分子生物学，农业和生物科学这两大学科的亚学科进行分析，结果如图 72 所示，在生物化学、遗传学和分子生物学中，发文主要集中在遗传学（23.78%），分子生物学（19.46%），综合生物化学、遗传学和分子生物学（14.59%），生物技术（9.19%），生物化学（8.11%），细胞生物学（7.57%），生理学（6.49%）等亚学科中。农业和生物科学学科的发文主要集中在植物科学（25.95%），农学和作物科学（11.89%），综合农业和生物科学（6.49%），昆虫科学（5.41%），生态、进化、行为与系统学（3.78%）等亚学科。

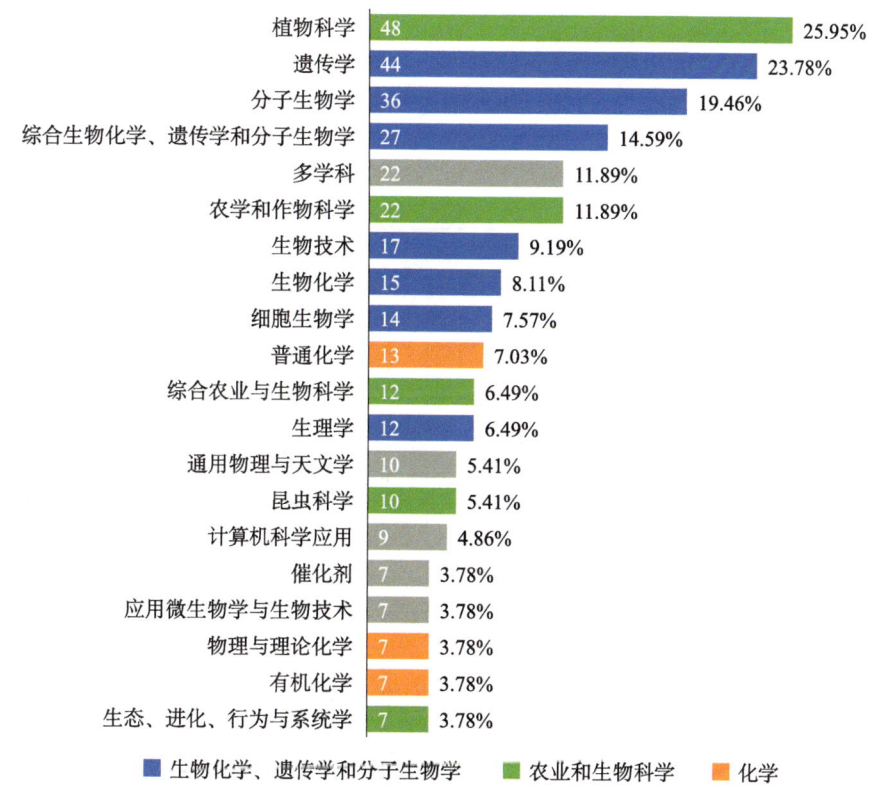

图72　深圳农业基因组研究所2017—2019年发文学科分布

2. 发文和引文主题分析

将文献按照主题组织，进行更细粒度的需求分析，是为了解决单纯按照学科为单元进行分析，针对性不强，导致资源建设成本高、利用不充分的问题。2017—2019年深圳农业基因组研究所发文共计涉及112个主题，通过相应的遴选指标，遴选出发文、引文涉及的主要主题（表68）。可以看出基因组所在"Rice; *Oryza sativa*; Cultivated rice"这个主题的发文和引文最多，由此判断该研究所较为侧重这一领域的研究，在该领域文献的需求强度也最高；该所在"ATP-Binding Cassette Transporters; ABC transporters; Multixenobiotic resistance"这个主题的发文占该主题全球同期论文的 1.83%，说明其在全球范围内对该领域的研究有较为突出的贡献；该所参与的最受关注、发展势头最好的主题为"Genome; Genes; Single guide"和"RNA, Long Untranslated; Neoplasms; Proliferation migration"，主题显示度值分别为 99.987 和 99.984；同时，该所发文具有较高引文影响力的主题也为"Genome; Genes; Single guide"，发文 FWCI 值是同类论文的 12.08 倍。综上，通过主题分析的结果不仅从各个角度反映出基因组所学科文献资源的精细化需求，同时也体现了研究所研究领域的分布态势，能够为其学科规划和发展提供参考。

表 68　深圳农业基因组研究所发文引文主要主题

主题	发文量	发文占主题同期论文比(%)	引文量	主题显示度	FWCI 值
Rice; *Oryza sativa*; Cultivated rice	9	0.73	351	98.470	3.92
Bacillus thuringiensis; Noctuidae; Zea Boddie	6	1.29	275	94.565	2.66
Genome; Genes; Single guide	6	0.10	198	99.987	12.08
RNA, Long Untranslated; Neoplasms; Proliferation migration	6	0.05	131	99.984	1.25
Rice; Drought; Lowland rice	5	0.85	71	95.657	0.88
Potatoes; *Solanum tuberosum*; Cultivated potato	4	1.68	29	87.619	2.71
Tomatoes; *Lycopersicon esculentum*; Tomato varieties	4	1.18	88	95.701	7.32
Nitrates; Nitrogen; Nitrate transporters	4	0.77	84	97.199	0.70
Bacillus thuringiensis; Proteins; Thuringiensis strain	4	0.71	188	94.640	1.65
Genome; Algorithms; Novo genome	4	0.20	160	99.448	1.34
Melons; *Cucumis melo*; Melon accessions	3	1.35	62	84.275	5.19
Succinic acid; Fermentation; Succinate production	3	0.85	82	96.593	1.96
Abscisic acid; Arabidopsis; Guard cells	3	0.34	111	98.300	2.93
Enterocolitis, Necrotizing; Infant, Premature; Necrotising enterocolitis	3	0.33	36	97.715	0.84
Genome; Exome; Variant calling	3	0.10	146	99.810	6.18

续表

主题	发文量	发文占主题同期论文比 (%)	引文量	主题显示度	FWCI 值
ATP-Binding Cassette Transporters; ABC transporters; Multixenobiotic resistance	2	1.83	48	83.055	1.57
Cucurbitacins; Cucurbitaceae; G2/M phase	2	1.07	37	83.993	0.67
Chloroplasts; Plastids; Chloroplast gene	2	1.01	40	90.641	1.23
Rice; *Oryza sativa*; Cooked rice	2	0.96	53	83.339	1.31
Ligases; Ubiquitin; Ubiquitin ligases	2	0.82	60	89.622	2.39
Plastids; Dinoflagellida; Complex plastids	2	0.59	27	95.738	0
Genes; Saponins; Ginsenoside biosynthesis	2	0.53	68	94.260	0.77
MicroRNAs; Muscle, Skeletal; Myogenic differentiation	2	0.46	34	94.784	0.57
RNA Editing; RNA; Adenosine deaminases	2	0.43	63	98.037	0.34
Gene transfer, Horizontal; Eukaryota; Transferred genes	2	0.41	26	98.438	0.09
Senescence; Transcription factors; Leaf senescence	2	0.32	70	96.753	0.53
Parasitic plants; Plant growth regulators; Root parasitic	2	0.28	106	98.368	3.04
Brassinosteroids; Arabidopsis; BR biosynthesis	2	0.26	70	97.909	0.58
Acetylation; Lysine; Acetylated proteins	2	0.24	43	99.261	0.12
Herbivores; Herbivory; Volatiles HIPVs	2	0.21	61	98.624	1.59
DNA Methylation; Methylation; Whole-genome bisulfite	2	0.21	55	98.483	0.73
Genes; Gene expression; Stable genes	2	0.19	77	96.751	2.95
5-Methylcytosine; Epigenomics; Cytosine modifications	2	0.18	59	99.497	0.84
Phytoremediation; Cadmium; Pot experiment	2	0.16	80	98.956	1.61
Anthocyanins; Transcription factors; Anthocyanin biosynthetic	2	0.13	36	98.997	1.42
MicroRNAs; RNA; Degradome sequencing	2	0.10	38	99.589	0.35
Metagenome; Obesity; Microbial composition	2	0.02	62	99.985	2.44

3. 需求期刊及保障情况

经引文分析得知深圳农业基因组研究所发文引用了 1 283 种外文期刊，与国家农业图书馆已订阅外文电子期刊品种进行比对，测算出其外文电子期刊全文保障率达到 91.99%，引文量前 40 的期刊见表 69。

表 69 深圳农业基因组研究所引文量前 40 期刊

编号	期刊名称	引用数量	是否保障
1	Proceedings of the National Academy of Sciences of the United States of America	346	是
2	Nucleic Acids Research	285	是
3	Nature	279	是
4	Bioinformatics	257	是
5	PLoS ONE	243	是
6	Science	239	是
7	Plant Physiology	235	是
8	Nature Genetics	208	是
9	Plant Journal	192	是
10	Plant Cell	184	是
11	PCR Methods and Applications	153	是
12	Nature Biotechnology	150	是
13	Scientific Reports	145	是
14	Theoretical and Applied Genetics	121	是
15	Genome Biology	115	是
16	Cell	114	是
17	BMC Genomics	108	是
18	Insect Biochemistry and Molecular Biology	102	是
19	Journal of Experimental Botany	101	是
20	Frontiers in Plant Science	98	是
21	Nature Communications	90	是
22	Journal of Biological Chemistry	85	是

续表

编号	期刊名称	引用数量	是否保障
23	Nature Methods	77	是
24	Molecular Biology and Evolution	70	是
25	PLoS Genetics	70	是
26	Journal of Physiology	68	是
27	Plant and Cell Physiology	67	是
28	Plant Molecular Biology	64	是
29	Nature Reviews Genetics	62	是
30	Journal of Economic Entomology	60	是
31	Molecular Plant	59	是
32	Genetics	57	是
33	BMC Bioinformatics	56	是
34	Annual Review of Plant Biology	53	是
35	Current Opinion in Plant Biology	52	是
36	Applied and Environmental Microbiology	51	是
37	Trends in Plant Science	49	是
38	Plant, Cell and Environment	47	是
39	Field Crops Research	46	是
40	Euphytica	44	是

4. 需求数据库分析

分析各直属研究所引用外文文献的来源数据库，从数据库层面把握各直属研究所需求，是外文全文数据库建设的重要依据，同时也为各直属研究所参与电子资源共建选择数据库提供参考。根据各直属研究所需求期刊分析结果，将其与国家农业图书馆订阅的27种外文全文数据库期刊目录进行比对，发现2017—2019年深圳农业基因组研究所引文主要来源数据库如图73所示，其中来源于ScienceDirect（25.35%）、OUP（16.75%）、Nature（16.04%）、Wiley（13.44%）和Springer（11.31%）的引用最多。

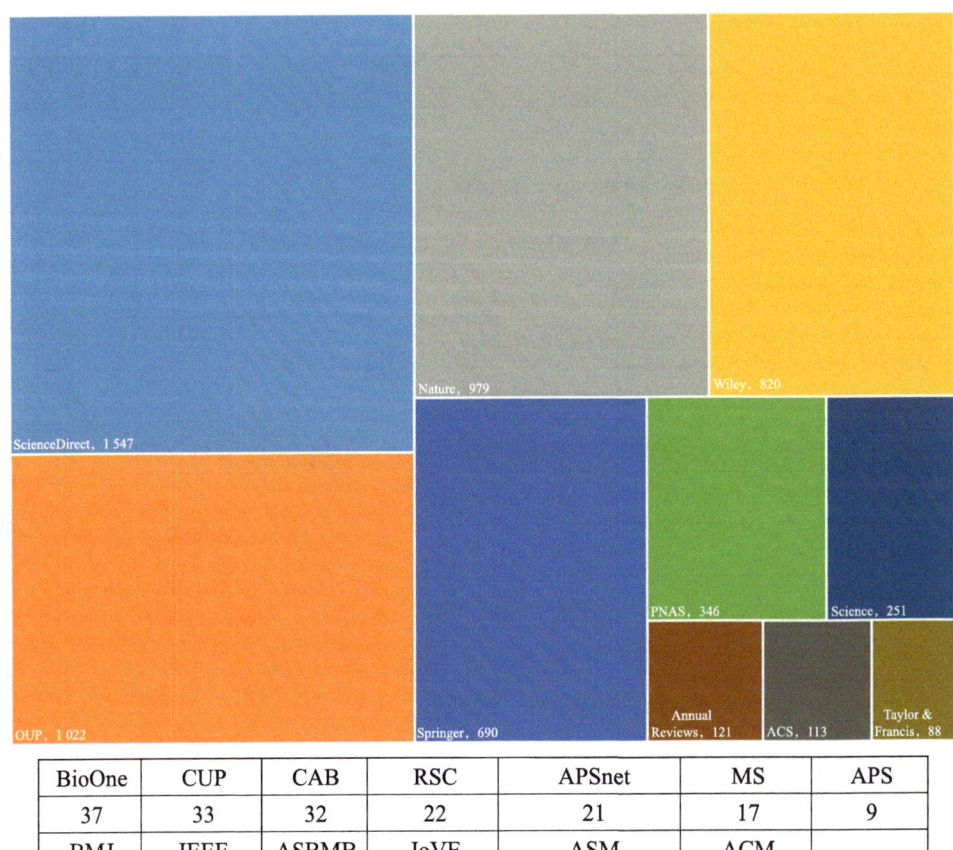

图 73 深圳农业基因组研究所引文来源数据库分布

总结和讨论

（一）中国农业科学院学科资源需求与保障特点

通过比较各研究所学科资源需求与保障情况，总结出三个特点。

（1）学科结构相对单一的研究所，像作科所、水稻所等保障水平较高，结构较多元的研究所，比如蜜蜂所、特产所等保障水平则偏低。对保障率偏低的研究所通过过去两年加强"交叉新兴"学科的资源建设，也使其保障率得到了一定的提升。而对于保障率较高的研究所，再想提升其保障水平较为困难，但通过需求分析也发现这些研究所对研究数据、软件、序列等资源有所需求，应当适当拓展非全文类型资源。

（2）保障率90%以下的10个研究所中，半数是从事畜牧兽医研究的研究所，其所需资源已随其学科的发展，逐渐超出传统畜牧兽医学的范畴，越来越多地涉及免疫与微生物学、医学、制药学等学科，针对这部分需求应当开展精准化需求分析，研究新的订阅模式，如采取单刊订阅等形式满足。

（3）由于学科交叉日益频繁，一些研究所产生了一系列新的需求，打破了外界对其学科方向的既定印象。例如随着作物组学的发展，棉花所、作物所等研究所出现了对计算机科学的需求；农经所涉猎环境监控、电子商务、甚至是云计算的农产品流通监测平台，需求外延至环境科学和工程学；资化所、草原所等开展可持续发展研究、农牧政策研究等涉及社会科学的资源。对于这些新出现的需求应当引起关注。

（二）中国农业科学院外文文献资源保障策略

1. 围绕学科体系，聚焦重大使命，深入开展需求分析强化文献保障

中国农业科学院文献资源保障体系构建应当以本机构"建成世界一流农业科研院所"的发展目标作为导向，不断进行优化调整，满足全院各个发展阶段科技创新、产业创新和宏观战略研究的文献信息需求。应充分发挥机构学科体系在科技文献资源整合、布局调整中的导向性作用，针对重点学科、优势学科、短板学科、特色学科以及亟须前瞻布局的新兴和前沿交叉学科，深入开展需求分析，强化文献保障。在"十四五"期间，尤其应当聚焦中国农业科学院粮食安全与重要农产品有效供给、农产品优质安全与营养健康、耕地保护与质量提升、动植物疫病防控与生物安全、农业绿色发展、农业机械化智能化、农业基础研究、前沿技术创新、乡村振兴与区域发展等重大使命进行科技文献资源优化配置，为各项重点任务提供更好的科技文献支撑。

2. 强化立体化的数字资源保障体系建设

随着全球科研范式和数字信息形态变革，科技信息资源呈现立体化特征。以往科技文献保障建设的重点是中外文期刊、会议、学位论文、科技报告等传统的一次、二次文献，本研究对中国农业科学院需求最集中（89%）的外文期刊全文资源保障现状进行分析得出，全院外文期刊全文保障率已经超过90%，剩余的10%需求也可以通过国家科技图书文献中心原文传递进一步得到满足。然而在语义出版、数据出版等背景下，农业科研用户信息需求逐渐超出传统文献资源的范畴，涉及越来越多的科学数据、可视化图谱等新兴资源，因此需要强化对富媒体学术资源、事实型数据资源、软件型工具资源等建设保障；并且针对农业产业创新信息需求，加强市场报告、产业分析、统计手册等资源建设保障，形成多元化载体和新型信息内容的立体化资源保障体系。

参考文献

[1] 王婷，颜蕴，王鸶飞，等. 中国农业科学院电子文献资源建设现状及发展策略 [J]. 农业图书情报学刊，2010，22（10）：32-34，56.

[2] 续玉红，颜蕴，王鸶飞. 基于引文分析的农业科研人员外文文献需求与保障研究 [J]. 农业网络信息，2010（5）：43-46，79.

[3] 王婷，颜蕴，续玉红. 基于引文分析的研究生文献需求研究——以中国农业科学院图书馆为例 [J]. 农业图书情报学刊，2011，23（11）：5-8，15.

[4] 王婷，颜蕴，续玉红，等. 交叉学科国外期刊需求分析方法探析 [J]. 数字图书馆论坛，2016（8）：50-53.

[5] 卢垚，王鸶飞，马鑫. 基于主题分析的交叉学科科技文献资源遴选方法研究——以蜜蜂学为例 [J]. 数字图书馆论坛，2020（11）：33-41.